Shakespeare's Sisters

Shakespeare's Sisters

How Women Wrote the Renaissance

❈

RAMIE TARGOFF

Alfred A. Knopf
NEW YORK 2024

THIS IS A BORZOI BOOK
PUBLISHED BY ALFRED A. KNOPF

www.aaknopf.com

Knopf, Borzoi Books, and the colophon are registered trademarks of
Penguin Random House LLC.

Library of Congress Cataloging-in-Publication Data
Names: Targoff, Ramie, author.
Title: Shakespeare's sisters : how women wrote the
Renaissance / Ramie Targoff.
Description: First United States edition. | New York :
Alfred A. Knopf, 2024. | Includes bibliographical references and index.
Identifiers: LCCN 2023013910 | ISBN 9780525658030 (hardcover) |
ISBN 9781984899514 (trade paperback) | ISBN 9780525658047 (ebk)
Subjects: LCSH: Pembroke, Mary Sidney Herbert, Countess of,
1561–1621—Criticism and interpretation. | Lanyer, Aemilia—Criticism
and interpretation. | Cary, Elizabeth, Lady, 1585 or 1586–1639—
Criticism and interpretation. | Pembroke, Anne Clifford Herbert,
Countess of, 1590–1676—Criticism and interpretation. |
Renaissance—England. | LCGFT: Literary criticism.
Classification: LCC PR2329.P2 Z88 2024 |
DDC 821/.309—dc23/eng/20230802
LC record available at https://lccn.loc.gov/2023013910

Jacket image: *Lady Mary Neville* (detail) after
Hans Eworth. Photo: National Trust Photographic Library /
Derrick E. Witty / Bridgeman Images
Jacket design by Jenny Carrow

Manufactured in the United States of America
First Edition

To Hannah

Contents

�

Family Charts

❈

Mary Sidney, Countess of Pembroke

SIDNEY/DUDLEY FAMILY

JANE DUDLEY, Duchess of Northumberland: Mary's grandmother

JOHN DUDLEY, 1st Duke of Northumberland: Mary's grandfather

ROBERT DUDLEY, 1st Earl of Leicester (second creation of the title*):
Mary's uncle

KATHERINE HASTINGS (née Dudley), Countess of Huntingdon: Mary's
aunt

LADY MARY SIDNEY (née Dudley): Mary's mother

SIR HENRY SIDNEY: Mary's father

SIR PHILIP SIDNEY: Mary's older brother

ELIZABETH SIDNEY: Mary's older sister

ROBERT SIDNEY, 1st Earl of Leicester (third creation of the title): Mary's
younger brother

BARBARA SIDNEY (née Gamage), Countess of Leicester: Mary's sister-in-
law (Robert's wife)

AMBROSIA SIDNEY: Mary's younger sister

SIR THOMAS SIDNEY: Mary's younger brother

HERBERT FAMILY

WILLIAM HERBERT, 1st Earl of Pembroke: Mary's father-in-law

HENRY HERBERT, 2nd Earl of Pembroke: Mary's husband**

WILLIAM HERBERT, 3rd Earl of Pembroke: Mary's son

KATHERINE HERBERT: Mary's daughter

PHILIP HERBERT, 1st Earl of Montgomery, 4th Earl of Pembroke: Mary's
son

* The title Earl of Leicester was renewed or "created" multiple times, as a result of the line dying
out without male heirs.

** To avoid confusion between Mary's father and husband—both named Henry—Henry
Herbert is referred to by his title, Pembroke. Otherwise, husbands and wives are referred to
throughout the book by their first names.

ANNE HERBERT: Mary's daughter

MARY HERBERT (née Talbot), Countess of Pembroke: Mary's daughter-in-law (William's wife)

SUSAN HERBERT (née de Vere), Countess of Montgomery: Mary's daughter-in-law (Philip's first wife)

ANNE CLIFFORD, Countess of Dorset, Montgomery, and Pembroke: Mary's daughter-in-law (Philip's second wife)

Aemilia Lanyer

BASSANO/JOHNSON FAMILY

BAPTISTA BASSANO: Aemilia's father

MARGARET JOHNSON: Aemilia's mother

ANGELA HOLLAND (née Bassano): Aemilia's sister

LANYER/FERRABOSCO FAMILY

NICHOLAS LANYER: Aemilia's father-in-law

ALFONSO LANYER: Aemilia's husband

HENRY LANYER: Aemilia's son

ELLEN FERRABOSCO (née Lanyer): Aemilia's sister-in-law

ALFONSO FERRABOSCO JR.: Aemilia's brother-in-law

Elizabeth Cary, Viscountess Falkland

TANFIELD/LEE FAMILY

SIR HENRY LEE: Elizabeth's great-uncle

SIR LAWRENCE TANFIELD: Elizabeth's father

ELIZABETH TANFIELD (née Symonds): Elizabeth's mother

CARY FAMILY

LADY CATHERINE CARY (née Knyvett): Elizabeth's mother-in-law

SIR EDWARD CARY, Master of the Jewel House: Elizabeth's father-in-law

HENRY CARY, 1st Viscount Falkland: Elizabeth's husband

LUCIUS CARY, 2nd Viscount Falkland: Elizabeth's son
LORENZO CARY: Elizabeth's son
EDWARD CARY: Elizabeth's son
HENRY CARY: Elizabeth's son
PATRICK CARY: Elizabeth's son
CATHERINE CARY, Countess of Home: Elizabeth's daughter
ANNE CARY, Dame Clementia: Elizabeth's daughter
ELIZABETH CARY, Dame Elizabetha Augustina: Elizabeth's daughter
LUCY CARY, Dame Magdalena: Elizabeth's daughter
VICTORIA CARY: Elizabeth's daughter
MARY CARY, Dame Maria: Elizabeth's daughter

Anne Clifford, Countess of Dorset, Montgomery, and Pembroke

CLIFFORD/RUSSELL FAMILY

FRANCIS RUSSELL, 2nd Earl of Bedford: Anne's maternal grandfather
WILLIAM RUSSELL, 1st Baron Russell of Thornhaugh: Anne's uncle
MARGARET CLIFFORD (née Russell), Countess of Cumberland: Anne's mother
GEORGE CLIFFORD, 3rd Earl of Cumberland: Anne's father
FRANCIS CLIFFORD, 4th Earl of Cumberland: Anne's uncle
HENRY CLIFFORD, 5th Earl of Cumberland: Anne's cousin

SACKVILLE FAMILY

THOMAS SACKVILLE, 1st Earl of Dorset: Anne's husband's grandfather
ROBERT SACKVILLE, 2nd Earl of Dorset: Anne's father-in-law
RICHARD SACKVILLE, 3rd Earl of Dorset: Anne's first husband
EDWARD SACKVILLE, 4th Earl of Dorset: Anne's brother-in-law
MARGARET SACKVILLE, Countess of Thanet: Anne's daughter
ISABELLA SACKVILLE, Countess of Northampton: Anne's daughter

HERBERT FAMILY

PHILIP HERBERT, Earl of Montgomery and Pembroke: Anne's second husband (see also "Mary Sidney, Countess of Pembroke," above)

Shakespeare's Sisters

October 1928

Newnham College and Girton College Cambridge University

Judith Shakespeare

In her 1929 feminist manifesto, *A Room of One's Own,* Virginia Woolf explored the reasons why over the centuries women had written so little compared to men. "A woman must have money and a room of her own," she famously pronounced, "if she is to write fiction." In lectures originally given in 1928 at Newnham and Girton Colleges (both women's colleges at Cambridge University), Woolf described her own circumstances—she had already written *Mrs. Dalloway* and *To the Lighthouse*—as a direct result of having inherited £500 a year from an aunt who died after falling off her horse in Bombay. Woolf got the news of her aunt's gift around the same time that women were given the vote, in early 1918. "Of the two—the vote and the money," she declared, "the money, I own, seemed infinitely the more important."

The most celebrated part of *A Room of One's Own* isn't Woolf's outrage over either women's erasure from the history books or the second-class treatment they receive in almost all aspects of their lives. What most readers remember from Woolf's polemical work is her account of Shakespeare's imaginary sister, Judith. If there had been a Judith Shakespeare endowed with a talent like her brother's, Woolf warned, she would have met with the darkest of fates. "Any woman," she exclaimed, "born with a great gift in the sixteenth century would certainly have gone crazed, shot herself, or ended her days in some lonely cottage outside the village, half witch, half wizard, feared and mocked at." For in spite of her genius, Judith Shakespeare "would have been so thwarted and hindered by other people, so tortured and pulled asunder by her own contrary instincts, that she must have lost her health and sanity." Had any woman survived these conditions, Woolf concluded that "whatever she had written would have been twisted and deformed, issuing from a strained and morbid imagination."

Woolf had good reasons for her pessimism. To be a woman in Shakespeare's England was to live a drastically reduced life. Girls were rarely permitted to go to grammar schools and were never allowed to attend university. Before marriage, they were supposed to serve and obey their fathers. Once married, women's obedience shifted to their husbands, who assumed possession of their wives' personal property and became their legal guardians under a doctrine called "coverture," which literally meant women were "covered" by the legal fiction that husbands and wives were one person. (This arrangement lasted until the passage of the Married Women's Property Act in 1870.) Renaissance women could not hold political office or vote. They could not become lawyers or doctors. They could not appear onstage in theaters. They were supposed to keep quiet in public, and disruptive behavior could lead them to be brandished as "scolds" and paraded through the streets wearing a heavy iron muzzle known as a "scold's bridle." Despite all of these restrictions and hardships, however, some women did learn their letters, read voraciously, and then take up the pen themselves. They weren't encouraged, and they rarely found even a shred of acclaim, but there were some women who managed to write.

When Woolf wrote *A Room of One's Own,* she knew almost nothing about the powerful literary works a small group of women had written—and in many cases, published—around the time of Shakespeare. These brilliant poems and plays, translations and histories, had been lost or forgotten for centuries. But Woolf had recently encountered one of these women's writing, which she peremptorily dismissed as trivial. In 1923, Woolf's lover Vita Sackville-West published the early diaries of Lady Anne Clifford, who had lived with her first husband, Richard Sackville, Earl of Dorset, at Sackville-West's childhood home at Knole. Sackville-

West saw in Anne a kindred spirit, a fellow reader and writer who was dissatisfied with the prescriptive role English society had carved out for her, and who had heroically found a way to fight back.

In 1605, the fifteen-year-old Anne Clifford, an aristocratic girl raised with all imaginable privileges of birth and wealth, was disinherited from one of the largest properties in England. Her father, George Clifford, Earl of Cumberland, a dashing courtier who was the Queen's Champion at the annual Accession Day jousts, had squandered away most of his money in his gambling debts and privateering ventures (he was famous for his capture of San Juan, Puerto Rico). When George died, he passed on both his debts and his vast estates, totaling roughly 90,000 acres, not to Anne—his only surviving child—but to his brother, Sir Francis Clifford.

Anne's response was to wage what would become one of the greatest inheritance battles England had ever seen, a nearly forty-year legal fight that brought her into direct conflict with the most powerful men in the kingdom. From her dramatic showdown in King James's private chambers at Whitehall Palace where, pressured to accept a substantial cash settlement, she brazenly declared to the king that she would never give up her lands "under any condition whatsoever," to her trespassing on her uncle's estates on horseback to persuade his tenants not to pay their rent; from her suffering at the hands of her profligate husband, who abandoned her for long stretches of time with the hope Anne would break down and put an end to her lawsuit, to her social ostracization from other ladies at court; through all of this, and much more, Anne kept herself going by keeping a diary. When she finally gained her father's lands after the death of her uncle and his only son, she also expanded her great diaristic project to write both a full memoir of her life and a massive history of the Clifford family from the Norman conquest through the present.

Anne would no doubt have been thrilled to know that a woman like Vita Sackville-West brought her writing back into the world. She would have been less pleased with Virginia Woolf's response. In her 1931 essay "Donne After Three Centuries," Woolf laid out the little she knew about Renaissance women writers. "If they wrote themselves," she claimed, and it is said that both Lady Pembroke and Lady Bedford were poets of merit, they did not dare to put their names to what they wrote, and it has vanished. But a diary here and there survives from which we may see the patroness more closely and less romantically.

"A diary here and there" brought Woolf to Anne, whom she described as "practical and little educated," someone who painstakingly restored her castles but "never attempted to set up a salon or to found a library." "A great heiress," Anne was "infected with all the passion of her age for lands and houses, busied with all the cares of wealth and property." She may have "read good English books as naturally as she ate good beef and mutton," but in Woolf's estimation, Anne's writing didn't deserve our attention.

Sackville-West saw it differently. She admired Anne's "sharp, vigorous mind, that had, so humanly, its sentimental facet on the opposite side to all its severity." She sympathized with Anne's early struggles—"restrained on the one hand by the severe and virtuous influence of an ever-present mother, and coloured on the other hand by the fable of an adventurous and almost legendary father"—and she conjured up the "neat and meticulous child, keeping her accounts in a note-book with that precision which followed her throughout life." She applauded the old woman (Anne lived to eighty-six) who kept her diary "with the same scrupulous care up to the day before her death," filling the pages with a fascinating combination of "gossip," "strong family feelings," "texts and maxims," and above all "coincidences," which she would "turn happily down any little by-path in order to ferret . . . out."

That Woolf couldn't grasp what was thrilling about Anne's diaries reflects her own tastes and biases—a topic beyond our interest here—but it also gives us a different perspective on the reasons she thought Judith Shakespeare couldn't have practiced her art. For it turns out Woolf's doomed vision of women writers in Renaissance England was horribly mistaken. Although she claimed to have heard of "Lady Pembroke" (whom she might more respectfully have called by her own name, Mary Sidney), she seems never to have read a word of either Mary's dazzling verse translation of the Psalms or her beautiful poems to Queen Elizabeth. She almost certainly hadn't heard of Aemilia Lanyer, the first Englishwoman to publish a book of original poetry in the seventeenth century, whose brilliant poem, "Salve Deus Rex Judaeorum," offers a feminist retelling of both Eve's fall and the Crucifixion. Woolf likewise knew nothing about Elizabeth Cary, whose stunning tragedy recounting the murder of the ancient Jewish princess Mariam at the hands of her tyrannical husband, Herod, was the first original play to be published by a woman in England. Revisiting many of the themes of Shakespeare's *Othello* written just a few years before, *The Tragedy of Mariam* bravely affirms a woman's right to follow her own conscience and speak her mind at whatever cost.

Mary Sidney, Aemilia Lanyer, Elizabeth Cary, and Anne Clifford were among a small but not insignificant group of Shakespeare's contemporaries who did what Woolf deemed impossible: they wrote works of poetry, history, religion, and drama when none was encouraged from their kind. They weren't professional writers who earned an income from their works, and however wealthy they may have been—three of these four women were very rich—they were far from free to dedicate as much time as they'd like to writing. Each had husbands and children to care for and households to run; they enjoyed bursts of great productivity and were beset by periods of stagnation; they wrote when their circumstances allowed. And yet, whatever limitations these women faced, their writing largely defined who they were and how they wanted to be remembered. Against all odds they found rooms of their own, if only to be buried inside them with their writing for hundreds of years before the doors were finally torn down.

Shakespeare's Sisters opens up Renaissance history to four extraordinary women for whom writing was their life force. Once we learn about these women and read their books after centuries of neglect, it's not only their names that we recover. Suddenly, there are new voices. We hear from teenage girls married off to men they would never have chosen; wives forced to tolerate their husbands' spending their money and taking lovers; mothers whose babies died before their first birthday, or whose children were taken away by their fathers as punishment for wifely disobedience. We hear from widows filing their own lawsuits in Chancery Court, opening charities and schools, traveling for pleasure to Europe, building their own houses, and erecting monuments. We hear a woman's perspective on the killing of Mary, Queen of Scots and the Spanish Armada; the Protestant wars in the Netherlands and the witchcraft trials in England and Scotland; the ongoing persecution of Catholics and the outbreak of the Civil War. We realize that however much we thought we knew about the Renaissance, it was only half the story. We begin to understand how much we've been missing.

CHAPTER ONE

April 28, 1603

Westminster, London

Queen Elizabeth

From above, it looked as if London had been taken over by an enormous black snake. Sixteen hundred participants marched in the somber procession, forming a cortege that stretched for half a mile. Together, they were wearing some 12,000 yards of black cloth, which had been distributed to the official mourners to make their own hoods and suits. Jostling for places in the streets, windows, and gutters were thousands of spectators eager to get a final glimpse of their queen. After ruling for forty-four years—a decade longer than the average life expectancy to someone born in the sixteenth century, and through the reigns of eight popes and four kings of France—Queen Elizabeth was being laid to rest.

Elizabeth's rise to power had been anything but smooth. When she was two years old, her mother, Anne Boleyn, was beheaded on charges of adultery and treason; shortly thereafter, the little princess was declared illegitimate. Kept in relative obscurity for much of her childhood, Elizabeth enjoyed a brief period of familial harmony when her father, Henry VIII, married his sixth—and final—wife, Katherine Parr. Katherine, who shared Elizabeth's youthful zeal for Protestantism, treated her lovingly and helped to ensure her restoration as one of Henry's heirs (she was third in line, after her half siblings, Edward and Mary). But Henry's death in 1547 brought more trauma to the fourteen-year-old girl, who became the victim of overt sexual advances at the hands of her stepmother's new husband, Thomas Seymour, whom Katherine had married with surprising haste only months after becoming a widow. Given that the new king—the ten-year-old Edward VI—had as his "protector" Seymour's older brother, Elizabeth had nowhere to turn.

Things only got worse for her with Edward's untimely death in 1553, leaving Mary—the Catholic daughter of Henry's first wife, Catherine of Aragon—the presumptive heir to the throne. Protestant plots to unseat her led to enormous political unrest in the kingdom, and relations between the two half sisters quickly deteriorated when Mary took the throne. In 1554, she had Elizabeth imprisoned in the Tower of London, after putting down a rebellion to overthrow her rule in which Elizabeth was directly implicated. In the next few years, around three hundred Protestants were burned at the stake. It was a miracle that Elizabeth survived. In 1558, Mary's health, which had always been frail, deteriorated rapidly following a flu epidemic; she died on November 17 at the age of forty-two. Suddenly, the disgraced Elizabeth would be queen. At her coronation on January 15, 1559, the path before her was fraught with perils: there were threats of invasions from Spain, ongoing wars with France and Scotland, a depleted treasury, and few trusted allies in sight. No one would ever have imagined she would rule for as long as she did.

Nearly half a century later, England was in a state of national grief as it prepared to bury its queen. Elizabeth had died on March 24 at the age of sixty-nine, after suffering from what was described as "a settled and unremovable melancholy" and poor physical health. During her final weeks, she leaned up against a pile of cushions and refused to eat or sleep. The actual cause of death was a combination of bronchitis and pneumonia, although some historians think she was poisoned by the toxins in the heavy cosmetics she wore throughout her reign (even on her deathbed, she apparently had an inch of makeup covering her face). She died at Richmond Palace in Surrey, where she and her court often passed the winter. Demolished fifty years later by an act of Parliament during the Civil War, the palace was a Renaissance jewel on the bank of the Thames, built in white stone with octagonal towers whose weathervanes were capped in gold and azure. It looked straight out of a fairy tale. Elizabeth loved Richmond for more practical reasons: it had both excel-

lent hunting grounds—she was a passionate hunter throughout her
life—and unusually good insulation compared to the drafty and
damp conditions of the other royal residences.

In the days before Elizabeth's death, the kingdom had been
in a state of high alert. Thousands of troops poured into London
to keep the peace in the city; ports were closed and the navy on
guard for fear of a foreign invasion. Any transition of power after
a forty-four-year reign was complicated; in this case the circumstances were unusually fraught. Normally the monarch's successor
would long have been known, but the childless queen had kept
her choice shrouded in mystery. She had good reason to do this,
knowing full well that once she named her successor the country's
attention to her would be compromised. The result of her canny
refusal, however, produced great instability in the state. In the final
years of her reign there were no fewer than twelve claimants to the
throne, including the Infanta Isabella, daughter of the Spanish king
Philip II—a possibility that sent waves of panic through the Protestant establishment.

Fully aware of the chaos she was creating but clearly preferring it to the alternative, Elizabeth found herself on her deathbed
without having made a will. It was only on the day before she died
that she finally communicated her wishes, and there are competing
reports of what happened. Either through a short verbal exchange
or with a mere gesture of her hand, she chose as her heir the man
long understood to be her favorite candidate: her cousin James VI
of Scotland. James's mother, the Catholic Mary, Queen of Scots,
was Elizabeth's lifelong enemy and had been executed for treason in
1587 following several decades of involvement in plots to assassinate
the English queen and replace her on the throne. The Protestant
James, who had quietly agreed to his mother's execution with the
lure of a "greater prize" that would await him, now took the throne
as ruler of the newly united Scotland, Ireland, and England.

Early on the morning of March 24, Elizabeth's privy councilors rushed from Richmond to London to announce the news. Surrounded by council lords, bishops, and scores of earls, barons, and
knights—there were some three hundred men in all—the secretary
of state, Sir Robert Cecil, made the official proclamation: the queen
was dead, long live the king. While the councilors were busy reas-

suring London citizens of a smooth transition, Elizabeth's servants
began preparing her corpse. Unlike most of her predecessors, Elizabeth had requested not to be embalmed—a process that, through
the removal of the viscera and stuffing of the cavities with sweet
spices, delayed the corpse's decay during the often lengthy period
between the monarch's death and burial. Instead, Elizabeth's corpse
was wrapped tightly in cerecloth, a special linen soaked in wax, and
then dressed in her formal robes. Before the body was closed off in
a wooden coffin, a death mask was made, preserving her face for
eternity.

Once the preparations of her corpse were finished at Richmond—the procedure took several days—Elizabeth's coffin made
its first public appearance as it journeyed down the Thames on
a barge, accompanied by a group of her gentlewomen and privy
councilors. The trip was made at night, and the banks of the river
flickered with torchlight. Its final destination was Whitehall Palace, where Elizabeth would lie in state until the funeral. The center of royal power since 1530, when Henry VIII appropriated the
already grand residence in Westminster from the fallen Cardinal
Wolsey, Whitehall, with its vast galleries, courtyards, staterooms,
and gardens, was one of the largest palaces in Europe. (In 1689, it
was destroyed by fire, leaving only the splendid Banqueting House
designed by Inigo Jones intact.)

The main approach to Whitehall was by water, with a double-
tiered pier connecting the Thames to the privy stairs of the palace. Once inside, Elizabeth's coffin was placed on a high bed in the
Withdrawing Room, where guests came to pay their final respects.
The room was draped in expensive velvets and satins that covered
the walls, windows, and the bed of state; dark tones of black and
purple were set off by rich gold and yellow. To the astonishment
of at least one of the visitors, the Venetian ambassador Giovanni
Scaramelli, the deceased queen was treated with the same ceremony
she enjoyed while alive. As he wrote in his April 12 dispatch to the
Doge of Venice, it was "as though she were not wrapped in a fold
of cerecloth, and hid in such a heap of lead, of coffin, of pall, but
was walking as she used to do at this season, about the alleys of her
garden." Elizabeth's coffin was waited upon with her full range of
servants and gentlewomen, who kept up their usual rituals: morn-

ing blessings and prayers, the Good Night ceremony each evening at 9 p.m., and so on. In what seemed to Scaramelli an elaborate farce, even Elizabeth's table service was fully maintained.

Keeping up the appearance of living grandeur was a task made more complicated by an unfortunate development: whoever had wrapped Elizabeth's corpse had skimped on the cloth—rumor had it that the man given the job had sold the extra fabric for profit—so that the seals were not airtight. As King Lear said of Gloucester, the queen "smell[ed] of mortality." This only added to the burdens confronting the ladies of the bedchamber who sat with the coffin night and day. These official members of Elizabeth's household were joined by other noblewomen who came to court for the period of mourning and rotated in and out of the privy chamber. According to the 1603 memoir of Anne Clifford, her mother, Margaret, Countess of Cumberland, was "sitting up with [the coffin] two or three nights." Like so many duties at court that seem to our eyes unappealing—the role of "groom of the stool" comes first to mind—it was considered a great honor to watch over the corpse, and the thirteen-year-old Anne complained about being kept out "by reason I was held too young." She spent her days at Whitehall instead in the gardens, where the talk was focused on the new king and queen.

The demanding work of maintaining Elizabeth's corpse finally came to an end on April 28, when the ceremony moved outdoors for the grand finale. The procession began with 260 poor women from London's almshouses, walking in rows of two. The inclusion of the poor in royal funerals was a long-standing English tradition: the wealth and status of the deceased was communicated in part through the number of social inferiors participating in the ceremony. For a king's funeral, there were only men from the charitable houses; for Elizabeth's funeral, the poor mourners were exclusively women.

Following the almswomen, who were typically paid a small fee for their presence, the procession moved through England's social hierarchy, beginning with members of the royal household marching in order of rank. The sheer scale and variety of the servants made visible to the public just how extensive an institution the royal court was—it was a world unto itself.

Almswomen leading the procession at Queen Elizabeth's funeral

There were porters for wheat and wine, children of the scullery and pastry furnace, conductors of the bakehouse, coopers and grooms, purveyors of poultry and wax, the master of spice-bags, cart-takers, apothecaries and surgeons, the chief clerk of the wardrobe, surveyors and supervisors of the dresser, sewers of the hall, sergeants of the woodyard and larder, gentlemen ushers and waiters, the clerk of the green cloth, the clerk of the privy seal, royal chaplains, and secretaries for the Latin and French tongues.

There were also clusters of court musicians, who—according to the detailed drawings of the event that have survived in the form of a long roll—held their instruments down as a sign of mourning. Music was likely played at some point in the procession (members of the children's choir, for example, are shown with open books of music in their hands), but the fact that all of the musicians and singers were at a good distance from the queen's coffin suggests there was a solemn silence surrounding her. This may have been to allow for the sounds of grief to reverberate through the streets: as one eyewitness described it, "there was such a general sighing, groaning, and weeping as the like hath not been seen or known in the memory of man."

Among the musicians was Aemilia Lanyer's husband, Alfonso, who was listed in the royal household's records as having received an allowance for "mourning livery" to wear at the funeral. Along with five of Aemilia's cousins, Augustine, Arthur, Andrea, Edward, and Jeronimo Bassano, the roughly thirty-year-old Alfonso was a member of the court's recorder ensemble. (Now largely demoted to use in children's musical instruction, the recorder was the most popular of all end-blown flutes in the Renaissance.) Aemilia may have had musical talent herself: her father, Baptista Bassano, hailed from a well-known Venetian family of musicians whose gifts seem to have been smoothly transmitted from one generation to the next. But there were no women musicians at court—these jobs were only for men. When Alfonso set off from their home in St. Botolph's parish in Bishopsgate to take his place in the procession, Aemilia and her ten-year-old son Henry would have been left to fend for themselves with the rest of London's citizens.

Following all of the members of the household and closer to Elizabeth's hearse, the status of the mourners steadily rose. Officers of the court and government, including the Lord Chief Justice, the Master of the Revels, and foreign ambassadors and agents, were followed by the Master of the Requests, the Lord Mayor and aldermen of London, and the Master of the Jewel House. This last position was held by Elizabeth Cary's father-in-law, Sir Edward Cary. Elizabeth had been married six months earlier to Sir Henry Cary, an ambitious courtier who would ultimately be "created" (or named) Viscount Falkland and become one of King James's privy councilors. It's not clear whether Elizabeth was herself present, as she was still living with her parents in Oxfordshire at the time, while Henry was in London pursuing his career. But given that the marriage had been arranged precisely to give her wealthy, self-made father, Lawrence Tanfield, access to the nobility, there would have been no better introduction to the splendor of the court than the funeral of the queen.

Immediately preceding the coffin were members of the male aristocracy—viscounts, earls, marquesses, and dukes—as well as church bishops and the archbishop of Canterbury. Mary Sidney's elder son, William Herbert, Earl of Pembroke, held the Great Banner of England, behind which came an open chariot drawn by four gray horses, each draped in black velvet, carrying the main attraction. The queen's coffin was covered in purple velvet, on top of which lay her life-size, eerily realistic effigy. The wax and wood statue wore Elizabeth's crown upon a wig of bright red hair and was dressed in her most formal robes; in the effigy's hands were the royal orb and scepter. Six knights bearing their coats of arms held up a canopy over the chariot, while twelve other knights carried heraldic banners that surrounded the coffin in a sea of vibrant color. For the throngs of onlookers in the streets, it would have been difficult to see anything but the colorful flags.

In the wake of the hearse, the aristocratic mourners abruptly switched from men to women. First came the Swedish-born Helena Snakenborg, Marchioness of Northampton. As the most senior lady of the bedchamber, Lady Helena was given the role of the chief mourner—a position always filled by someone of the same sex as the deceased—after King James's cousin Lady Arbella Stuart turned the honor down. James, who was in charge of making the choice, had approached Arbella as a way of compensating her for Elizabeth's poor treatment. Like James himself, Arbella was a direct descendant of Henry VII's daughter Margaret Tudor; since she was English (and not Scottish) born, many had in fact regarded her as Elizabeth's rightful heir. Many, but not the queen, who had banished Arbella from court late in her reign after she was seen flirting with Elizabeth's favorite, Robert Devereux, Earl of Essex. More worrying than her jealousy over Essex was the queen's concern that Arbella might make a marriage that could threaten Elizabeth's plans for her successor; months before Elizabeth's death, Arbella was discovered plotting a potential match with another possible heir to the throne, Edward Seymour. After receiving James's invitation to be the funeral's leading lady, Arbella apparently responded that since

Noblewomen and maids of honor at the queen's funeral,
wearing their expensive mourning gowns

she had been denied access to the queen during Elizabeth's lifetime, she wouldn't "after her death be brought upon the stage for a public spectacle."

Lady Helena was followed by the fourteen "countess assistants" to the chief mourner, a group of the highest-ranking noblewomen in the country; these included Mary Sidney, who had recently been widowed and hence was now Dowager Countess of Pembroke, and Anne Clifford's mother, Margaret. The rest of the female aristocracy—the remaining countesses and viscountesses, the earls' daughters and baronesses, and finally the maids of honor of the privy chamber—brought up the rear.

The procession ended at Westminster Abbey, where the crowds were left outside as the official mourners filed into the church. Compared to the extraordinary procession outdoors, the church service was surprisingly simple. An organ played a fanfare, the queen's almoner delivered a sermon, and the traditional liturgy for burial was performed. Scaramelli, the Venetian ambassador, didn't attend for fear of angering the pope (such were the dangers of entering a Protestant church), but his source told him "little else was done except the chanting of two psalms in English and the delivery of a funeral oration."

A more conspicuous absence than Scaramelli's was that of England's new king. There's no clear answer as to why James wasn't present at Elizabeth's funeral, but he had certainly received mixed messages. On the one hand, some English councilors had encouraged him to come and took his absence as a sign of disrespect, an impression confirmed by his decision not to wear mourning clothes or to allow others in his court to do so. When the French king Henry IV sent a special envoy to Scotland to congratulate James, he was told on arrival that "no one, whether ambassador, foreigner or English, was admitted . . . in black." On the other hand, the royal household had been so consumed with tending to Elizabeth's corpse that Cecil remarked, "the State could not attend both the performance of that duty to our late sovereign, and of this other of his Majesty's reception."

Meanwhile, around the time of the funeral London was struck with bubonic plague, which ravaged the city in a manner unseen over the previous forty years. Plague was a regular occurrence in

Renaissance England, with outbreaks roughly once a decade throughout Elizabeth's reign, but the 1603 plague was one of the most devastating, killing nearly a quarter of London's population. Under these circumstances there was no way to welcome the new king with the pomp and ceremony he expected, and James, understandably cautious, took his time in making the long journey from Scotland to the English capital. At Westminster Abbey on July 25, four months after Elizabeth's death, he was finally crowned. An era had ended. But a legacy—one that would define English politics and culture for generations—was just beginning.

Mary Sidney, Aemilia Lanyer, Elizabeth Cary, and Anne Clifford: four women who were born during Elizabeth's reign and knew no other ruler. What did Elizabeth's life—or her death—mean to them as women? Over the course of her forty-four years in office, Elizabeth had repeatedly defied the country's expectations for a female monarch. As the seventeenth-century philosopher and statesman Sir Francis Bacon declared, no one could have imagined so fierce a nation "could be swayed and controlled at the beck of a woman." During the reign of Mary I, some outspoken Protestants dared to challenge whether women could ever rule by divine right. In his treatise published shortly before Mary's death entitled *The First Blast of the Trumpet against the Monstruous Regiment of Women,* the Scottish Protestant John Knox argued that a female monarch was both "repugnant to nature" and a violation of God's will. Women, Knox exclaimed, were "weak, frail, impatient, feeble, and foolish, and experience hath declared them to be unconstant, variable, cruel, and lacking the spirit of counsel." Little did he know that within months a queen of his own faith would take over the kingdom, making his words less than opportune. His friend John Calvin quickly jumped in to try to cover up the offense, but the explanation he gave only made matters worse. In a letter to Elizabeth's secretary of state, Sir William Cecil, Calvin affirmed Knox's general position—he even likened women's rule to slavery, calling them two evils God had delivered to punish mankind—but he conceded that there were some women specially endowed with "the singular blessing of God." Elizabeth, in short, was an exception to the rule.

The idea of Elizabeth as an exception did nothing to change the period's general perceptions of women. Far from being held up as a role model, she was merely set apart from the rest of her sex. The queen's own rhetoric affirmed her unique status, framing her gender as something to be overcome. On some occasions, she defined herself as essentially male. "I know I have the body but of a weak and feeble woman," she proclaimed before her troops at Tilbury in 1588, "but I have the heart and stomach of a king." At other times, as in her "Golden Speech" to Parliament in November 1601, she declared that her unusual talents came directly from God: "should I ascribe any of these things unto my self or my sexly weakness, I were not worthy to live."

If Elizabeth's public speeches tended to deny her "sexly weakness," her personal appearance oddly pulled in the opposite direction—she was nothing if not a bundle of contradictions. As confirmed even on her deathbed, she wore an extravagant amount of makeup, covering her skin with the whitest of powders; she dyed her hair and also had a variety of red and blond wigs; she carried herself in a coquettish manner. As she grew older, her love of clothing became ever more of an obsession: by the end of her reign she had over three thousand dresses in the Great Wardrobe at Westminster. After a private audience with the sixty-four-year-old queen at Whitehall in 1597, the French ambassador André Hurault reported that Elizabeth had left her gown open in front so that he could see "the whole of her bosom," which, he noted, was "somewhat wrinkled." Her face, he added, "is and appears to be very aged," while her teeth were "yellow and unequal, with many of them missing." This may have been a tactless account, but to judge from Elizabeth's portraiture, you would never have known of any flaws. In her last painted image, the so-called Procession Picture from 1601, the nearly seventy-year-old queen appears as a much younger woman dressed in virgin white, her rosy cheeks and fair complexion unmarred by the ravages of time.

Even without hearing Elizabeth's misogynistic speeches or seeing her age-defying portraits, sixteenth-century Englishwomen would have been well aware that they shared very little with their queen. Elizabeth occupied neither of the roles that defined most women's lives: those of wife and mother. She was never forced to submit to the will of a husband who had legal rights over her body and property; she never suffered the pains of childbirth or experienced, as so many women had, the death of a beloved son or daughter. Not only did she lack personal experience of marriage and childbirth: she showed very little interest in understanding what the lives of most women in her kingdom were actually like.

In her personal embrace of chastity, Elizabeth routinely opposed the marriages of the women around her. In 1585, one of her favorite gentlewomen in the privy chamber, Frances Howard, wrote to her future husband, Edward Seymour, Earl of Hertford, that the queen spoke to her using "many persuasions . . . against marriage and the inconvenience thereof" and claimed she would herself care for Frances more than he ever could. As a result of responses like this, Elizabeth's women frequently married without consulting her. When they were later found out, the queen's reaction could be violent. Upon discovering, for example, that her second cousin and member of her privy chamber, Mary Shelton, had secretly married Sir John Scudamore in 1574, Elizabeth angrily sent her away from court after breaking Mary's finger with a hairbrush. As late as 1597, the courtier William Fenton declared that "the Queen doth still much exhort all her women to remain in virgin state as much as may be."

Whether Elizabeth actually made an affirmative decision never to marry remains a mystery. On the one hand, in her first speech before Parliament in February 1559, she announced that she was "already bound unto a husband, which is the kingdom of England," and held out her hand to show her inauguration ring. "Reproach me so no more that I have no children," she declared, "for every one of you, and as many as are English, are my children." The twenty-five-year-old queen concluded the speech by conjuring up her epitaph: "when I have expired my last breath, this may be inscribed upon my tomb:

'Here lies interred Elizabeth
A virgin pure until her death.'"

On the other hand, in response to a petition from Parliament in 1563 urging her to take a husband—one of multiple petitions of this kind issued between 1559 and 1576—she remarked: "If any think I never meant to trade that [single] life, they be deceived." At stake in these discussions was nothing less than the future of the kingdom. Without children of her own, Elizabeth's rule was destined to be haunted by the question of succession, creating no end of anxiety and paranoia among the English people, who were wary of a foreign king.

During the first decades of her reign, Elizabeth dangled the possibility of marriage before both the nation and a string of suitors. The first serious contender was Mary Sidney's uncle Sir Robert Dudley, widely considered the queen's favorite courtier, whom she created Earl of Leicester in 1564. When Elizabeth came to the throne it was widely rumored the two were lovers: Robert lived at court in a suite of rooms suspiciously close to the queen's and was never far from her side. After his wife died in 1560, having apparently fallen down a flight of stairs—following a lengthy investigation, the coroner ultimately deemed it a "death by misadventure"—he began an active suit to marry Elizabeth that lasted well into the 1570s.

In the meantime, a series of Catholic princes from the Continent came and went. Among the serious contenders were Charles II, Archduke of Austria; Henry, Duke of Anjou (later Henry III of France); and Henry's younger brother, Francis, Duke of Alençon and Anjou. Francis came the closest to winning Elizabeth's hand, despite their significant age difference: when he came to England in the winter of 1579, he was twenty-one and she was forty-five. By all accounts Elizabeth was very fond of Francis—she affectionately called him "my frog"—and even at one point agreed to a formal engagement before calling it off the next morning. This was a huge relief to the more fiercely Protestant members of the Privy Council, who under no circumstances wanted to see a Catholic match. After Francis's departure from England in 1582, the prospect of the queen's ever marrying came to a definitive end. This didn't stop her from engaging in lengthy flirtations with younger courtiers—most spectacularly Sir Walter Raleigh and Essex—through her final years. But the role Elizabeth chose to play above all had already been anticipated in her 1559 address to Parliament. She wanted to be known as the Virgin Queen.

Elizabeth was both a woman and more than a woman, or no woman at all. Rejecting identities of wife and mother, she embraced those of military leader and religious icon, roles out of reach for all but her. Indeed, she showed no interest in constructing an image of herself that was either relatable or aspirational to Englishwomen. She may have broken through the glass ceiling, but she didn't care whether others followed suit.

There was one way, however, in which the queen provided a strong positive example for women like Mary Sidney, Aemilia Lanyer, Elizabeth Cary, and Anne Clifford. This was in her role as a writer. From early in her childhood, Elizabeth had been encouraged not only to study a wide range of languages but also to write things of her own. Her personal tutor, the celebrated Cambridge teacher of Greek and Latin Roger Ascham, taught his young pupil to master her linguistic skills by doing "double translations": Elizabeth would first translate a passage from Greek or Latin into English and then translate it back into the original tongue. By comparing her two compositions, she honed her skills in both languages. The results of these and other exercises, Ascham claimed in his 1570 best-selling book, *The Schoolmaster,* were nothing short of extraordinary. There were "few in number in both the universities [Cambridge and Oxford] or elsewhere in England," Ascham boasted, "that be in both tongues comparable with Her Majesty." "It is your shame (I speak to you all, you young gentlemen of England)," he declared, "that one maid should go beyond you all in excellency of learning and knowledge."

As a young girl, Elizabeth put her intellectual talents to good use within the royal household. For the traditional exchange of gifts with her family members at New Year's, she took to preparing translations of learned texts. For her father, Henry VIII, she translated her stepmother Katherine Parr's book of English prayers into three different languages: French, Latin, and Italian. To her brother, the future Edward VI, she gave a translation into both Latin and English of an Italian sermon by the Protestant reformer Bernardino Ochino. For Katherine, whose own education and passion for Protestantism made her a crucial role model, Elizabeth prepared two very special gifts. The first was a prose translation of a spiritual poem written in French by Katherine's fellow Protestant queen, Marguerite of Navarre. This beautiful little book, which Elizabeth wrote out in her own perfect Italic hand, and whose cover she personally embroidered, is one of the treasures of the Bodleian Library at Oxford. It's hard to imagine a comparable example of three powerful Renaissance women—two queens and a princess who would herself become a queen—connected through a single object. In her dedicatory letter to her stepmother, the eleven-year-old Elizabeth remarked that the mind risks becoming dull if it isn't "always occupied upon some manner of study."

As proof of Elizabeth's commitment to maintaining her mind, the following year she gave Katherine another impressive translation from French: the long first chapter of Calvin's *Institutes* (roughly seventy pages in its modern edition). In the three-page dedicatory letter accompanying this gift—written in perfect French—she declared that of "all the arts and sciences, the invention of letters seems to me the most intellectual and spiritual, excellent and ingenious." Elizabeth didn't simply have a talent for writing: she worshipped at its altar.

As queen, Elizabeth made no effort to hide her intellectual interests from her subjects. Following in the footsteps of Katherine, whose 1547 devotional work, *The Lamentation of a Sinner,* was the first book bearing a woman's name to be published in England, Elizabeth published a book of prayers entitled *Precationes privatae* in 1563. The first part of the book consisted of Latin prayers she had written to express her gratitude for two major events in her life: her recovery from smallpox in 1562, and her safe delivery from prison in 1555 after her sister Mary had suspected her of treason. She also included a prayer thanking God in the frankest of terms for her birth as a royal woman. "Thou hast willed me," she wrote, "to be not some wretched girl from the meanest rank of the common people who would pass her life miserably in poverty and squalor, but to a kingdom."

Such a sentiment certainly wouldn't have endeared Elizabeth to the poor women in her kingdom, but she could safely assume that few of them would be able to read at all, let alone in Latin. It's very hard to calculate literacy rates for this period, as many people knew how to read but not how to write, and yet estimates are typically based on whether someone could sign his or her name. But historians believe around thirty percent of Englishmen were literate, with the figure dropping to ten percent for women living in London, and lower for women outside of the metropolis.

The second part of Elizabeth's 1563 book consisted of 259 *"Sententiae"*—pithy sayings from scripture, classical authors, and Christian writers—which Elizabeth had translated from Latin to English. In entries entitled "On Justice," "On Mercy," and "Of Counsel," she displayed her extensive learning on good government; in paired sections "Of Peace" and "Of War," she showed her pragmatism as a military leader, despite belonging to the "unwarlike sex." Under the guise of scholarly translations, Elizabeth was establishing her credentials to rule.

What was already visible in this early publication became more pronounced in Elizabeth's later works: namely, her use of writing as a powerful tool to respond to the challenges she faced. In 1593, when her most important Protestant ally in Europe, the French king Henry IV, decided to convert to Catholicism (this was the occasion for his famous utterance, "Paris is worth a mass"), Elizabeth comforted herself by translating Boethius's *Consolation of Philosophy,* a medieval Latin dialogue that argued against the pursuit of worldly fortunes in favor of trusting in God. Five years later, she turned to an essay by Plutarch known by its Latin name, *"De curiositate,"* a study of how spying, rumormongering, and slandering might affect social and political harmony.

These were themes close to Elizabeth's heart throughout her reign, but they were especially relevant in 1598 following the death of Sir William Cecil, who had been Elizabeth's principal adviser since she came to the throne. In the power struggle that ensued between Cecil's son Robert, who took over as secretary of state, and Elizabeth's volatile favorite, Essex, both parties set up their own spy networks for gathering intelligence. In addition to finding whatever solace she could from the ancient Greek philosopher (whom she read in a Latin translation by Erasmus—her Greek was presumably rusty), she gave herself an extra challenge, converting Plutarch's essay from prose into verse. The choice in part reflected Elizabeth's childhood training. In *The Schoolmaster* Ascham described making his young pupil transform texts from one genre—as well as one language—to another. It also reflected another side of her intellectual life: her love of writing poems.

It's impossible to know how often Elizabeth wrote poetry to work through crises in her life, but several powerful examples have survived. First, when Mary put her under house arrest at Wood-stock in 1554 after her release from the Tower of London, Elizabeth wasn't allowed either to receive visitors or to have pen, paper, or ink. She responded to this hardship by scribbling a poem on the window frame in her chamber with a piece of charcoal. "O Fortune," the poem begins, "thy wresting, wavering state / Hath fraught with cares my troubled wit." This poignant confession of her suffering gives way to Elizabeth's desire to be avenged: the ten-line poem concludes with her prayer that God would "grant to my foes as they have thought," an enigmatic way of wishing they might reap what they have sown. In the same room, on the glass of a window, Elizabeth used a diamond to inscribe this terse, defiant couplet: "Much suspected by me / Nothing proved can be," under which she carved her name, "Elizabeth the prisoner."

In the aftermath of Mary, Queen of Scots' escape into England in 1568 and the 1570 defeat of a rebellion of powerful Catholic earls supporting her, Elizabeth turned to poetry again. In her poem known by the first half of its opening line, "The Doubt of Future Foes," Elizabeth warns her enemies that their plots would be discovered and their traitorous heads chopped off (a threat that ultimately came to fruition, at least for Mary):

> *Their dazzled eyes with pride,*
> *Which great ambition blinds,*
> *Shall be unsealed by worthy wights*
> *Whose foresight falsehood finds . . .*
> *My rusty sword through rest*
> *Shall first his edge employ*
> *To pull their tops who seek such change*
> *Or gape for future joy.*

After circulating widely in manuscript copies—ten different copies from the period have survived—Elizabeth's poem was published in 1589 in George Puttenham's *Arte of English Poesie,* a handbook of literary terms and technique that became indispensable reading for aspiring poets. In an obviously absurd compliment—this was the era of Spenser, Marlowe, and Shakespeare—Puttenham named the queen "the most excellent poet" alive, whose "learned, delicate, noble muse" surpassed everything that has been written "before her time or since." Perhaps not, but what couldn't be doubted was how much writing poems meant to the queen in times of strife.

Elizabeth didn't write only political poems: she also used verse to express her struggles with love. "I grieve and dare not show my discontent," one such poem begins, written after the departure of her favorite foreign suitor, Francis: "I love and yet am forced to seem to hate." Nowhere else did she reveal so plainly the sadness she felt at the failure of her marriage negotiations or admit how much she hid beneath her steely surface. "Some gentle passion slide into my mind," she implores later in the poem, "For I am soft, and made of melting snow." On another occasion, Elizabeth put into verse her sorrow over losing suitors as she grew older and her regret that she had sent them all away: "For I did sore repent that I had said before, / 'Go, go, seek some otherwhere; importune me no more.'"

A final poem from late in Elizabeth's life suggests her desire to withdraw from all of the "vain pleasures" that had brought her nothing but pain:

> Now leave and let me rest, Dame Pleasure, be content.
> Go choose among the best; my doting days be spent.

None of these accounts of herself would have been familiar to those around her, who saw an invulnerable monarch who neither accepted her age nor desisted in her flirtations. Elizabeth kept nearly all these poems very private: unlike "The Doubt of Future Foes," they weren't printed in her lifetime, and they appeared in only a handful of manuscripts, suggesting she shared them with a very small number of people, if at all. It's possible there are more poems about her love affairs that have been lost in the archives. But from the few she left behind, we hear a different voice from this strong queen: the voice of an anguished woman.

On May 15, 1603, James gave the order for Elizabeth's coffin to be buried following several weeks of its display in Westminster Abbey; her effigy was removed from view a week or so later. Nearly half a century after her coronation, the queen had finally exited the London stage. With her death, Englishwomen were stripped of a complicated role model whose accomplishments went far beyond anything they were taught to imagine as possible. There's no way to know what impact Elizabeth's writing may have had on ambitious and well-educated women like Mary, Aemilia, Elizabeth, and Anne, or how much of her writing they knew; all four of them, as we'll see, had interactions of one kind or another with the queen. However much or little of Elizabeth's writing they may have read, the queen set a precedent for using her pen both to connect to the world outside her and to express her innermost fears and desires, something that all four women at the heart of this book would also do. To have been born into a country with a queen of great intellectual ability was to have seen from earliest girlhood the potential of a woman's mind. Elizabeth's death was a loss, but it was also an opportunity.

CHAPTER TWO

October 27, 1561

Tickenhill Palace, Worcestershire

Mary Sidney

In the fall of 1561, while Sir Robert Dudley was in hot pursuit of the new young queen, his sister Lady Mary Sidney temporarily left her post as one of Elizabeth's gentlewomen to give birth to her fourth child. Her daughter Mary Sidney was born on October 27 at Tickenhill Palace in the area between Wales and England known as the Welsh Marches. Wedged between rugged mountains and gentle river valleys, this was a wild landscape made up of moors, woodlands, and farms; the villages were filled with half-timbered houses, the borders lined with castles. Tickenhill sat above the bustling market town of Bewdley on several acres of land adjoining a wooded park that, by the end of the sixteenth century, had more than 3,000 oak trees and 150 red deer. This was about as far from the queen's privy chamber as Lady Sidney could be.

For Lady Sidney's husband, Sir Henry Sidney, the palace was a rural retreat from his administrative base at Ludlow some fifteen miles away. Elizabeth had named Henry president of the Council of Wales and the Marches in 1560—a major position that made him her deputized ruler in the region—and his work involved frequent travel between his various seats. Lady Sidney was herself away much of the time fulfilling her duties for the queen (the couple had the Renaissance equivalent of a commuter marriage). Her position at court was both unpaid and demanding: the gentlewomen of the

privy chamber were Elizabeth's constant companions, helping her
to dress and apply her cosmetics, sitting with her during her meals
and evening entertainments, and even taking turns sleeping at her
side (the unmarried queen never slept alone). When Elizabeth
and her thousand or so household members moved from palace
to palace every few months—the court changed residence more or
less seasonally—Lady Sidney was expected to accompany her. The
queen resented her women leaving her side for anything but the
most urgent business, a status she grudgingly granted to childbirth.

The younger Mary Sidney's birth was inscribed in the family's
unofficial book of records: a fifteenth-century Psalter nearly two feet
in length in which important dates were jotted in the margins next
to the appropriate month in the calendar for reading the Psalms.
There were no birth certificates at the time—these were introduced
in England only in the nineteenth century—so the exact birthdates
for most people in the period are unknown; the best estimates are
church records for baptism. Mary had two older siblings: Philip,
born in 1554, and Elizabeth, born in 1560; another sister, Margaret,
had died before her second birthday in 1558. It's hard to fathom how
Mary dealt with the death of Elizabeth in 1567; the two girls were a
year apart and would have been constant companions. By that time,
two more siblings had arrived: Robert in 1563 and Ambrosia a year
or two later (her birthdate is not recorded). The family's last child,
Thomas, was born in 1569.

It's surprising how many children Sir Henry and Lady Sidney
managed to have, given the challenges they faced. Not only did
they often live apart, but Henry also claimed to have lost all physical interest in his wife after her bout with smallpox, an illness that
in his eyes stripped her of her beauty. In October 1562, Lady Sidney
had been recalled from Wales to nurse the queen, who was ill with
the highly contagious disease. In later centuries, smallpox would
be responsible for the death of millions of people: records suggest
that in the 1700s it killed between six and ten percent of London's
population. In the mid-sixteenth century, the disease had not yet
developed its virulent strain and was rarely fatal; the primary concern was to keep victims from being disfigured. Smallpox typically
began with a rash that spread all over the body, transforming itself
into bumps and then pustules that ultimately turned into scabs;

when the scabs fell off, they left the pockmarks that gave the disease its name. Given how quickly the disease could spread—scientists now understand it traveled through air droplets as well as through contact with the patient's rash, bodily fluids, or clothing—nursing someone with smallpox was more or less a guarantee of infection.

However much Lady Sidney may have wanted to refuse the invitation to attend the queen on her sickbed, she had no choice but to comply. There was no Renaissance equivalent of maternity leave, and her infant daughter was in the care of a wet nurse (almost no women of the upper classes nursed their own children). Thus, shortly before Mary's first birthday, Lady Sidney returned to the queen. Working alongside the royal physicians, who used the Japanese "red treatment" that had become popular in Europe beginning in the twelfth century, she helped wrap Elizabeth in a scarlet blanket thought to heal the rash and laid her on a mattress before a burning fire. After a little more than a week, Elizabeth recovered with only minor scarring, but Lady Sidney was much less fortunate. As Henry recounted with chilling frankness in a letter twenty years later: "When I went to Newhaven [in 1562] I left her a full fair lady in mine eye at least the fairest, and when I returned, I found her as foul a lady as the smallpox could make her, which she did take by continual attendance of her majesty's most precious person."

Henry's bitterness toward "her majesty's most precious person" wasn't due only to her having ruined his wife's complexion: he also felt the queen was burdening him with too many responsibilities, for too little pay. In 1565, in addition to his demanding post in Wales and the Marches, Elizabeth named him lord deputy of Ireland. The English had been officially ruling the Irish since the Anglo-Norman invasion of Ireland in the twelfth century, but they had never conquered the powerful Irish chieftains who controlled the local clans. Tensions between the two parties worsened dramatically in the mid-sixteenth century when the English tried to enforce their new state religion of Protestantism on their fiercely Catholic subjects. As Henry soon discovered, being lord deputy of Ireland was the political equivalent of nursing the queen with smallpox: it was a prestigious but utterly thankless job. Adding insult to injury, he was personally forced to pay the enormous expense of shuttling the entire Sidney household between Dublin and Wales.

Given the demands of her parents' day jobs, Mary was raised largely at the hands of servants. When they weren't on the move, the Sidney children spent much of their time at Ludlow Castle. Perched on a steep rock face over the River Teme, the fortress dated back to the time of the Normans, who used the strong defensive location and formidable curtain walls to fight off their fierce Welsh enemies. For Mary and her siblings, the castle was the stuff of medieval romance. They could climb the treacherously narrow staircase to the top of the thirteenth-century tower or run through the imposing gateway across the castle moat to the grassy field of the outer bailey; they could sit and read on the stone seats lining the windows of the North Range or say their prayers in the freestanding Chapel of Saint Mary Magdalene, whose unusual round nave dated back to the eleventh century. It's impossible to know just how such an evocative place may have shaped the young girl's imagination, but its ruins today have a haunting beauty.

Mary's other childhood home was the palace that Henry had inherited outright from his father (and that wasn't connected to his post as lord deputy): the magnificent Penshurst Place in Kent. Built in local sandstone in the mid-fourteenth century and fully fortified some fifty years later, the estate was given to Mary's grandfather as a gift from Edward VI in 1552; it has remained in the Sidney family ever since. If Ludlow is the stuff of feudal romance, Penshurst epitomizes Renaissance civility. The elegant manor house and grounds sit on a level plain in the Medway valley thirty miles southeast of London, with open views to the south and west and woodland to the north. Thanks to renovations undertaken by Mary's father, it has one of the earliest classical loggias in England as well as a spectacular Italian parterre designed to be viewed from the home's formal staterooms. Ben Jonson, who wrote a poem about the house ("To Penshurst") in the early seventeenth century, when it belonged to Mary's brother Robert, Earl of Leicester, famously praised it for its grandeur without ostentation. "Thou art not, Penshurst, built to envious show," Jonson begins, "but stand'st an ancient pile."

When Mary was three, her ten-year-old brother, Philip, left Ludlow for the nearby Shrewsbury School, across the road from Henry's administrative seat at Shrewsbury Castle, an impressive timber fortress built at the time of the Saxon settlement. Centuries later, Shrewsbury School would welcome the young Charles Darwin, who was born in the town. After four years at Shrewsbury, Philip began his studies at Christ Church, Oxford. There were no comparable milestones for Mary: her education took place entirely at home. Not only were girls barred from higher education at the universities, but they were also kept out of nearly all primary schools. There were a few exceptions: the Banbury Grammar School in Oxfordshire, for example, ruled in 1594 that girls above the age of nine (or at whatever age they could read English) were not to be admitted, which meant very young or illiterate girls would have been allowed to attend. But instruction beyond basic literacy—and especially any learning of Latin—was out of the question.

Given these restrictions, whether a girl received any kind of education in Renaissance England depended entirely on her family circumstances. In this respect—as in so many—Mary was lucky in her birth. First and foremost, she came from a line of well-educated women. Her maternal grandmother, Jane Dudley, Duchess of Northumberland, was known at the court of Henry VIII for her impressive mastery of foreign languages and her passion for Protestant reform. Later in life, the duchess developed interests in the natural sciences and even commissioned two treatises from the celebrated mathematician and astronomer John Dee: one on the origins of heavenly bodies, and another on the subject of "floods & ebbs." Lady Dudley had eleven sons and two daughters, but she made sure the girls weren't left behind their brothers: Lady Sidney and her sister Katherine, the future Countess of Huntingdon, were taught French, Italian, and possibly Latin; they were also trained to be good Protestants and knew the Bible well.

This impressive intellectual pedigree laid the groundwork for Mary's own learning. The best-known book for female education in the period, the Spanish humanist Juan Vives's *Instruction for Christian Women,* proclaimed that it was up to mothers to teach their daughters not only "the skills proper to their sex: how to work wool and flax, to spin, to weave, to sew," but also the art of letters. "A pious mother," Vives wrote, "will not think it a burden to consecrate some moments of leisure to literature or to the reading of wise and holy books." Vives's book was commissioned in 1523 by Henry VIII's first wife, Catherine of Aragon, who employed Vives as a tutor for the young Princess Mary; he was operating under the assumption that upper-class women had little to do outside of tending to their children. In Mary Sidney's case, it's not clear how large a role her mother could have played in teaching her to read and write, given Lady Sidney's obligations to the queen. But even if she was frequently away, she saw to it that her daughters received a first-rate education at home. Family account books confirm that private tutors were hired for the girls as well as for the boys: payments were made to "Mr. Lodwicke," referred to as Ambrosia's "schoolmaster" but likely also Mary's; to Thomas Thornton, a tutor with unspecified duties; to "Mistress Maria, the Italian"; and to Jean Tassel, the children's tutor in French.

There's no way to know exactly what subjects Mary was taught, but a book published in 1605 to teach French to English "ladies and gentlewomen," Pierre Erondelle's *The French Garden,* described what a typical day in the Sidney household may have been like. Erondelle conjured up a conversation between a wealthy mother and her daughters. "At what hours do your Masters come?" the mother asks, to which her daughter Charlotte responds: "Our dancing Master cometh about nine a clock, our singing Master, and he that teacheth us to play on the virginals, at ten; he that teacheth us on the Lute and the Viol de Gamba, at four a clock in the afternoon; and our French Master cometh commonly between seven and eight a clock in the morning." From seven in the morning until eleven, and then beginning again at four in the afternoon, the girls were busy learning the skills that would be expected of them as members of the English aristocracy.

What's conspicuously missing from Erondelle's list of the girls' lessons is what would be regarded today as academic instruction—apart from the hour of French, there was no reading or writing involved. The girls' brothers, by contrast, whom Erondelle refers to as "scholars," spent their time "well employed as to their books." This is how it went: unless you were a royal princess being groomed potentially to rule the kingdom, girls generally learned to dance and speak French while boys studied Latin and philosophy. From the records that have survived, the Sidney children seem to have followed a similar program. Even before Philip left for Shrewsbury, the family physician, Thomas Moffett, recorded that the young boy was provided with tutors "in languages, veneration of God, literature, public affairs and virtuous action"; no such curriculum is mentioned anywhere for Mary or Ambrosia. It's hard not to imagine that Mary read alongside her brothers—especially Robert, for whom "great books" were purchased during the exact years she was being tutored at home. The best evidence for what she ultimately learned, however, lies in the writing she did as an adult. There, her obvious mastery of literature and theology went far beyond what the girls in Erondelle's treatise were ever taught.

In the spring of 1575, Mary's life took a dramatic turn. The year began tragically: following a serious illness that also afflicted Lady Sidney, Ambrosia died in Ludlow at the age of ten. This was the second sister Mary had lost in her short thirteen years, and once again there's no way to know how she managed her grief. The news of Ambrosia's death traveled quickly to the queen, who sent an unusually heartfelt condolence letter to Sir Henry:

> Yet for as much as we conceive the grief you yet feel thereby (as in such cases natural parents are accustomed) we would not have you ignorant (to ease your sorrow as much as may be) how we take part of your grief upon us.

She then made what she hoped would be a welcome proposal. "God hath yet left you," she reminded Sir Henry,

> the comfort of one daughter of very good hope, whom if you shall think [it] good to remove [her] from those parts of unpleasant air (if it be so) into better in these parts, & will send her unto us before Easter, or when you shall think good, assure yourself that we will have a special care of her.

Mary was to become one of Elizabeth's maids of honor.

To be a royal maid of honor was the most prestigious position a girl could have in Renaissance England. However aristocratic the family, there was nothing like sending your daughter off to live with the queen—this was the ultimate finishing school. The maids, who were typically around fifteen or sixteen when they arrived at court and by definition unmarried, didn't have the finest room and board:

they slept in a crowded dormitory known as the Coffer Chamber where they shared narrow beds, and they ate second-class food (often leftovers) at a long communal table set apart from the queen and her gentlewomen. They were also kept on a short leash by the "Mother of Maids," one of the queen's ladies appointed to make sure they kept quiet at night—apparently they often made a racket—and more important stayed out of trouble, a job usually performed with middling success. Besides carrying Elizabeth's train, waiting on her at table, fetching miscellaneous things at her every whim, and keeping her entertained with music or dance, the girls spent much of their time simply being seen by the dashing courtiers coming in and out of the palace. Some of these men were officially in search of brides; many others were seeking less permanent arrangements. The inevitable affairs that took place were ignored unless the maid got pregnant, which happened quite frequently and led to strong recriminations of all parties. With luck a marriage might be arranged, but whatever the outcome the maid—no longer a maid—was forced to give up her position at court. Not surprisingly, the maids of honor had the highest turnover of anyone in the queen's privy chamber.

Whatever the risks involved, the opportunity for Mary to exchange the Welsh Marches—in Elizabeth's words, "those parts of unpleasant air"—for life at court seems to have come as a pleasant surprise to her parents. In recent years, their relationship to the queen had been under even more strain than before. First, the expenses Henry incurred in Wales and Ireland were growing all the time. In addition to paying for the costly moves back and forth, the castles he lived in desperately needed repairs, and he found himself deeply in debt. When he appealed to Elizabeth for help, she blamed him for spending more money than she had ever anticipated and refused to increase his salary. Things were so bleak that when the queen offered Henry a peerage in 1572—she wanted to give him a barony, the lowest of the aristocratic titles but certainly a step up from his status as a gentleman—he didn't have enough money to pay the accompanying expenses. Not only were there fees for the creation of the title itself and gratuities (more or less bribes) to reward the supporters, but the newly made peer was also expected to pay for elaborate celebrations to mark the promotion; Sir William Cavendish's creation as baron in 1604, for example, cost him close to £3,000 (roughly equivalent to £400,000 today). Swallowing her pride, Lady Sidney wrote to the queen's Master of the Rolls, Sir William Cordell, to explain the dilemma. Describing herself as "a poor, perplexed woman (to see her husband this hardly dealt with)," she suggested that an increase in Henry's stipend would allow him to accept the honor. Nothing came of her request, and Henry was forced to turn the barony down. He remained a mere "Sir" for the rest of his life.

Lady Sidney, for her part, could barely afford her expenses at court. Though to modern ears her position as one of the elite women inside the queen's privy chamber would seem to guarantee at the very least a comfortable standard of living, this shockingly wasn't the case. In 1573, she was reduced to borrowing £10 from her steward John Cockram to pay for gloves, hats, and some medical bills. "I am already very near moneyless," she wrote to Cockram, whom she addressed as her "loving servant," imploring him to send whatever he could "this night though you strain your uttermost credit." Shortly thereafter, Lady Sidney fell ill and left court to recover; upon her return in early 1574 at Elizabeth's order, she discovered that the well-insulated rooms she had long occupied had been given to someone else. "Her Majesty hath commanded me to come to the court," she complained to her brother-in-law Thomas Radcliffe, Earl of Sussex and the queen's lord chamberlain, "and my chamber is very cold and my own hangings very scant and nothing warm." (With no central heating, rooms were kept warm by a combination of fire and heavy cloths hung on the walls.) She asked Sussex for "three or four lined pieces of hangings," a request he cruelly refused. Whatever loyalty he may have felt to the Sidney family—his wife was Henry's sister—was trumped by his strong opposition to Lady Sidney's brother Robert Dudley, who had been created Earl of Leicester in 1564 and had become Sussex's enemy at court.

In a further effort to sabotage Lady Sidney's position, Sussex accused her of having stolen several items from the queen's private wardrobe. Lady Sidney had in fact borrowed some things in 1569 before the birth of her youngest child, Thomas, who, according to the Sidney family Psalter, was born near London; as she explained, she "had no stuff of my own nearer than Wales or Ireland." She claimed to have promptly returned the items with a servant, who must have taken them for himself. There were no consequences to this particular accusation, but Lady Sidney's reception at court was far from what it had been a decade or so earlier. Indeed, ever since she had nursed the queen back to health from smallpox, she'd been treated with palpable coolness. Who knows if Elizabeth allowed herself to feel guilty about Lady Sidney's physical marring, but perhaps the last thing the queen wanted was a reminder of her own battle with the disease.

Given all of these circumstances, Elizabeth's invitation to bring the Sidneys' daughter to court may have seemed to them like a peace offering. Whatever ambivalence Lady Sidney felt about life in the queen's privy chamber, she understood what an enormous opportunity it was for Mary to be included among the maids of honor. She also knew that, unlike her own lifetime appointment, Mary's post would by definition be temporary, ending ideally with her marriage.

Sometime in the spring of 1575, Mary set out from Ludlow to London. The journey of roughly 150 miles would have taken between three and five days, depending on how frequently the horses were changed and how many stops were made. There's no record of whom Mary traveled with—presumably at least a handful of servants—or the route she took, but there was an extensive network of old Roman roads between Wales and the capital. Based on the maps that have survived, the itinerary may have passed through Hereford, Gloucester, Woodstock, and Oxford, with overnights wherever the family had friends or relations (an aristocratic girl like Mary would never have slept in an inn).

When Mary got to London, she may well have felt like something of a country bumpkin. There's no record of her having been at court before this, and neither the rustic castle at Ludlow with its Norman walls nor the quiet splendor of Penshurst was a match for the glamor of Elizabeth's palaces. Depending on exactly when Mary arrived, she may have joined the court at the well-insulated Richmond Palace, which Elizabeth preferred in the winter months, or at Whitehall for Easter, or at any of the other royal residences. Both for purposes of sanitation—each castle had to be regularly cleaned and aired out—and to suit the queen's mood, the court regularly moved from castle to castle. Assuming Mary was settled at court by May, she may have been aware of the queen's visits to her friend

Catherine Talbot, Countess of Pembroke, who lay on her deathbed at her London residence of Baynard's Castle. Of course, she could hardly have imagined how much her own future would be tied up with this particular story, as we'll see.

Whatever Mary's first impressions of life at court during the spring of 1575 may have been, she received a full education in royal politics and spectacle that summer when she joined the queen on what turned out to be one of the most memorable royal "progresses" of Elizabeth's reign. During the unpleasant and hot months, health conditions in London tended to deteriorate rapidly. Although bubonic plague often made a first appearance in the winter, it was slow to develop until temperatures rose in June or July, when it would spread like wildfire through the city. Smallpox was also rife in densely populated areas, and the throngs of servants, lords, and ladies bustling through the royal palaces were by no means immune. So Elizabeth was naturally eager to get out. The progresses also allowed her to visit England's rural population, who lined up to see her as she made her way through the towns and villages dotting the countryside. The queen didn't travel light: she was accompanied by hundreds of staff as well as advisers and courtiers. In modern terms, it was as if the royal household went on tour. The highest-ranking members of the court typically resided in the main house of their hosts while the servants slept in tents on the property or in nearby inns and private homes. The success of the progress depended entirely upon the hospitality of Elizabeth's wealthy subjects, who were forced to provide for the queen and her enormous entourage in the grandest style they could afford.

Detailed records of the planning for Elizabeth's proposed visit in 1594 to the home of the Lord Keeper of the Great Seal, Sir John Puckering—a visit that in the end never took place—give some idea of the preparations involved. In a document entitled "Memorial of things to be considered of, if her Majesty should come to my Lord's house," Puckering's steward spelled out the decisions and tasks that lay before him:

1. The manner of receiving [the queen] both without the house and within, as well by my Lord as by my Lady.
2. What present shall be given by my Lord [to the

queen], when and by whom it shall be presented, and whether any more than one.

3. The like for my Lady.

4. What presents my Lord shall bestow on the Ladies of the Privy Chamber or Bed-chamber, the Grooms of the Privy Chamber, and Gentlemen Ushers and other officers, Clerks of the Kitchen, or otherwise.

5. What rewards shall be given to the Footmen, Guards, and other officers.

6. The purveyed diet for the Queen, wherein are to be used her own cooks.

7. The diet for the Lords and Ladies, and some fit place for that purpose specially appointed.

8. The allowance for diet for the Footmen and Guards.

9. The proportion of the diet, fitted to each place of service: plate, linen, and silver vessels.

10. To furnish how there will be upon a sodden [boiled] provision of all things for that diet made, and of the best kinds.

11. As it must be meats, so in like sort for bread, ale, and wines of all sorts.

12. Great care to be had, and conference with the gentlemen ushers, how her majesty would be lodged for her best ease and liking, far from heat or noise of any office near her lodging.

13. The sweetening of the house in all places by any means.

This impressive to-do list didn't even touch upon the question of keeping Elizabeth entertained during her stay. It's no wonder that many noblemen actually fled abroad the minute a progress was announced in their county to avoid the economic disaster that even a brief stop at their home would inevitably bring. A visit from the queen was the most expensive compliment a courtier could ever receive.

During the summer of 1575, the queen traveled northwest from London to Warwickshire, where her destination was Mary's uncle Leicester's home at Kenilworth Castle. Elizabeth had given him the

castle in 1563, exactly a decade after it passed in and out of possession of his father, John Dudley, Duke of Northumberland. One of
the most powerful men in England under Edward VI—and one of
the most unscrupulous—the staunchly Protestant Northumberland
had plotted his way to become the protector of the realm while
Edward was still too young to govern; he then convinced the sickly
Edward to name the piously Protestant Lady Jane Grey his heir in
place of Edward's half sister, the ardently Catholic Mary. To confirm
his control of the future kingdom, Northumberland hastily married
his oldest son, Guildford, to Lady Jane.

Following King Edward's death in 1554, Northumberland's
scheme worked for around a week before Jane was removed from
the throne—she's known to history as the "Nine Days' Queen"—
and heads began to roll. Northumberland, Guildford, and Lady
Jane were all executed, and Leicester and his other brothers were
put in the Tower of London. Kenilworth, meanwhile, was seized
by the Crown. Elizabeth's return of the splendid estate to Leicester was thus a symbolically loaded gift—a quiet redemption of his
father's dramatic fall—and Leicester dedicated enormous amounts
of time and capital to making it one of the most impressive (or, in
the eyes of many contemporaries, the most pompous) residences in
the kingdom.

Leicester's not-so-secret agenda in renovating Kenilworth was to
create both a luxurious haven for the queen and a place to propose
marriage to her. Following a visit in 1568, when Elizabeth deemed
her accommodations unsatisfactory, he even built a new lodging
designed specifically for her comfort. After fifteen years of wooing
Elizabeth, the 1575 progress would be his last sustained attempt to
win her hand; the nearly three-week-long visit, estimated to have
cost up to £1,000 a day, could be regarded as an extravagant marriage proposal. In fact, Leicester may have already given up any real
hope of marrying Elizabeth but wanted to display in the grandest style possible his uncompromised devotion to her. The previous
year he had fathered a son with Lady Douglas Sheffield, and he was
also widely rumored to be involved with Elizabeth's former gentlewoman of the privy chamber, Lettice Knollys, Countess of Essex,
whom he would marry in 1578, much to the queen's distress. Leicester was hedging his bets.

There's really no modern equivalent to what Mary Sidney witnessed in 1575 at Kenilworth. From the moment the queen and her
court arrived at the castle gates, they were in the grip of a seemingly endless spectacle. Elizabeth was greeted by a group of women
dressed as the ancient Sibyls, followed by a large man disguised as
Hercules, who played the role of the castle porter. The giant initially
pretended to be angered by the large group of visitors until he took
in the queen's "beauty and princely countenance," at which point he
handed her the keys to the castle while pronouncing a set of crude
but flattering verses. Once inside the estate, there were fireworks
and water pageants, hunts and bearbaiting, folk plays and courtly
masques. Mary listened to the Arthurian enchantress known as the
Lady of the Lake recite elegant poetry to the queen as she floated
across an artificial lake on a movable island lit with torches; she
heard the sea god Proteus sing a beautiful melody while lying on a
twenty-four-foot-long mechanical dolphin whose belly contained a
large group of musicians.

Many of the entertainments were not so subtly organized
around the theme of marriage. One afternoon a rustic wedding feast
known as a "bride ale" was held for a local couple, which involved
hours of running at the quintain (tilting against a wooden shield on
a post) and Morris dancing. The bride was thirty-five years old—a
hint to the forty-one-year-old Elizabeth that there was still time
for her—although the comparison wouldn't have been welcome:
an eyewitness described the woman as "ugly, foul, ill-favored" and
"ill-smelling." On a loftier level, the poet George Gascoigne, whom
Leicester had employed for the occasion, wrote a masque staging
the conflict between love and chastity in which a virgin maiden
of the goddess Diana named Zabeta (a variant on Elizabeth) was
ultimately handed over to Juno, the goddess of matrimony. This
particular piece was cancelled before it could be staged—officially
on account of poor weather, but rumor had it that Elizabeth had
received word of the plot and refused to attend.

The Kenilworth entertainments didn't persuade Elizabeth to
marry Leicester: if this was in fact his goal, the visit was an expensive flop. But for the thirteen-year-old Mary Sidney, there could
have been no better introduction to the power of theater and poetry
at the Elizabethan court. In ways she could never have learned from

her private tutors, she witnessed elegant performances of flattery, persuasion, and seduction; she saw how words, like lances or swords, could be wielded as courtly weapons. Twenty-five years later, Mary would put some of the lessons to good use in her short play, or dialogue, *Astrea,* written to welcome Elizabeth to her own home.

At the end of the summer progress of 1575, the court spent a month at Woodstock as the guests of Sir Henry Lee, a trusted courtier whom the queen had named as lieutenant and steward of the royal manor where she'd been kept under house arrest twenty years earlier. Lee's entertainments were geared toward a very different purpose from those of Leicester: instead of pushing Elizabeth toward marriage, his goal was to encourage her to embrace the role of virgin queen. On one particular afternoon well documented for posterity, Elizabeth and her ladies were taken to an elaborately decorated banqueting house on a hill in the woods; the structure, built of packed earth and boughs of greenery, had been erected just for the occasion. There, Elizabeth was greeted by a woman dressed as the Fairy Queen, who arrived in a wagon of state drawn by six children.

This seems to have been the first time Elizabeth was identified with the allegorical queen, one of the many myths that arose around her self-image as a virgin ruler. Unlike her cultivation of herself as a kind of secular Madonna, this association was distinctly pagan: the Fairy Queen was a native English figure, the benevolent ruler of fairies and elves who dwelt deep in the woods. The role also tied Elizabeth to the magical world of King Arthur, whom she wanted to claim as her distant ancestor. Elizabeth's identification with the Fairy Queen would be immortalized in English literature in Edmund Spenser's epic poem written in the 1590s; *The Faerie Queene* both affirmed Elizabeth's fictionalized lineage—"Thy name, O sovereign queen, thy realm and race / From this renowned Prince [Arthur] derived are"—and created a powerful alter ego for her. Spenser wasn't alone in conjuring up a fairy world for Elizabeth: Shakespeare created his own version in *A Midsummer Night's Dream,* but his Fairy Queen, Titania, would never have won Elizabeth's praise. Neither a virgin nor chaste, the bewitched Titania ends up falling in love with a "rude mechanical" named Bottom while he bears the head of an ass.

For Mary, the occasion at Woodstock was memorable not only for the magical appearance of the Fairy Queen, the splendid trees glistening with golden ornaments, and the banquet table shaped like a crescent moon. It was also the day she received a short poem—in fact, a single couplet—written especially for her. After the Fairy Queen finished her lengthy address to Elizabeth, the other female guests received "fine-smelling nosegays made of all colors," to each of which was attached a "posy of two verses." There's no description of Mary's bouquet, but her "posy" read as follows:

Though young in years yet old in wit, a guest due to your race,
If you hold on as you begin, who is't you'll not deface?

Mary's youth and pedigree (here referred to as her "race") were things about her that anyone could have known. But in these two short lines, the anonymous poet perceived something else. In the highly competitive world of the Elizabethan court, Mary seemed well equipped to rise to the top. If she could only "hold on" to her lead, the posy suggests, she might "deface" the many male courtiers who would be disappointed in their desperate wooing. She might also "deface" (in the sense of "outdo") the other ambitious maids around her. In practical terms, this meant only one thing. Just as the middle-aged Elizabeth started to settle into her role as a virgin queen, the adolescent Mary was poised to make an enviable marriage.

Less than two years after her arrival at court, the posy's prediction came true. Sometime in early 1577 the fifteen-year-old Mary became engaged to the thirty-eight-year-old Henry Herbert, Earl of Pembroke, who was newly widowed; his wife, the queen's friend Catherine Talbot, had died the previous May. Pembroke's father, William Herbert, was the kind of ruthless and cunning man who had thrived under Henry VIII. Having arrived at Henry's court as an untitled Welshman with no significant wealth, William ended up an earl with vast estates in Wiltshire and Glamorgan. The jewel of his properties was the ancient abbey of Wilton, which he received as part of Henry VIII's sweeping dissolution of the monasteries. Sitting on 46,000 acres of land in Salisbury, Wilton had been the royal seat of the Saxon kingdom of Wessex, founded in the sixth century. When William died in 1570, his son inherited his title and lands. Pembroke became one of the most desirable husbands in the kingdom.

For Mary's father, the prospect of her marriage to Pembroke was a dream come true. Despite his prominent positions in Elizabeth's government, Henry Sidney had remained without either a title or wealth; the marriage would bring both into the family. For Mary, apart from the possible allure of becoming a countess, the prospect of marrying Pembroke had little appeal. Twenty-three years her senior, he had been married twice before, and by all accounts was neither handsome nor brilliant. Mary, by contrast, was widely regarded as a beautiful woman: her earliest portrait, a miniature by the famous Nicholas Hilliard, shows her with striking reddish-blond curls and a perfect complexion. She was also known for her wit and charm. Pembroke, however, wasn't particularly interested in her personal qualities. Having no children from either of his earlier marriages, he was desperate for an heir. Like a young mare, Mary was picked to breed.

As the most powerful member of the Sidney/Dudley clan, Mary's uncle Leicester was entrusted with negotiating the terms of the marriage. For upper-class Englishmen, these negotiations were closer to hammering out a political treaty between nation-states than making a private agreement between families. After months of back-and-forth, Leicester presented Mary's father with the terms he and Pembroke had agreed upon. On the surface, they looked very favorable to Mary: she was to receive an enormous jointure (the provision for a wife should she outlive her husband) consisting of life interest in Pembroke's manors in Dorset, Wiltshire, Devon, Glamorgan, and Monmouth, which together generated more than £1,000 of annual income. In return, Pembroke demanded a "portion," or dowry, of £3,000.

For Henry, the sum was impossibly high. In an anguished letter to Leicester dated February 4, 1577, he acknowledged that the marriage would do "great honor to me, my mean lineage and kin" and claimed to be so overjoyed for "my dear child [to have] so happy an advancement as this is" that he would "lie a year in close prison rather than it should break." And yet, his enthusiasm unfortunately didn't match his purse. In brief, he confessed, "I am poor." Although he had reserved £2,000 for Mary in his will, he didn't have the money at hand. As "your Lordship knoweth," he wrote to his brother-in-law, "I might better spare [it] when I were dead."

Henry even petitioned the queen for help, complaining about her failure to compensate him for various expenses he had incurred in Ireland and explaining that he needed the funds "not to enrich myself," but only to pay what he owed to Pembroke "for my daughter." Elizabeth didn't budge: she resented the sheer amount of money required to maintain the peace in Ireland and refused to recognize how much of the cost came out of Henry's pocket. In the end, he managed to raise the sum, borrowing from friends and family members to make the final payment in February 1578. Meanwhile, Pembroke agreed to proceed with the marriage before the full portion was raised. No doubt confident Henry's connections would ultimately prevail, he was clearly anxious to move forward with his primary purpose of securing his legacy. Although only in his late thirties—life expectancy for an adult male of his class was around fifty-five—he may have felt he was racing against time.

Mary and Pembroke were married on April 21, 1577. According to the record book of the Chapel Royal, the ceremony was held in the queen's "closet," a small chapel inside Elizabeth's private chambers where only a handful of weddings were celebrated over the course of her reign. The only other record regarding the wedding that has survived is an itemized list of clothes purchased for Mary's trousseau: a skirt embroidered in purple and gold, another skirt embroidered in black and silver, two undescribed smocks and handkerchiefs, and a pair of "night court shoes" (pumps with low heels). Once the wedding was over, Mary traveled with Pembroke to her new home at Wilton. If they made the trip from London during the day, she would have passed the stone monument of Stonehenge on the Salisbury Plain before turning south to approach the idyllic landscape of Wiltshire. There were lush valleys by the Nadder and Wylye Rivers, filled with chalk streams and bubbling springs; grassy fields that in spring were as green as emeralds; stunning chalk ridges and downs dotted with an extravagant variety of wildflowers. As Mary's brother Philip succinctly put it, "all things conspire together to make this country a heavenly dwelling."

It's hard to imagine Mary's reaction when she first laid eyes on Wilton, whose severe monastic foundations had been transformed into one of the grandest residences in the kingdom (viewers of *The Crown* will have seen its interiors disguised as Buckingham Palace).

Elizabeth Bennet's response in *Pride and Prejudice* to Mr. Darcy's far more modest Pemberley comes to mind. "She had never seen a place for which nature had done more," Jane Austen wrote; "at that moment she felt that to be mistress of Pemberley might be something!" Even if the young bride had spent much of her childhood in castles, she had never before been the lady of the house with two hundred servants at her command. The adjustment must have been daunting.

The next mention of Mary at court was from the royal account books for Christmas in 1577, when, as was the widespread custom among the nobility, she and her husband exchanged gifts with the queen. Elizabeth's subjects made a ceremonial display of their loyalty, and the queen responded by rewarding them with treasure from the Jewel House. Pembroke gave Elizabeth £20 in gold, while Mary gave her a linen garment embroidered in gold and silver and lined with yellow taffeta. In return, the queen gave them each a silver-gilt bowl weighed according to their rank. As yet another reminder of the marital hierarchy, Pembroke's bowl weighed thirty ounces, Mary's only twenty-four. The only other mention of Mary during this period was her presence at celebrations for Elizabeth's forty-fifth birthday in September 1578; a friend of Philip's mentioned to him in a letter that the queen "bestows the greatest care" on both his mother and his sister.

There's no way to know how Mary felt at the queen's various festivities or what it was like for her to return to court in a higher social position than her own mother. As is so often the case for Renaissance women's lives—even aristocratic and reasonably well-documented lives like Mary's—her impressions of the world around her haven't survived (for this, she would have needed to keep a diary). The one exception to this general void was a letter Mary sent to Leicester in August 1578. Written in her own hand—and not, as would often have been the case, by a secretary—it revealed something of the sixteen-year-old's experience as a new wife to her much older husband. The context for the letter was Pembroke's illness that summer, about which Mary had notified Leicester in a previous letter (now lost). Leicester responded by sending his own physician to Wilton, but by the time he arrived, Pembroke had already recovered.

At this point Mary made a social blunder: she failed to let

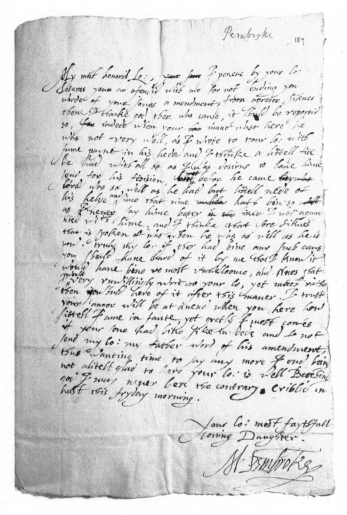

A letter hand-written by Mary Sidney
soon after her marriage, signed with her new title

Leicester know about her husband's improvement, and the subsequent letter that has survived opened with an apology for not
keeping her uncle better informed. "My most honored Lord," Mary
began, "I perceive by your Lordship's letters you are offended with
me for not sending you word of your son's amendment." Calling
Pembroke Leicester's son was somewhat comical (the two men were
six years apart), but having negotiated the terms of the couple's mar-

riage, Leicester occupied the symbolic role of father to both bride and groom. Mary then explained what had happened—the illness, it turned out, was no more than a "little fit"—and she concluded by declaring, "I trust your anger will be at an end when you hear how little I am in fault." She signed the letter "Cribbled in haste this Friday morning, Your lordship's most faithful loving daughter."

The description of the writing as "[s]cribbled," borne out by the multiple deletions and corrections she made to the letter, gives the impression that Mary wrote in great haste: she had just received an irate letter from one of the most powerful men in the kingdom and presumably didn't want to keep him waiting—again—for her reply. It also seems clear she hadn't yet mastered the etiquette required by her new position: when someone sends his own private physician to take care of your husband, you thank him right away and keep him apprised of all developments. Putting aside the various faux pas, there's something both brave and honest about Mary's tone, which was ultimately more explanatory than apologetic. However flustered she may have been, the young countess was learning to stand her ground.

By the summer of 1579, Mary was pregnant. On April 8, 1580, she gave birth to a son, who was named William after Pembroke's father. Pembroke treated William's arrival as a major historical event, installing a substantial marble plaque in the local church of St. Mary's and inviting the entire parish to a celebratory dinner. As a sign of the importance of the infant heir to the Pembroke title, the queen agreed to be the boy's godmother. For Mary, it had been a dizzying time. Only five years earlier she had left the comforts of her childhood home to live at court; two years later, she became the wife of an earl and the mistress of the spectacular Wilton. And now, six months before she turned nineteen, she had fulfilled the purpose of her marriage and given birth to a healthy boy.

The pregnancy hadn't only been the occasion for Mary to produce a much-desired heir. It was also the beginning of a different creative process for her. Just before she gave birth to William, her brother Philip came to keep her company. He ended up staying at Wilton through the summer. The two siblings hadn't spent much of their childhood together—they were seven years apart and Philip was often away at school—but around this time, they discovered their shared passion for literature. With Mary at his side Philip began to write what became his best-known work, a long prose romance named for her, *The Countess of Pembroke's Arcadia*. The Renaissance equivalent of a novel, the *Arcadia* recounted the adventures of the Greek princes Pyrocles and Musidorus, who disguised themselves, respectively, as an Amazon woman and a shepherd in pursuit of the two daughters of the Duke of Arcadia. The tale involved political unrest, peasant uprisings, cross-dressing, mysterious prophecy, and sexual violence. Rounding out the complicated plot were intervals of pastoral poetry and song.

The genre of romance was often associated with women—it was considered frivolous reading—and Philip claimed to have written it at Mary's request: "You desired me to do it and your desire to my heart is an absolute commandment." In his dedicatory letter addressed to "My Dear Lady and Sister, the Countess of Pembroke," he described his writing as having taken place either "in your presence," or "the rest, by sheets, sent unto you as fast as they were done." He also professed he'd written it "only for you, only to you." It's not clear how much Mary may have helped shape the complex plot as she read along, and it's possible she was a true collaborator. But whatever her involvement may have been, the presence of Philip at Wilton writing this work gave her a powerful vision of what it meant to give birth to ideas, and not just to children. As the next decade would show, this would become her lifeline.

CHAPTER THREE

April 11, 1576

St. Botolph's Without Bishopsgate, London

Aemilia Lanyer

On the other side of London, far from the gilded halls where Mary Sidney was serving as a maid of honor for the queen, the seven-year-old Aemilia Lanyer was at home in the parish of St. Botolph's Without Bishopsgate mourning the death of her father. Baptista Bassano had immigrated to England from Venice with four of his brothers in 1540 at the invitation of Henry VIII. A well-known musical family—Baptista's father was a sackbut player (an early form of trombone) and instrument maker for the Venetian doge, and his sons were all talented musicians—the Bassanos formed a recorder ensemble at the English court, lured by attractive salaries and spacious lodgings in a dissolved Carthusian monastery (also known as a Charterhouse).

Although the Bassanos seem to have been practicing Catholicism in Venice, circumstantial evidence suggests they may have been of Jewish origin: Bassano was a common Jewish name, there are links between the family and other known Jewish Venetians, and the Bassano coat of arms displayed silkworm moths and the silkworms' favorite tree—the mulberry—which suggested ties to the Jewish-dominated silk industry. Who knows if Henry VIII appreciated the possible irony of giving the Bassano brothers the former dwellings of Catholic monks, but the cells had private gardens and unique supplies of water, making them unusually comfortable places to live. In 1545, Baptista and his brothers became legal "denizens" of England, a status between being an official subject of the Crown and being a "stranger." Denizens could own but not inherit property; they could vote, but they couldn't be members of Parliament or hold civil or military office. As the famous eighteenth-century jurist Sir William Blackstone put it, "A denizen is a kind of middle state, between an alien and a natural-born subject, and partakes of both." This "middle state" is the world Aemilia grew up in, with relatives who had lived most of their lives in England but never fully belonged.

In 1552 the Bassanos left the Charterhouse to take up residence in private homes in the northeast of London. By the time of Aemilia's birth in 1569, Baptista had been settled for roughly a decade in St. Botolph's, a densely populated and rather unsanitary part of London in the eastern ward of Bishopsgate. (The ward is divided into "Bishopsgate Without," or outside the city wall, and "Bishopsgate Within.") The thirteenth-century parish church where Aemilia was baptized, built on ruins dating to before the Norman invasion, was right next to the town ditch. Originally dug for defensive purposes, the ditch had become a pestilent site. According to John Stow's 1598 *Survey of London,* it was full of "unsavory things, to the danger of poisoning the whole city." Danger of another sort loomed nearby: just down the road from the church was Bedlam Hospital for "distracted people," where, in Stow's words, those who "be distraught in their wits are, by the suit of their friends, received and kept." In 1569 Bishopsgate became the site of an overflow burial ground for parishes within the city walls that had run out of room in their churchyards; an acre of ground next to the hospital was walled in to receive the London dead. Today the neighborhood is filled with gleaming modern skyscrapers, but a few surviving narrow stone alleys and timber-framed houses evoke the world Aemilia would have known.

It was no coincidence that Baptista settled in Bishopsgate: this was an area popular with immigrants who generally couldn't afford to live in the more expensive inner wards of the city. There were also more prominent inhabitants, including in the early seventeenth century Sir Paul Pindar, a successful merchant who became King James's ambassador to the Ottoman Empire. (In 1596 Shakespeare was recorded as living in the tiny parish of St. Helen's Bishopsgate, just on the other side of the city walls and only a few minutes' walk from St. Botolph's.) According to the records of the fees that "strangers" were required to pay, foreigners made up roughly ten percent of the parish's population, among whom were many Dutch and Italian workers in the silk industry. The Italian merchants in Bishopsgate, most of whom were Venetian, apparently liked to meet outside to conduct their business. As one Venetian observer related, the men closed off the street with chairs so that horses and carts couldn't enter in order to create a space—a local Rialto, as it were—to "make their deals."

Nearly all of the Italians in London were officially Protestants, as were Baptista and his brothers by the time Elizabeth came to the throne (if the family was originally Jewish, there would have been two conversions—first to Catholicism in Venice, and then to Protestantism in England). There were even several Italian Protestant churches in London where Italians could pray in their own tongue. These churches drew both native speakers and also many Englishmen, who came, as Elizabeth's childhood tutor Roger Ascham complained, "to hear the Italian tongue naturally spoken, not to hear God's doctrine truly preached"—the services were an occasion for free Italian lessons. It's possible Baptista occasionally worshipped in one of these churches, but all records link him to the local parish church of St. Botolph's. Whatever ties he had either to Judaism or to Catholicism were nowhere to be seen once he settled in England.

Although the Bassanos seem to have given up their religion—or religions—of origin, they didn't give up their native language: there are surviving letters in Italian exchanged among family members through the end of the sixteenth century. At home, however, it's unlikely Aemilia had much access to her father's native tongue, especially after his death: her mother, Margaret Johnson, was a Protestant Englishwoman who seems to have had very little education. When it came to signing her last will and testament, Margaret marked it with an "X," suggesting she was either illiterate or at least had not mastered even the most rudimentary skills in writing.

In his will, dated January 3, 1576, Baptista referred to Margaret as his "reputed wife," which meant the couple had been joined in a common-law marriage rather than one consecrated in the church. In practical terms, this usually meant the union had been ratified simply by sexual consummation. Such a bond was recognized by the courts in terms of the legitimacy of any offspring—Aemilia and her two siblings (an older sister, Angela, and a younger brother, Philip, who died in 1573 at the age of two) had been baptized in the Protestant church—but the marriage itself was of questionable social status. As the seventeenth-century writer Edward Waterhouse explained, "though the Church of God and the laws of men may allow the issue of reputed marriage to be lawful . . . yet generally the laws of God and men abhor them."

For aristocrats like Mary Sidney and Pembroke, a de facto union of this kind could never have happened: nothing could be left undocumented in the complex transfer of wealth, title, and land that accompanied the blessings of the church. Gentry families with small amounts of property or some social standing in their community also tended to have church ceremonies. The middle-class Shakespeare, son of a glover and alderman, and Anne Hathaway, daughter of a yeoman farmer, were married in church despite their union having already been consummated: Anne was several months pregnant at the time of the wedding, which took place after a single reading of the banns instead of the usual three in order to hurry the process. The fact that Aemilia's parents were joined without any such ceremony suggests both that Margaret had no dowry to bring to the match—in that case, some provision would have been made for her jointure or inheritance if she outlived her husband—and that Baptista may not have been fully settled in a religious community at the time. This was a mixed marriage, in effect, between an Englishwoman and an Italian immigrant; they may have felt like outsiders.

However unglamorous her surroundings at home, Aemilia spent her early years at one short remove from the queen. Baptista and his brothers had remained in service to the Crown through the turmoil of the 1550s—regardless of changes in regime, the recorder consort played on—and the Bassanos were listed as members of the royal household when Elizabeth came to the throne. According to Baptista's brother Augustine, the queen shared her father Henry VIII's love of the recorder and requested that the brothers attend her on a daily basis. In a letter sent to Elizabeth in 1568, written in Italian, they reassured her they were "raising [their] children to be virtuous so that they will be able to serve your majesty." Aemilia, of course, wasn't included among the future musicians, and even if Baptista had lived, he would never have trained her as her uncles were training their sons. Watching all the men in her family set off for court while she was stuck at home may have fueled her own ambition to rise from her humble origins. This ambition, as we'll see, would be one of the great themes in her adult life.

Aemilia may have also been allured by the stories her father told her about his time with the queen. Of all the Bassano brothers, his ties to Elizabeth were particularly close. Sometime between 1545 and 1552, Baptista may have served as the young princess's Italian tutor and taught her to play the lute. In 1565, the royal account books list him as having given the queen a Venetian lute as a New Year's gift. Everyone from the lowest scullery maids to the highest members of the aristocracy gave Elizabeth New Year's gifts—we saw that Mary Sidney, having just become Countess of Pembroke, presented the queen with an embroidered linen garment in 1577—so there was nothing unusual about Baptista's participation in this annual ritual. But it's hard not to see the specific choice of the Venetian instrument as an unusually personal gesture.

With Baptista's death in 1576, Aemilia's link to the queen came to an abrupt end. She and her mother, Margaret, were left without either Baptista's courtly connections or his solid income of £30 a year (to put this in perspective, the average shoemaker made £4 a year, and the average brewer made £10). Because Aemilia's older sister was already married—according to Baptista's will, Angela was the "wife of Joseph Holland, gentleman"—whatever remained of his estate was directed to Margaret and Aemilia. As Aemilia later related, the inheritance was much smaller than it would have been had Baptista not fallen upon hard times: "the wealth of her father failed before he died," she reportedly said, "and he began to be miserable in his estate." To Margaret, Baptista left the "rents, issues, and profits" on three properties he held with long-term leases; to Aemilia, he gave "one hundred pounds of lawful money of England to be paid at her full age of one and twenty years or day of marriage [whichever] shall happen first." By the standards of the aristocracy, the sum was a pittance—Mary Sidney's dowry, we will recall, was £3,000—but given that it reflected more than three years of Baptista's salary, it spoke to his strong desire to provide for Aemilia's future. In a hint of his own financial hardships, he stipulated that were Aemilia to die before her twenty-first birthday, the money should be used toward "payment of my debts."

In addition to leaving Aemilia as much money as he could, Baptista had also thought about the best plans for her care, stipulating in his will "that my said executrix shall have the keeping and bringing up of the said Aemilia, her daughter, and the bestowing of her in marriage." It would have been entirely possible—and perhaps advantageous—to name one of his brothers who still served at court as Aemilia's legal guardian; his entrusting her to Margaret (his "executrix") suggests both his confidence in her judgment and his desire to keep mother and daughter together. It also meant Baptista wasn't particularly concerned with Aemilia's education: there was no chance Margaret could follow Vives's advice in his *Instruction for Christian Women* that mothers teach their daughters to read literature and study "wise and holy books." If Baptista's will had been strictly followed, Aemilia's prospects for becoming well-educated would have been grim.

What happened next falls into the category of unexpected events that dramatically change the shape of a person's life. No doubt with Aemilia's best intentions in mind, Margaret seems to have violated Baptista's will. Sometime after her husband's death, she sent Aemilia away from home to be, as Aemilia later put it, "brought up with the countess of Kent." The practice of sending one's daughter to be raised in a household of means was relatively widespread at the time: since girls were denied access to formal education, it was one of the only forms of upward mobility available. Ambitious parents generally sought high-ranking families who might give their daughters opportunities they couldn't themselves provide. Mary Sidney's invitation to live at court was the placement of dreams— the Renaissance equivalent of admission to the most exclusive university.

Depending on her social status, a young girl's position in her new household could be anywhere between surrogate daughter and lady's maid. After the death of his wife, the Sidney family's secretary Sir Edmund Molyneux, for example, sent two of his young daughters to live with his cousin so they might learn "to play the gentlewomen and good housewives, to dress meat and oversee their households." Lady Sidney's sister, Katherine, Countess of Hunting-don, who had no children of her own, ran an establishment for girls like the Molyneux sisters. "I think there will be none make ques-tion," she boasted to her friend Sir Julius Caesar, "but I know how to breed and govern young gentlewomen."

No evidence has survived to explain how Aemilia came to the attention of Susan Bertie, Countess Dowager of Kent, but the most likely connection was through Susan's mother. Katherine Wil-loughby, Duchess of Suffolk, was the only child born to a wealthy English baron and a Spanish noblewoman who had loyally served Catherine of Aragon. Despite her mother's lifelong alliance with the Catholic queen, Katherine became one of the great early champions of Protestantism. In addition to her passion for religious reform, she and her first husband, Charles Brandon, Duke of Suffolk, were enthusiastic patrons of music at the royal court, where they would almost certainly have known Baptista and his brothers. The duch-ess was also possibly connected to Baptista and Margaret through the family of Anne Vaughan Lock, a radical Protestant writer who dedicated her translation of Calvin's sermons to Katherine in 1560. Anne's brother, Stephen Vaughan, was a close friend of Baptista and Margaret's, and hence the seemingly enormous distance between the countess and the Bassanos was reduced to a few small degrees of separation.

Susan Bertie was Katherine's daughter from her second mar-riage, when the duchess chose as her husband someone far beneath her social rank. After becoming a widow in 1545, she waited roughly seven years before marrying her gentleman usher, Richard Bertie. Shakespeare's Malvolio may fantasize about marrying his aristo-cratic mistress, Olivia, in *Twelfth Night,* but in reality, such matches were few and far between. It's tempting to think Susan's knowledge of her own father's background may have made her sympathetic to a girl like Aemilia. Susan herself had experienced more hardship than most aristocratic children during her childhood. When she was an infant, her Protestant parents fled with her to the Continent to escape persecution at the hands of Mary I; after a harrowing journey through Europe that lasted nearly two years, they finally took up residence in Samogitia, Lithuania, as the guests of King Sigismund II Augustus of Poland. The family returned to England once Elizabeth was securely on the throne—a letter Katherine wrote to Elizabeth from Samogitia congratulating her on her accession has survived—and by the summer of 1559 they had returned to Katherine's ancestral home, the thirteenth-century castle of Grimsthorpe in Lincolnshire.

In 1570, the sixteen-year-old Susan married Sir Reginald Grey, Earl of Kent, who died three years later, leaving her childless. Since there was no direct male heir, Kent's title and estates passed to his brother. At this point Susan seems to have moved to London to live at court, where she remained on and off until her remarriage in 1581 to Sir John Wingfield of Withcoll, Lincolnshire. It's not clear exactly when she would have taken Aemilia in, but given both the lack of evidence that Aemilia ever lived in Lincolnshire and her reference to Susan as "the countess of Kent," it's likely to have been between Baptista's death in 1576 and Susan's remarriage five years later. This is confirmed in an undated poem Aemilia wrote much later in her life. Addressed to "The Lady Susan, Countess Dowager of Kent," she looks back at Susan's role as a surrogate mother:

> Come you that were the Mistress of my youth,
> The noble guide of my ungoverned days,
> Come you that have delighted in God's truth,
> Help now your handmaid to sound forth his praise.

Whether Susan's role as "Mistress of my youth" included giving Aemilia formal instruction can't be known for certain, but somewhere along the way she acquired an excellent humanist education. In her poem to Susan, she focuses on the countess's having shaped her character:

> And as your rare perfections showed the glass
> Wherein I saw each wrinkle of a fault;
> You [were] the Sun's virtue, I that fair green grass,
> That flourished fresh by your clear virtues taught.

Under Susan's care, the "ungoverned" Aemilia learned to behave like a gentlewoman.

The decade or so after Aemilia's likely departure from Susan's household has left almost no traces. The only record involving Aemilia to survive is her mother's last will and testament, dated June 27, 1587, and probated eleven days later. Married women were generally not allowed to make wills—they could only designate gifts of their own with their husbands' permission—but as a widow Margaret was in a position to dispose of the property she inherited from Baptista as she liked. Naming her "well-beloved daughter" Aemilia as her heir, she bequeathed to her "all my leases, goods, and chattels" upon the condition that Aemilia continue to pay her brother-in-law, Joseph Holland, and his son Philip £10 a year from the income she received until she married. (There was no marriage prospect in sight at the time, but the assumption was that everyone would ultimately get married—except, of course, the queen.) Once married, Aemilia's husband was to pay £200 to Joseph and Philip to discharge the annual payments. Margaret also stipulated that Aemilia would pay whatever debts Margaret had left behind "with the pawn of goods and chattels which I shall leave unto her"; these particular possessions weren't described.

Thus, in the summer of 1587, Aemilia was an eighteen-year-old orphan with a small inheritance and a blank future before her. It was far from an ideal moment to be venturing out in the world, especially for someone eager, as she seems to have been, to make a life at court. Tensions were unusually high at the time over plots both domestic and foreign to topple Elizabeth's reign and return England to Catholicism. The previous fall, Elizabeth's spymaster, Sir Francis Walsingham, had uncovered an elaborate plan—known as the Babington plot, after its chief conspirator—to assassinate the queen and put Mary, Queen of Scots on the throne. As a Catholic member of the royal family with a strong claim to the English Crown, Mary had been at the center of a series of attempts to replace her Protestant cousin, often involving Spanish allies. Despite being kept under house arrest since shortly after her escape to England in 1569, the former Scottish queen managed to be implicated in one plot after another.

In September 1587 at St. Giles Field in London, Aemilia might have seen the brutal execution of Babington and thirteen fellow conspirators, who were hanged, drawn, and quartered before a large group of spectators. This was Elizabethan England at its most savage: the first seven men were taken down from the gallows to be "drawn," or disemboweled, while they were still conscious. After the normally bloodthirsty crowd reacted with horror, the executioners adjusted the order of things for the next batch of men to avoid any sympathy for the victims. Four months later, Mary, Queen of Scots, who had been privy to the plans and made clear her support in a letter intercepted by Walsingham's agents, was beheaded at Fotheringhay Castle in Northamptonshire. It famously took three blows of the ax to sever her head—the first blow shockingly missed her neck entirely, and even the second blow didn't complete the job. Adding to the already botched spectacle, the executioner who finally raised Mary's head to the crowd found himself holding only a red wig, as Mary's gray-haired head slipped from his grasp onto the ground.

In the end, the killing of Elizabeth's long-term enemy brought little relief from the nation's larger anxiety about its ongoing conflict with Spain. While English troops were fighting alongside their Protestant allies in the Spanish-occupied Netherlands, rumors were swirling over Spain's plans for a naval invasion of England. King Philip had begun several years earlier to prepare a massive fleet with an aim of finally conquering his long-term Protestant enemy. In a preemptive move to ward off the attack, the English admiral Sir Francis Drake had led a successful raid in April 1587 in the Bay of Cádiz that plundered and sank two dozen of Philip's ships, a triumph that Sir Francis Bacon famously described thirty years later as "the singeing of the king of Spain's beard." Drake's success may have slightly delayed the invasion and reduced the fleet, but by the summer of 1588 the seemingly formidable Spanish Armada was sighted off England's southern coast.

What exactly Aemilia was doing while London braced for war isn't certain, but somehow in the midst of the chaos this daughter of an Italian (and possibly also Jewish) immigrant found her way back into the upper echelons of English society. This time, she was not the young ward of a countess, but the mistress of a very prominent lord. Henry Carey, Baron Hunsdon, was no ordinary courtier: the son of Anne Boleyn's sister, Mary Boleyn, he was the queen's first cousin. Given that his mother had a notorious affair with Henry VIII a decade or so before the king married Anne, it was rumored that Hunsdon may in fact have been Henry's illegitimate son. It's therefore possible he was both Elizabeth's cousin and her half brother.

Hunsdon joined Elizabeth's household while she was still a princess, and he remained her faithful servant through his long career. His older sister, Lady Katherine Knollys—who may also have been fathered by Henry VIII—served Elizabeth as a lady of the bedchamber until her death in 1569, despite competing obligations to her enormous family (she had sixteen children). The presence of Mary Boleyn's two children within Elizabeth's inner circle wasn't coincidental: this was part of a larger pattern in which Elizabeth quietly sought to redeem the Boleyn family from the ignominy of her own mother's execution.

Around the time of her coronation, the queen raised Hunsdon's social status by first knighting him and then giving him his new title (it was at this point he became Baron Hunsdon); he now had as his principal seat the manor of Hunsdon in Hertfordshire, a palatial estate created by Henry VIII replete with a moat and an impressive deer park. In addition to the splendid manor, Elizabeth gave Hunsdon a grant of lands in Kent and Essex. Altogether the properties generated a staggering income of around £4,000 a year.

In 1568, Hunsdon became governor of Berwick in the northernmost part of England, a position that led to his heroic role in crushing the Northern Rebellion of Catholic earls in 1570, one of the occasions behind Elizabeth's celebrated poem "The Doubt of Future Foes." In 1577 Elizabeth named him to the Privy Council, and in 1585 he became her lord chamberlain. As chief officer of the royal household, Hunsdon was in charge of the clerical and medical staff; the gentlemen guards for the queen; the waiters, carvers, and servers; and all branches of entertainment, including the royal musicians. He also was a great patron of the theater, who formed a company of players (or actors) that came to be known as the Lord Chamberlain's Men. In 1594 Hunsdon absorbed some of the key figures in Lord Strange's company, Lord Strange's Men, when Strange suddenly died. This company included the great actor Richard Burbage, and Shakespeare himself.

There's no record of how Hunsdon and Aemilia met, but six of her Bassano relatives worked directly for him: five cousins played in the court's recorder consort, and one had ventured away from the family's traditional instrument to join the flautists. It's also possible Aemilia had established some of her own ties at court from her time with Susan Bertie; in this case, she might have been introduced to the lord chamberlain at one of the many festivities over which he presided. All that's known for certain is that, in 1597, Aemilia described herself as having been "favored much of her majesty and of many noblemen," suggesting both that the queen knew her personally and that she had ties to courtiers beyond Hunsdon. She also declared that "the old lord chamberlain kept her long" and "loved her well."

Affairs between male courtiers and Elizabeth's unmarried gentlewomen and maids were very common; this is the fate, as we've seen, that Mary Sidney so successfully avoided. When these relationships were discovered—usually due to the woman's becoming pregnant—the results ranged from threats of litigation or violence to secret marriages. In 1581, for example, when one of the queen's maids of honor, Anne Vavasour, gave birth to a son in the maids' own chambers at court, her uncle Sir Thomas Knyvett challenged the child's father, Edward de Vere, Earl of Oxford, to a duel. Both men were badly injured, and the conflict ended with Oxford's return to his long-estranged wife, while Anne married an untitled gentleman some years later. In the late 1580s, Sir Walter Raleigh had an affair with another of the queen's maids, Elizabeth, or Bess, Throckmorton. After Bess became pregnant, she and Raleigh married without informing the queen, incurring her great fury; both husband and wife were promptly sent for a few months to the Tower of London. Mary Sidney's son William met a similar fate when he impregnated the queen's former maid of honor Mary Fitton. When William refused the queen's command to marry Mary—as the heir to his father, the Earl of Pembroke's title and fortune, he had hopes to make a greater match—he was sent to Fleet prison before being banished to the family home at Wilton, where he stayed until the queen's death. The list goes on.

No such drama can be reported about Aemilia's relationship with Hunsdon. Forty-five years her senior and married with many children (his wife bore him ten sons and three daughters), Hunsdon certainly wasn't husband material. Even if he had been a bachelor, their difference in status would have made the match impossible. The fact that Aemilia wasn't one of the highly visible maids of honor, but was instead on the outside of elite circles, with no official place at court, no doubt helped to keep the affair secret. From Aemilia's account—the only record we have—this was neither a brief nor a superficial relationship. In addition to her claim that "the old lord chamberlain kept her long," she boasted that he "maintained [her] in great pomp." Given Hunsdon's significant wealth and power, we might imagine this "pomp" to include valuable jewels, clothing, and gifts of all sorts, which would have made her appear far above her station. This crossing of class lines was officially illegal in Renaissance England, where sumptuary laws governed the type of fabrics—silks, velvets, satins, etc.—and colors that could be worn by different classes of people. Purple was restricted to the royal family, whereas cloth of gold was allowed in the doublets and sleeves of dukes and marquesses; imported wool, meanwhile, was forbidden to be worn by anyone "under the degree of a baron, unless he be a knight, that is companion of the Garter." In 1636, King Charles would even forbid the buying, selling, or wearing of imitation jewelry.

Aemilia seems to have fully enjoyed whatever arrangement she had with Hunsdon, and it may have lasted even longer if she hadn't—like Bess Throckmorton at almost the same moment—become pregnant. If Aemilia had hailed from a powerful family with a stake in maintaining her honor, Hunsdon could easily have found himself in a mess, if not in the Tower of London. But as an orphan with no one to protect her, she seems to have agreed to Hunsdon's terms. The solution he apparently came up with was typical for affairs between male masters and their female servants. Records of a legal proceeding, for example, in 1606 between one Margaret Wall and her wealthy employer, Mr. Millington, reported that after Margaret became pregnant with Millington's child, he offered to marry her to another servant and sweetened the deal with a one-time payment of £200.

Hunsdon was not Aemilia's employer, but, like Millington, he arranged for Aemilia to take a member of his staff as her husband before the baby was born. The chosen groom was someone with a background nearly identical to her own. Around two years Aemilia's junior, Alfonso Lanyer was a recorder player at court whose father had been a French flautist employed alongside Baptista; the two men would certainly have known each other well, and the children may also have met. Whether or not Aemilia and Alfonso knew one another before, the match was certainly not their choice. Born to one musician in the court's recorder consort, she was now to be married to another. Whatever dreams Aemilia had of moving up the social ladder seemed permanently dashed. Who knows if she knew anything about the prodigious literary talent she had within her, or if she had tried at this stage in her life to write poems of her own. For this side of her to flourish, she would need the companionship of women.

CHAPTER FOUR

November 17, 1588

Ludgate Hill, London

Mary Sidney

While Elizabeth's privy councilors spent the spring of 1588 bracing for a Spanish invasion—blocking the Thames with barriers of chains and cables, barricading London's busy streets, and mustering even the weakest of men—Mary Sidney was hidden away in Wiltshire in the former Augustinian priory of Ivychurch. With her at the pastoral retreat that belonged to her husband's family were her three children, William, Anne, and Philip Herbert; her younger brother Thomas Sidney; and her brother Robert Sidney's wife, the Welsh heiress Barbara Gamage, with her infant daughter, Moll (the future poet Lady Mary Wroth). However safe the bucolic countryside may have seemed from the approaching Armada, plans were in place for a quick escape should the enemy make its way inland. In a letter written to Barbara in August from his post in Flanders, Robert asked her to "send me word what my Lady of Pembroke's determination is; if the enemy come not, I will send for you, and if he do, I will send you money to provide for your going into Wales."

As Robert's letter makes clear, Mary was left in charge of the group while he and Pembroke were away preparing for war. Having recently been named to his father-in-law Sir Henry Sidney's former post as president of the Council of Wales and the Marches, Pembroke was not only tasked with fortifying ports and raising troops;

he was also asked to help with efforts to keep any sympathizers with Spain from defecting to the enemy side. In a letter sent to him in January 1588, the Privy Council warned that many Welshmen "most obstinately have refused to come to the church to prayers and divine services," suggesting they were secretly practicing Catholicism at home. These men, the queen advised, "should be looked unto and restrained." In addition to fulfilling his obligations in Wales, Pembroke made a huge personal contribution to the Crown, offering 800 of his own men as soldiers—300 on horse and 500 on foot—furnished with arms at his own cost.

The Spanish army never made it anywhere near Ivychurch, and Mary and her relatives remained safely in Wiltshire through the tense summer of naval conflict. Between late July, when the Armada first began its advance up the English Channel, and mid-August, when it became clear to the Spanish commanders that they had lost any chance of victory at sea, England's future as a nation was on the line. The fleet of 132 vessels carrying 20,000 soldiers and 8,000 sailors was fueled by Philip II's decades-old desire to reconquer the lost English kingdom he had ruled alongside his wife, Elizabeth's half sister, Queen Mary, for a brief four years. Before the Armada took to sea, Pope Sixtus V renewed his papal bull excommunicating the Protestant Elizabeth and absolving her English subjects from their oaths of obedience, raising hopes of an internal rebellion to match the Spanish invasion. On August 9, Elizabeth addressed the English troops at Tilbury in what would become her most celebrated speech. "Let tyrants fear," she boldly declared:

> I am come amongst you, as you see, at this time, not for my recreation and disport, but being resolved, in the midst and heat of the battle, to live and die amongst you all.

This was also the occasion for her gender-defying assertion about having the body of a woman but the heart and stomach of a king.

The dazzling size and strength of the Armada turned out to be insufficient against the far more maneuverable English fleet. In a victory they proudly explained as a result of both naval prowess and divine providence, the English routed the "invincible" Armada with surprising ease. After battling horrible storms and impossible headwinds, with losses of roughly one-fifth of his men and nearly all his munitions, the Spanish commander Alonso Pérez de Guzmán, Duke of Medina Sidonia, began his long retreat home.

Making matters much worse, the course that Medina Sidonia chose—to the north around Scotland and Ireland before taking a starboard tack to Spain—turned out to be disastrous. Five of his enormous cargo ships, known as Levanters (originally built to sail in the Mediterranean), made for Ireland's western coast in hope of procuring food and water; only two managed to get away. Thousands of Spaniards drowned at sea, and many of those who got to shore were brutally murdered. In a letter sent from London in November to the Spanish ambassador in France, the Portuguese spy Antonio de Vega delivered the latest news: "A fresh report has just come from Ireland saying that many ships of the Spanish Armada have been lost on that coast, and that many persons have been beheaded and others taken prisoners." The violent killings were blamed on the Irish, who were consistently treated as wild savages, but in fact it was mostly English soldiers, or Irishmen in English pay, who were responsible.

While the Spanish were taking stock of their horrendous losses and mourning their dead, England gave itself over to celebration. De Vega described the "great preparations" in London for the annual joust on Accession Day—a national holiday honoring the date Elizabeth became queen (November 17)—made all the more spectacular in 1588 by the addition of a second day devoted to national thanksgiving. Never one to play down the symbolic potential of her victories, Elizabeth rode through the city gates in what the sixteenth-century historian John Stow described as a "chariot throne" modeled on those of the ancient Roman emperors; all of the London guilds were assembled in full livery to greet her, and the enormous crowd in the streets produced an "unceasing uproar" of jubilation. Outside St. Paul's Cathedral, whose lofty interiors were adorned with the banners of the defeated Spaniards, fifty or so clergymen waited for the queen's arrival, which was followed by a sermon delivered in the churchyard that she heard from a special "closet" made for the occasion. After the festivities were over, she returned to Whitehall Palace by torchlight.

As it happened, Elizabeth was not the only woman to come through London's gates in grand style for the festivities. According to de Vega's report, "the wife of the earl of Pembroke made a superb entrance into this city." As a sign of Mary Sidney's position at the pinnacle of English society, de Vega treated her arrival as a major event. Following directly upon his report of the Spanish naval losses and the return of the explorer Sir Thomas Cavendish from his 782-day circumnavigation of the globe, he gave a detailed account of her appearance as a triumph of its own:

> Before her went 40 gentlemen on horseback, two by two, all very finely dressed with gold chains. Then came a coach in which was the Countess and a lady, then another coach with more ladies, and after that a litter containing the children, and four ladies on horseback. After them came 40 or 50 servants in her livery with blue cassocks.

De Vega referred to Mary as Pembroke's wife—at this point she hadn't yet done anything to distinguish herself otherwise—but he didn't realize the livery her servants wore belonged to the Sidneys, not the Herberts. As we'll see, this choice wasn't accidental.

To the extent that Mary's appearance at court in November 1588 was newsworthy, it had to do with her absence for several years even before the threat of the Spanish invasion. This had been for her a period of nearly uninterrupted mourning. After giving birth to three children in a space of four years—following William's birth in 1580, Katherine was born in 1581, and Anne in 1583—Katherine died on the same day in 1584 that a second son, Philip, was born. In the family Psalter where all births and deaths were recorded, the three-year-old girl was poignantly described as "a child of much promised excellency if she might have lived." Although Mary was still young at the time—she was not quite twenty-four—she bore no further children, or at least none that survived long enough to be mentioned in the family annals.

Roughly a year and a half after Katherine's death, Mary's father, Henry, died at the age of fifty-six. Following the queen's orders, his heart was buried at Ludlow Castle and the rest of his corpse laid to rest in the family's chapel in St. John the Baptist Church at Penshurst. Henry never imagined he would die before his wife, who had been in poor health since her bout with smallpox in 1562 after nursing the queen. In a 1583 letter to his friend Sir Francis Walsingham, whose daughter Frances was to marry Mary's brother Philip later that year, Henry even described his hopes for his own eventual remarriage. Despite being "toothless and trembling," he cruelly proposed that he was himself not yet "so old, nor my wife so healthy, but that she may die, and I marry again and get children." In the summer of 1586, some three months after Henry's death, Lady Sidney joined her husband in his Penshurst tomb.

Still reeling from these deaths, in October 1586 Mary received another horrendous blow. After incurring serious wounds in September fighting the Spanish alongside his fellow Protestants at the Battle of Zutphen in the Netherlands, her brother Sir Philip Sidney was dead. Struck by a musket just above his knee—either to increase his mobility or in an act of gallantry so that he wouldn't be better protected than his own men, he had apparently removed his thigh armor—the thirty-one-year-old Philip had lain languishing in bed for twenty-five days before it became clear he had developed gangrene. By this point the infection had progressed too far for the leg to be amputated. On October 16, Philip sent a desperate letter to the Dutch physician Jan Wier begging him to come at once; on October 17 he died.

In early November Philip's corpse was returned to England, where it lay in state at the church of Holy Trinity, Minories, for around three months. During this time, his father-in-law, Walsingham, tried to settle the enormous debts Philip had left behind, which were believed to have reached the sum of £6,000. As his dire financial situation suggests, Philip had been both one of Elizabeth's most promising courtiers and one of the most disappointed. Although he served as a diplomat on several European missions and in 1585 had been named governor of Flushing (one of three Dutch cities placed under English rule by their Protestant allies), he never achieved a status that matched his combination of pedigree, brilliance, and charm.

Many of Philip's failures were in fact due to his volatile relationship with the queen. During the negotiations in 1579 for her marriage to the French duke of Anjou, Philip earned Elizabeth's wrath by circulating a letter strongly opposing the match on religious grounds. This injudicious expression of his Protestant fervor was followed by his public quarrel on the tennis court with the Catholic-leaning Earl of Oxford, Edward de Vere (the same man who would infuriate the queen by impregnating one of her maids several years later). Regardless of who was at fault, Elizabeth ordered Philip to apologize to Oxford, given the earl's superior rank. Far from taking the appropriate steps to repair things, he stubbornly responded by withdrawing from court.

Philip's political career may have been mixed at best, but there was another realm in which he unquestionably thrived: he was one of the greatest writers of the era. In addition to the romance he wrote for—and with—Mary while at Wilton in 1580, *The Countess of Pembroke's Arcadia,* he was the author of the first major sonnet series in English, *Astrophil and Stella.* Following closely on the model of the Italian poet Francesco Petrarch's sonnets for his beloved Laura (whom, as it happens, the poet didn't know personally—he once greeted her in a piazza but otherwise admired her from afar), *Astrophil and Stella* told the story of Philip's thwarted love for Penelope Devereux, the sister of the Earl of Essex. Penelope broke Philip's heart when she married Robert Rich, Earl of Warwick, in 1581. Around the same time—likely 1582 or 1583—Philip also wrote *The Defence of Poesie,* one of the strongest arguments that had ever been made for the power of imaginative literature.

Unlike his fellow poet Edmund Spenser, Philip never published any of his writing, choosing instead to circulate it privately among friends in manuscript copies. This decision can be explained in part by the so-called stigma of print common among English aristocrats at the time—the idea that there was something vulgar about sharing your writing with the world at large—and in part by Philip's ambivalence about being a writer in the first place. Focused on his advancement at court, he claimed he had accidentally "slipped" into writing. At the same time that he disavowed his role as a poet—he called it his "unelected vocation"—he achieved real fame as a writer among the English elite, who feverishly shared his works among themselves, creating a private world of secret readers. Around a dozen manuscripts containing selections of Philip's poems have survived, and this likely represents only a fraction of the number circulating during his lifetime. When the first edition of *Astrophil and Stella* appeared in 1591, its publisher claimed it had already been widely "spread abroad in written copies," and Philip's close friend Fulke Greville noted that the original was "so common, or widely available, that it wasn't worth printing."

Whatever fame and glory Philip enjoyed in life increased exponentially with his death. As tensions continued to rise between England and Spain in 1587, his sacrifice for the Protestant cause on the battlefields of the Netherlands cast him in the role of national hero. Eight days after Mary, Queen of Scots lost her head at Fotheringhay Castle—and possibly scheduled to detract attention from that controversial event—Philip was honored with one of the most extravagant funerals ever held for anyone outside the royal family (modern historians have compared it to the funeral for Winston Churchill). A procession of seven hundred mourners marched through London to St. Paul's Cathedral, where the ceremony was held; according to one eyewitness, the streets were "so thronged" with ordinary citizens paying their respects that the official participants "had scarcely room to pass." In the months to come, books of commemorative poetry written in both Latin and English appeared from the presses at both Cambridge and Oxford University, with contributions from nearly all the major authors of the era. In addition to poems by Spenser, Ben Jonson, and Sir Walter Raleigh, there was even an elegy for Philip written by James VI of Scotland, England's future king.

Mary wasn't an official mourner at Philip's funeral: an Elizabethan ordinance stipulated that "a man being dead, he [was] to have only men mourners at his burial," which meant that even wives weren't allowed to serve as mourners for their own husbands. (The same was true for male mourners at a woman's funeral: men were barred from playing a formal role.) But whether or not Mary attended Philip's funeral as a bystander, her principal mourning was conducted in private over the space of many years. The bond she had developed with her brother after her marriage, when he spent long stretches of time with her at Wilton during his exile from court, was unquestionably one of the closest of her life. Writing about the Sidney pair a century later, the gossipy biographer John

Aubrey went so far as to claim that "there was so great love between Sir Philip Sidney and his fair sister that I have heard old gentlemen say that they lay together, and it was thought the first Philip earl of Pembroke [Mary's second son] was begot by him." There's absolutely no evidence to support the idea that the relationship was incestuous, and Aubrey was in general an unreliable source. But behind the unfounded report lay Mary's deep attachment to her brother and her admiration for his intellectual gifts. Following his death, she transformed this admiration into a vocation of her own. Her magnificent return to London in 1588 wasn't only a way of signaling to the world that her mourning had ended. It was also her way of announcing her intention to become Philip's literary heir.

What did it take for a woman in Renaissance England to enter the overwhelmingly male world of literature? Even more than her education and the wealth and title brought by her marriage, it depended for Mary on having a gifted brother whose death made space for her. For it was through Philip's legacy that Mary paved her own way, beginning her own literary career by editing and publishing his works. Not surprisingly, she started with *The Countess of Pembroke's Arcadia,* which felt almost like personal property. It was also the messiest of the manuscripts Philip had left behind, and she was not the only one trying to clean it up. After finishing the first version of the romance sometime shortly after his long sojourn with Mary in 1580, Philip had expanded the tale to create a much darker and more complicated story roughly twice the length of the original—and it wasn't even finished. When he set out on his fatal trip to the Netherlands, he gave the new manuscript to Greville with instructions for further revisions.

In 1590, Greville published Philip's *Arcadia* with his own editorial changes (this edition is referred to today as the *New Arcadia*), but he kept the trappings of the original work, including the dedicatory letter to Mary and the original title bearing her name. This framing of the book as a private exchange between the aristocratic siblings no doubt added to its popular appeal: readers were given the sensation of being let into a secret book never meant for them to see. For Mary, the experience of being used as a marketing draw was clearly less agreeable. It motivated her to get to work. Three years after Greville's version of the *Arcadia* appeared in print, Mary published her own edition. The title page declared that the romance had been "augmented and ended" in comparison to Greville's 1590 publication. In addition to Philip's dedication to her, which described the *Arcadia*'s "chief protection" to be its "bearing the livery of [Mary's] name," Mary included a letter addressed "To the Reader" written by her husband's secretary Hugh Sanford. Sanford, who had helped her edit the book, began by accusing Greville of having contaminated the original text. "The disfigured face," Sanford wrote,

> wherewith this work not long since appeared to the common view, moved that Noble Lady, to whose Honor [it was] consecrated, to whose protection it was committed, to take in hand the wiping away those spots wherewith the beauties thereof were unworthily blemished.

Subtly tweaking Philip's own words to Mary about his composition (he had claimed, as we've seen, that he wrote it "only for you, only to you"), Sanford described the book as "by more than one interest The Countess of Pembroke's Arcadia; done, as it was, for her; as it is, by her." The letter ended by announcing Mary's intentions to publish more of Philip's writing, "which the everlasting love of her excellent brother will make her consecrate to his memory." As Sanford made clear to the world, Mary was just getting started.

By 1598, Mary had edited all of Philip's major works, which she published in a single volume that became the definitive collection for centuries to come. While she was busy editing her brother's writings, she also began to forge a creative path of her own. The earliest mention of Mary's talents as a poet came from none other than Edmund Spenser, who dedicated his 1591 elegy for Philip, "The Ruines of Time," to her. In the poem, Spenser exclaims to Philip's spirit:

> *Then will I sing: but who can better sing*
> *Than thine own sister, peerless Lady bright*
> *Which to thee sings with deep heart's sorrowing?*

Four years later, Spenser included another elegy for Philip that was almost certainly written by Mary, "The Doleful Lay of Clorinda," in his collection *Astrophel,* named for the lovestruck speaker of Philip's sonnets. In his introductory lines preceding the poem, Spenser attributed what followed to Astrophel's sister, "the gentlest shepherdess that lives this day." Written in the voice of the so-called Clorinda, "The Doleful Lay" lamented the death of her beloved Astrophel. "What cruel hand of cursed foe unknown," Clorinda asks,

> *Hath cropped the stalk which bore so fair a flower?*
> *Untimely cropped, before it well were grown,*
> *And clean defaced in untimely hour.*
> > *Great loss to all that ever him did see,*
> > *Great loss to all, but greatest loss to me.*

The highly artificial language of pastoral poetry was at the time one of the most popular vehicles for expressing grief: the deepest personal feelings were channeled through what may sound to our ears like impersonal and formal utterances.

In later centuries, "The Doleful Lay" was routinely attributed to Spenser, with one critic from the early 1900s even claiming that Spenser was "impersonating the Countess of Pembroke" by the "cloaking of his tone to something more feminine and tenuous." Who knows how many works by Renaissance women were mistakenly credited to the men around them—we'll see a few more examples ahead. Among Mary's own circle of acquaintances, however, there was no mistaking her authorship of the poem. In both the depth of her lamenting Philip's loss and her commitment to his writing, she discovered her own voice as a poet.

After finishing the elegy for Philip, Mary's next steps were in the sphere of translation. As modeled by the queen herself, aspiring women writers routinely began by translating the works of others, a practice that allowed them simultaneously to show off their talents and remain hidden behind the original (typically male) author. In 1590, Mary took on the task of translating two different works from French. The first, *Excellent discours de la vie et de la mort,* was written by a close friend of Philip's, Philippe du Plessis Mornay, who was a celebrated Protestant theologian and scholar. The two men had met in 1572 during Philip's only trip to Paris, where he'd gone for the wedding of the Protestant king Henry of Navarre (who would later become the king of France, as Henry IV), and the Catholic princess Marguerite of Valois. The match was an attempt to end the ongoing French religious wars between Catholics and Protestants, who were known in France as Huguenots, but the occasion was forever tainted by the horrific St. Bartholomew's Massacre that occurred six days after the marriage. On August 24 some three thousand Huguenots, many of whom had come to Paris to attend the ceremony, were brutally slaughtered in a plot generally blamed on Marguerite's mother, Catherine de' Medici. Catherine had apparently persuaded her son, the French king Charles IX, that this was the best way to deal with the continuing Huguenot threat (she clearly didn't put too much stock in her daughter's marriage, which she later tried to have annulled). The streets and gutters of Paris were flooded with blood, the Seine full of floating corpses. The massacre then spread out from the capital into the provinces, where an estimated fifty thousand Huguenots were killed.

Philip and Mornay weren't together during the actual massacre: Philip was safely sheltered in the home of Walsingham, who was then serving as the French ambassador, while Mornay moved between hiding places, including staying for some time in a small space between two roofs. But the experience ignited Philip's passion for the Huguenot cause and drew him closer to his new friend. When Mornay and his wife came for a long stay in England in 1577 in hopes of gaining Elizabeth's support, Philip was often at the couple's side; he also became godfather to their daughter, born in London in the spring of 1578 and baptized in the French Protestant church on Threadneedle Street. There's no specific record of Mary's knowing Mornay, but given her husband's involvement in the Protestant faction to which Philip belonged, it's likely she would have had occasion to meet Mornay in London, where the men often gathered.

In translating Mornay's *Excellent discours,* Mary was fulfilling Philip's dream of disseminating his friend's writing as widely as possible. (He had himself translated another of Mornay's treatises, which is now lost.) The treatise Mary chose was less political than philosophical in its message: it argued for stoical resolve in the face of death. As rendered in Mary's English version, Mornay asked his readers: "What good, I pray you, is there in life that we should so much pursue it? Or what evil is there in death, that we should so much eschew it?" This combination of classical indifference to life's pleasures and Christian hopefulness in salvation must have appealed to Mary in the aftermath of so much personal loss. She may have found comfort above all in Mornay's assurance that "death can be but sweet and agreeable, knowing that through it [we] enter into a place of all joys."

According to a note scribbled on her original manuscript, Mary completed *A Discourse of Life and Death* in May 1590. By November of that year, she had finished her second French translation. This time she turned her hand to a literary work: Robert Garnier's 1578 *Marc Antoine*. A "closet drama"—meant to be read silently or in a small group rather than performed in a theater—Garnier's tragedy about the death of the ancient Roman general and triumvir was part of a continental vogue for highly rhetorical plays in which the action took place offstage.

The taste for this nondramatic model of theater—more high-brow poetry than entertainment—was very different from what was playing at the time in London. In the late 1580s, English audiences were enthralled by Christopher Marlowe's action-packed *Tambur-laine,* a whirlwind epic filled with blood and gore, and gripped by his dark comedy, *The Jew of Malta.* By the early 1590s, they were lured into the Machiavellian plots of Shakespeare's *Richard III* and reeled from the brutal violence of his earliest revenge tragedy, *Titus Andronicus.* What Mary thought about this far more sensational model of theater isn't known, but Philip, who died before Marlowe or Shakespeare could have convinced him otherwise, was prejudiced against it. In *The Defence of Poesie,* he expressed his preference for plays with "stately speeches and well sounding phrases, climbing to the height of Seneca his style, and as full of notable morality." Without his ever having read *Marc Antoine,* Philip's description captured its style more or less perfectly.

What drew Mary to Garnier's drama was not only or perhaps not even primarily its correspondence to Philip's literary ideals. As with Mornay's treatise, *Marc Antoine* provided her with an opportunity to think seriously about the art of dying. In this case, the choice had the extra advantage of including a female character who displayed the virtues of classical stoicism. Although its official subject is Mark Antony, the play is equally interested in Antony's lover, Cleopatra. Unlike the seductive and morally complicated figure Shakespeare made famous twenty years later, Garnier's Cleopatra is unequivocally heroic. Following Antony's death, she bravely prepares for her own, instructing her children to "learn to endure," whatever their fate may be. The play ends before Cleopatra applies the asp to her breast, so that her suicide—anathema to Christian readers—doesn't compromise her moving and noble farewell to the world. In Garnier's Egyptian queen, Mary found a powerful female model for both eloquence and courage in the face of death.

Two years after completing her translations, Mary did something Philip had never done. She decided to publish her work. In 1592 a single volume containing both *A Discourse of Life and Death* and *Antonius* appeared in print, with Mary's name—or at least her title—proudly displayed on its title page. This bold embrace of the world of print was unprecedented for a woman of Mary's status. The only other women to publish translations before her weren't members of the aristocracy: Anne Lock had published several of Calvin's sermons in 1560 (this was the book dedicated to Katherine Willoughby), and Margaret Tyler's translation of a Spanish romance, *The Mirror of Princely Deeds and Knighthood,* appeared in 1578. Neither of these women, however, had their names on the title page; the printers used only their initials.

Of the two works Mary published, it was *Antonius* that enjoyed immediate success. By 1595, a second edition of the play appeared on its own with the more descriptive title *The Tragedie of Antonie.* The quick reissuing was almost certainly in response to the 1594 publication of a sequel, *Cleopatra,* written by the poet Samuel Daniel. In 1592, Daniel had earned a place as a tutor to Mary's children after dedicating his sonnet series, *Delia,* to her. In that dedication, he referred to Mary as "the happy and judicial patroness of the muses." In his 1594 dedication of *Cleopatra,* he addressed Mary in an entirely different fashion, thanking her for having "called up my spirits from out their low repose to sing

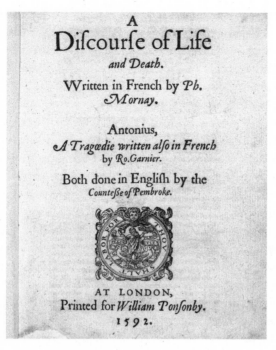

The title page for Mary Sidney's first publication

of state, and tragic notes to frame." Over the course of two years, Mary had been transformed in Daniel's eyes from patron to fellow poet.

Daniel's admiration for Mary's poetic gifts wasn't limited to her *Antonius*. In the *Cleopatra* dedication, he also praised her for an ambitious new project. Among the unfinished works Philip had left behind was a translation of the 150 Hebrew Psalms into English poetry. In her greatest act of posthumous collaboration, Mary began by revising the 43 psalms that Philip had drafted. She then decided to finish off the remaining 107 psalms on her own. Of all the books of Hebrew scripture, the Psalms were often considered the most difficult to translate due to the mystery surrounding their form. As Philip put it in *The Defence of Poesie,* they were "fully written in meter, as all learned Hebricians agree, although the rules be not yet fully found." It would be several centuries before the English bishop and scholar Robert Lowth discovered that the Psalms were actually not written in verse but structured around a practice of parallelism: the idea expressed in one line is balanced by a parallel idea in the next. Philip and Mary were no "learned Hebricians"—it's not clear if they knew any Hebrew, and their translations were based on earlier versions in Latin and French. What likely drew them to the Psalms was the opportunity to combine religious faith and poetic talent.

The decision to transform the Hebrew Psalter into a sophisticated book of poems represented a major departure from the English translations available at the time. In the standard English versions of the Bible introduced after the Reformation—before then, the Bible was available almost exclusively in Latin—the Psalms were printed as prose paragraphs. The only complete Psalter in English verse before Mary's, known as Sternhold and Hopkins, was made to facilitate the singing of psalms during church services. Psalm-singing had become all the rage in England after Protestant exiles returned from Lutheran communities on the Continent, where hymns were a regular part of public worship (Protestant English services up to this point had been far more somber affairs). As the bishop of Salisbury, John Jewel, remarked with astonishment in 1560: "You may now sometimes see at Paul's Cross, after the service, six thousand persons, old and young, of both sexes, all singing together and praising God." All 150 Psalms in the Sternhold and Hopkins Psalter were done in "common meter," a simple ballad form consisting of alternate lines of eight and six syllables ("Amazing grace, how sweet the sound / That saved a wretch like me!").

Anyone who has taken even the most cursory glance at Mary and Philip's translation will grasp that it wasn't competing with Sternhold and Hopkins. The Sidney Psalter bears no relation to liturgy: it's a work of literature. In the 107 psalms Mary translated on her own, there are 128 different combinations of stanza and meter, suggesting a truly remarkable command of poetic form. Among many examples: Psalm 55 is written in twelve-line stanzas made up of three different rhymes that form two six-line palindromes, creating a dizzying rhyme scheme of *abccbaacbbca;* Psalm 76 plays with triple rhymes (involving all three syllables of a word), such as "signify/dignify," "glorified/historified," "furious/injurious"; Psalm 140 contains an elaborate chain of internal rhymes so that the end of each line rhymes with the opening phrase of the next line ("set me free / From men that be"; "how they may / My steps betray"); Psalm 78, the second longest of all the psalms, is in the sophisticated Italian form of *ottava rima* (*abababcc*); and the list goes on.

As the first person—male or female—to translate the entire Book of Psalms into English poetry, Mary secured a hallowed place for herself in the annals of literary history. In the history of women's writing, her contribution takes on even more significance. Not only did she produce a dazzling poetic translation of the sacred book, but she also brought to these supremely patriarchal texts a distinctly female voice. There's no definitive answer to the authorship of the Psalms: in the Geneva Bible, the English translation done by Protestants in exile during the 1550s, the majority of psalms are attributed to King David, with the rest assigned to a range of authors including Moses, Salomon, Asaph, and the sons of Korah. No women, needless to say, appear on the list. When women are referred to within the Psalms, however, Mary found a way to draw those moments out. In Psalm 51, for example, David exclaims: "Behold, I was born in iniquity, and in sin hath my mother conceived me." Mary uses the occasion to reflect on the love a mother feels for her unborn child:

> *My mother, lo, when I began to be,*
> *Conceiving me, with me did sin conceive:*
> *And as with living heat she cherished me,*
> *Corruption did like cherishing receive.*

As a good Protestant, she couldn't eliminate the notion that sin was transmitted from mother to child in the womb, but she softens the blow by referring twice to the gift of maternal "cherishing."

Likewise in Psalm 48, the very odd comparison between what enemy kings felt at the daunting sight of Jerusalem and the pain a woman experienced in labor—"Fear came upon them, and sorrow, as upon a woman in travail"—expands in Mary's version to this:

> *So they fear, and so they fare,*
> *As the wife,*

> *Whose woeful care*
> *The pangs of childbed finds.*

It's the phrase "woeful care" that makes the difference, conjuring up the complicated mingling of physical pain and emotional worry that a woman might feel when labor begins. As someone who had given birth to at least four children, Mary understood this metaphor in a way no male author ever could have done.

Possibly the most revealing moment in her translation comes in Psalm 45, traditionally understood as a wedding song for King Solomon and his young Egyptian bride. Addressing the princess directly, the psalmist urges her to leave her family behind:

> Hearken, O daughter, and consider, and incline thine ear: forget also thine own people and thy father's house. So shall the king have pleasure in thy beauty: for he is thy Lord, and reverence thou him.

In Mary's translation, these verses become:

> *O daughter, hear what now to thee is told;*
> *Mark what thou hear'st, and what thou mark'st obey:*
> *Forget to keep in memory enrolled*
> *The house and folk where first thou saw'st the day.*
> *So in the king, thy king, a dear delight,*
> *Thy beauty shall both breed, and bred maintain.*
> *For only he on thee hath lordly right,*
> *Him only thou with awe must entertain.*

First, Mary's adds to the command to "consider, and incline thine ear" a warning about wifely duty: "mark what thou hear'st, and what thou mark'st obey." Next, she intensifies the already inflexible marital hierarchy by changing "he is thy Lord, and reverence thou him" to the more insistent, even chilling lines: "For only he on thee hath lordly right / Him only thou with awe must entertain." "Only he," "Him only": the oppression of the marriage bond quietly but unmistakably seeps through. Finally, she expands the instruction to "forget also thine own people and thy father's house" to emphasize the anguish of leaving one's childhood home. Not only is the bride reminded that her "father's house" is also her birthplace ("where first thou saw'st the day"), but this wrenching separation from "house and folk" is invoked again later in the psalm. With no basis in the original, Mary slips in these lines of comfort to the homesick princess:

> *Then let no grief thy mind, O queen, annoy,*
> *Nor parents left [behind] thy sad remembrance sting.*
> *Instead of parents, children thou shalt bring,*
> *Of partaged earth the kings and lord to be.*

To Mary, the young woman's having been ripped away from her family to enter the king's palace isn't, as the Hebrew psalmist would have it, a moment for "gladness and rejoicing." It is instead a moment of "grief," which became a "sad remembrance." It's hard not to hear in these words Mary's own bitterness about being sent off at the age of fifteen to marry an older man, something she otherwise never expressed in her surviving letters or poems. In translating ancient scripture, Mary found a way to describe what it felt like to be a bride, a mother, and above all, a woman. She also gave a sense of this biblical woman's plight where none had previously existed.

In the eyes of her contemporaries, Mary's Psalms were considered an extraordinary accomplishment. Daniel was the first to offer elaborate praise, describing her voice as immortal:

> *Those Hymns that thou dost consecrate to heaven*
> *which Israel's singer to his God did frame*
> *unto thy voice eternity hath given*
> *and makes thee dear to him from whence they came.*

A similar note arose in the Herbert family physician Thomas Moffett's 1599 publication, *The silkewormes and their flies: lively described in verse,* which he dedicated to Mary, whom he addressed as "the most renowned patroness, and noble nurse of learning." "O Thou," he proclaims,

> *Whose sweet and heavenly tuned Psalms*
> *The heavens themselves are scarce enough to praise!*

Whose pen divine and consecrated palms
From wronging verse did royal singer [King David] raise.

John Donne later followed suit with the most celebrated homage, which was at least partly responsible for the translation's fame in subsequent centuries. As the title of his poem—"Upon the translation of the Psalms by Philip Sidney and the Countess of Pembroke his Sister"—makes clear, he credited Philip far more than was due. But Donne was also generous in expressing admiration for Mary. Dubbing her a new Miriam (the sister of Moses), he describes her Psalms as transforming English worship: "They show us Islanders our joy, our King / They tell us why, and teach us how to sing."

So impressive were the Sidney Psalms that some readers strained to believe they could have been written by a woman. Pembroke's godson Sir John Harington credited Mary's chaplain, Gervase Babington, for having done much of the work. "It was more than a woman's skill," Harington avowed, "to express the sense so right as she hath done." Harington may have questioned Mary's authorship, but this didn't stop him from wanting the translation to be published. It was a pity, he declared, that these Psalms "lie still enclosed within those walls like prisoners, though many have made great suit for their liberty."

The prison Harington invoked was nothing other than the manuscript form itself. Mary had allowed handwritten copies of her translation to circulate among her family and friends—hence its finding its way to Harington—but she stopped short of bringing it to a wider public. Several of the manuscripts that have survived erased her authorship altogether, with title pages announcing, "The Psalms of David translated into English verse by that Noble and Virtuous Gent: Sir Philip Sydney," or "The Psalms metaphrased into sundry kindes of verse, By the noble and famous gent. Sir Phillip Sidney, knight." Given both Mary's willingness to print the Mornay and Garnier translations with her name prominently displayed and her interest in attaching her own reputation to Philip's, it's puzzling she didn't want to ensure the Psalms were properly attributed to the two of them. Judging from the clues she left behind, she may have been waiting for one particular stamp of approval.

THE

PSALMS of DAVID

TRANSLATED

INTO

ENGLISH VERSE

BY

That Noble and Virtuous Gent:

Sʳ PHILIP SYDNEY.

A late-sixteenth-century copy of Mary's translation
that erases her work in favor of her more famous brother
(Cambridge, Trinity College, MS O.1.51, f.1r)

In the summer of 1599, Mary was expecting a several-day visit from the queen at Wilton. This was to be the first time Elizabeth visited Pembroke's grand estate since his marriage to Mary in 1577; she was last at Wilton during the summer progress of 1574. To welcome Elizabeth, Mary had a gift far more personal than the gold posset-bowl and pot encrusted with agates, for example, that Pembroke gave to the queen at Windsor in 1593. She had prepared a beautiful manuscript of her Psalms.

There are two nearly identical surviving manuscripts—both large, expensive folios—that are candidates for this gift. The first, known as the Tixall manuscript and made by an unknown scribe, is held today at the Bodleian Library at Oxford; the other, known as the Penshurst manuscript and written by the great calligrapher John Davies of Hereford, is still owned by the Sidney family. Only the Tixall manuscript includes two dedicatory poems, which may have been removed at some point from the Penshurst copy (it's conspicuously missing a few pages in the front). One of the two dedications, "To The Angel Spirit of the most excellent Sir Philip Sidney," shows Mary's abiding concern with her brother's memory. Unlike her earlier elegy to Philip, "The Doleful Lay," this poem is concerned less with her grief than with her indebtedness to Philip's talent. In a way that feminist readers might rightly find maddening, Mary credits Philip with everything that was "divine" about the translations, begging his forgiveness for her inferior contributions:

> *Pardon, blest soul, presumption overbold,*
> *If love and zeal hath to this error run:*
> *Tis zealous love, love that hath never done,*
> *Nor can enough, though justly here controlled.*

The entire project, she declares, was done for him: "to thee alone addressed / Is this joint work, by double interest thine."

The second dedicatory poem looks not toward the past, but instead at the immediate present. Addressed to the queen, for whom the manuscript was probably made in the first place, "Even Now That Care" uses the occasion to measure Elizabeth's success as an earthly ruler. Comparing Elizabeth to King David, Mary judges their accomplishments to be equally impressive: "Thus hand in hand with him thy glories walk." She also draws attention to Elizabeth's having earned the respect of kings across the Continent, overcoming all predictions of the kind Calvin and Knox, among others, had articulated: "Kings on a queen enforced their states to lay / Men drawn by worth a woman to obey." The poem ends by gently advising Elizabeth to "Sing what God doth and do what men may sing." Underlying all of this—the compliments of Elizabeth's rule, the analysis of her reception on the world stage, the encouragement that she behave in such a way to be both a vehicle for God's word and an inspiration for poets to write about her—was a quiet bid for the queen's support. Mary certainly didn't need Elizabeth's patronage in the form of money. But she may well have hoped that Elizabeth's endorsement of the translation, perhaps by sharing the manuscript within her own circles or ultimately printing it with the royal imprimatur, would bring Mary an entirely new level of recognition.

The Psalms were not the only poetry Mary planned to give to Elizabeth during her intended visit to Wilton. In the spirit of the entertainments she had seen at Kenilworth and Woodstock in the summer of 1575, she wrote a short pastoral play, *Astrea*. Named for the Greek goddess who symbolized innocence and justice, *Astrea* was based on the myth of the Virgin Queen that had come to dominate Elizabeth's self-representation in the final decades of her rule. Far from being full of extravagant praise for Elizabeth, as both Leicester and Sir Henry Lee's entertainments had been, *Astrea* takes as its topic the limitations of praise as a way of honoring the queen. To each of the compliments the fulsome shepherd Thenot makes in the dialogue, the level-headed Piers responds by accusing him of speaking falsely. Elizabeth is not a "field in flowery robe arrayed" or a "maiden bay, her verdure never dying": these, Piers retorts, are empty metaphors that don't come close to capturing Astrea's qualities. Piers ends the dialogue by declaring the impossibility of ever adequately praising Astrea:

> *Words from conceit do only rise*
> *Above conceit her honor flies*
> *But silence, naught can praise her.*

On the one hand, Mary maintains Elizabeth's inestimable worth beyond what human words could ever capture. On the other hand, an entertainment meant to flatter the queen that concludes by declaring the task impossible can hardly be seen as a great success, especially given that queen's long-established taste for flattery. If Mary was hoping to win Elizabeth's patronage for her poetic work, *Astrea* was a risky gambit.

As it happened, Elizabeth never made it to Wilton in the summer of 1599: her annual progress was drastically scaled back due to crises both political and personal. Rumor had it that the Spanish were readying their fleet for another attack on English shores, and Elizabeth and her ministers were scrambling to prepare the country for a second Armada. As the great chronicler of the era John Chamberlain wrote from London to his regular correspondent, the diplomat Sir Dudley Carleton, "we are all here in a hurle [commotion] as though the enemy were at our doors."

Less well known was that the sixty-five-year-old queen was physically ailing. According to a letter sent July 21 by the Catholic spy William Sterrell to an agent in Venice:

> Some suppose [the curtailed progress] is by occasion of the news of this fleet, but rather as I have heard some courtiers relate, it is an indisposition of her Majesty's body, now grown in years, and unable to endure travel, insomuch as they have affirmed that when she rideth to take air, a mile or two in the park (which now she seldom doth), always she complaineth of the uneasy going of her horse, and when she is taken down, her legs are so benumbed that she is unable to stand.

The letter was intercepted by Elizabeth's agents, and to contradict its account she insisted on resuming plans for all of her intended progress's stops, including Wilton. In the end she made it only to Thomas Cecil, Lord Burghley's estate at Wimbledon, a visit that was delayed so many times that Burghley complained to his brother, Sir Robert Cecil: "Her Majesty's so often coming and not coming so distempers all things with me . . . I do nothing but give directions into the country for new provisions: most of the old thrown away by reason of the heat of the time." He was especially irate about having to discard the by-then-spoiled bucks he'd slaughtered specially for her meals.

There's no way to know how disappointed Mary was to have missed the chance to have *Astrea* performed before the queen; it's not even clear if she ever gave her the more significant gift of the Psalter. The Tixall manuscript ended up in the hands of the diplomat Sir Walter Aston of Tixall, Staffordshire (hence the name), who was a friend of Mary's elder son, William; by the mid-eighteenth century, the manuscript had passed into the hands of the Clifford family. When I pored over it under heavy supervision in the Bodleian Library, I was astonished to see that someone along the way—perhaps one of Anne Clifford's descendants—had used the magnificent book to press flowers. Running across the pages of elegant calligraphy are sepia shadows of long stems and delicate blooms, often landing in the most provocative of places. Just below the plaintive cry of Psalm 51—"My mother lo, when I began to be / Conceiving me, with me did sin conceive"—is the trace of what looks like a pair of roses.

Having lost her chance to entertain the queen in person, Mary seems to have given up hope of gaining her patronage. The only further trace of contact between the two women was a letter Mary sent to Elizabeth in late 1600 or early 1601 thanking her for welcoming William at court (this was just before the scandal broke over William's impregnating Mary Fitton). This is the sole letter between them that has survived, and its tone is strikingly different from both "Even Now That Care" and *Astrea*. When addressing the queen outside the medium of poetry, Mary's voice became obsequious. Calling herself Elizabeth's "humblest creature" who, along with her husband, "humble ourselves at your highness's feet," she described her "trembling hand offer[ing] these worthless words to your excellent eyes," and praised the queen—in terms her shepherd Piers would have openly mocked—as the "sun which evermore hath power to perfect the greatest imperfection." In asking a favor for her son, Mary also reminded Elizabeth of her own past at court as a maid of honor: "I, who by a more particular bond, was born and bred more your Majesty's than any other creature do, I protest, desire to live but to serve and observe you."

No one reading this letter could possibly imagine how powerful a figure Mary was at the time in the world of English letters. The poet Nicholas Breton compared her to Elisabetta Gonzaga, Duchess of Urbino, the heroine of Baldassare Castiglione's best-selling *Il Cortegiano* (known in English as *The Book of the Courtier*): "Who hath read of the Duchess of Urbino may say the Italians wrote well; but who knows the Countess of Pembroke, I think hath cause to write better." For Francis Meres, the author of one of the most popular literary commentaries of the period, Mary was "a most delicate poet"; to Thomas Nashe, a prose writer and dramatist, she was "a second Minerva." Several poets added Mary's name to the titles of their works: Breton's *The Countess of Pembroke's Love* followed on the heels of his rival Abraham Fraunce's *The Countess of Pembroke's Emmanuel* and *The Countess of Pembroke's Ivychurch*. All of these writers were seeking her patronage, and some sought employment of one kind or another at Wilton. According to Aubrey, "Wilton

House was like a college, there were so many learned and ingenious persons." This account was certainly exaggerated: Daniel was the only well-known poet to live there, and this was in his capacity as a tutor to Mary's children. But Aubrey's conclusion that Mary "was the greatest patroness of wit and learning of any lady in her time" was almost certainly true. As the new century began, she seemed poised to have an extraordinary career as both a writer and patron of English literature.

And then everything changed. If her brother Philip's death had opened the door to Mary's literary ambitions, her husband's death closed it. On January 19, 1601, Pembroke died at Wilton at the age of sixty-two. According to Chamberlain's account in a letter to Carleton, Pembroke "left his lady as bare as he could and bestowing all on the young lord, even to her jewels." This account of Mary's financial position was vastly exaggerated: she received a respectable inheritance of £3,000 in plate, jewels, and household goods (around £400,000 today), as well as life interest in her valuable jointure properties so long as she remained "solo and unmarried." But what Chamberlain didn't anticipate was the far more damaging loss that widowhood would bring to Mary's intellectual life.

Although Pembroke never shared Mary's literary interests, he had given her an unusual degree of independence to pursue her passions. With his death, she lost not only her title—when William married, his wife would become the new Countess of Pembroke—and her principal home at Wilton, where she had lived for more than twenty years. She also lost the crucial support of a husband whose position in the world had enabled her blossoming. As it turned out, many of the poetic dedications to Mary were meant to attract Pembroke's attention; once his fortune was no longer fully available to her, a whole generation of writers eager for support turned elsewhere (including to her own two sons).

More surprising (and more depressing) is that Mary seems at least for the time to have stopped writing. The fact that someone as well placed in society as Mary didn't keep going once she was widowed gives us some inkling of how difficult it was for women writers living in less fortunate circumstances—or, indeed, without the "cover" of a powerful husband. The obstacles were nearly insurmountable.

And yet: however much Mary may have faded from view in literary circles at court, her accomplishments were by no means erased. Her works continued to circulate, her name continued to garner praise, and her example continued to inspire. When Aemilia Lanyer picked up her pen to write in the 1610s, it was Mary whom she imagined leading the way. But this is getting ahead of our story.

CHAPTER FIVE

Unknown date, 1595

New Woodstock, Oxfordshire

Elizabeth Cary

Elizabeth Cary was almost certainly one of the only girls in England whose education included examining a witch. In 1595 her father, Lawrence Tanfield, a lawyer and MP for New Woodstock in Oxfordshire, conducted a formal interrogation of an old woman charged with bewitching a man to death. Witchcraft prosecutions had been raging in England for several decades, following Parliament's passage of a law in 1563 that made it a felony to conjure evil spirits for any reason; this was an intensification of the 1542 law, which forbade practicing witchcraft or sorcery in order to hurt a person's body or goods, find treasure, or for any other "unlawful purposes." Across the country, trials of women—mostly poor, and mostly old—accused of using curses, charms, and potions to perform *maleficium* (literally, mischief or wrongdoing) were heard in both ecclesiastical and civil courts. Capital punishments were reserved for witches responsible for human deaths, with lesser fines for maiming people, damaging property, or killing animals.

Queen Elizabeth wasn't particularly caught up in the hysteria—she was too preoccupied with the seemingly unending threats of Spanish invasions and Catholic assassination plots to worry about witches—but her future heir in Scotland was very much under the witchcraft spell. In the early 1590s James VI personally oversaw a trial of three witches accused of trying to kill him. In gripping testimony produced under torture—in this case, the authorities used both a thumbscrew and the binding or winching of the accused's head with a cord—one of the women, Geillis Duncan, was found with a "devil's mark" (usually imagined as an extra nipple or teat) on her body, confirming her guilt. She then named several of her accomplices, including one Agnes Sampson, who, under torture, described traveling in a kitchen sieve across the sea along with two hundred other witches to meet the Devil in the church of North Berwick in East Lothian, on the shore of the Scottish Firth of Forth. There, she related, the Devil asked them to "kiss his buttocks, in sign of duty to him" and declared that James VI was "the greatest enemy he hath in the world." Agnes confessed to have taken steps to wreck the king's ship upon his return from his wedding celebrations in Denmark in the spring of 1590; she explained that she had first christened a cat to which she attached several parts of a dead man's body and then thrown the cat and human limbs into the sea to produce a wild storm.

Agnes and the others were burned as witches. But the killing of this group of women hardly reassured James that his problems were resolved. Indeed, the fact that James believed Agnes's account—the winds around his ship had seemed to him particularly fierce compared to the other ships traveling nearby—shows the extent to which even those in the highest positions could be made to feel vulnerable to the threat posed by these disenfranchised members of society. In response to a 1584 book, *The Discovery of Witchcraft,* by the skeptic Reginald Scot—Scot claimed that witches existed only in the realm of the imagination—James wrote a work of his own. Published in 1597, *The Demonology* outlined in great detail the powers that witches had over the mind, body, and elements. For James, who dealt with all sorts of serious political intrigue and religious conflict, witchcraft was one of the greatest dangers to the realm.

The case brought before Lawrence Tanfield in 1595 was typical of the accusations that arose in local communities where neighbors blamed one another for everything that went wrong in their lives. Butter that wouldn't set, crops that didn't thrive, children that mysteriously fell ill, cattle that suddenly died: all of this was the work of witches. On this occasion, the woman being examined—and probably tortured—was accused of causing a man's death by means of a "familiar in the shape of a black dog, a hare, or a cat," which had "licked [the man's] hand, or breathed on him, or stepped over him," after which the man "came home sick and languished away." The details were admittedly fuzzy, but the implication was clear: the witch had been engaged by the Devil to do his bidding through her "familiar" (usually a household pet that served as the witch's attendant). As with the great majority of witchcraft accusations, the witness didn't need to have seen the witch actually do the killing to charge her with the crime. Indeed, one of the most insidious features of the witchcraft craze was the total lack of evidence required to make an accusation, since witches were rarely imagined to lay hands directly upon their victims.

After hearing the witness's testimony, the accused fell prostrate before Lawrence, and "quaking, begging pardon, [she] acknowledged all and the same of each particular accusation." Normally, a confession of this kind would have been a death sentence, and the confirmed witch would be brought to the gallows (in Scotland, witches were routinely burned; in England they were usually hanged). But luckily for this woman, the ten-year-old Elizabeth Cary was in the audience, no doubt gripped if not terrified by what was unfolding. "Seeing the poor woman in so terrible a fear, and in so simple a manner confess all," she suspected her words bore no relation to the truth. The young girl quickly came up with a plan, whispering to her father to ask the woman whether she had also "bewitched to death Mr. John Symonds." John was Elizabeth's uncle, who—unbeknownst to the accused—was standing nearby. "Yes," the woman quickly admitted, she had killed Mr. John Symonds "just as she had done to the rest, promising to do so no more if they would have pity on her." Laughter broke out as Lawrence revealed that her supposed victim was in the room, alive and well. The case was dismissed, and the woman set free. How much Elizabeth took in of the complexity of it all—the would-be witch at once declared innocent and impotent, stripped of her magic powers and made the object of collective derision—can't be known. But the trial was a fascinating introduction to one of the only ways a woman in Renaissance England could regularly threaten the world of men. Later in her life, as we will see, Elizabeth would develop a few ways of her own.

The story of Elizabeth's heroic turn as girl detective in a witch-craft trial has been preserved in her 1645 biography, *The Lady Falkland, Her Life,* written by several of her children. Unlike the "Lives" of so many men from this period, Elizabeth's didn't see print for hundreds of years. In the mid-nineteenth century the manuscript of *The Lady Falkland* was found in an archive in the north of France not far from where four of Elizabeth's daughters, Anne, Elizabeth, Lucy, and Mary, had lived as nuns at the Benedictine convent in Cambrai. The book was a collaborative project: Lucy was the principal "scribe," with additions and corrections made by Mary and one other unidentified hand; later emendations were done by the girls' brother Patrick, who came to France in the late 1640s after spending more than a decade at the English College in Rome. Whoever its principal author may have been, *The Lady Falkland* shows signs of having originated in a convent, often sounding like a hagiography in its lavish praise of Elizabeth's sacrifices for her children and her faith. It is also the richest possible source for the experiences Elizabeth must have recounted to her daughters, who in turn made the wildly unusual decision that their mother's life was worth remembering.

According to *The Lady Falkland,* Elizabeth's intervention in her father's witchcraft trial was one among many examples of her precocious intelligence. By the time she was four, she had learned to read; by adolescence she had taught herself French, Spanish, Italian, Latin, and a little Hebrew. At some point in her childhood her parents had a visitor from Transylvania, and she took it upon herself to learn his native tongue—presumably Romanian or Hungarian—although she admitted to forgetting it soon after he left (to be fair, she had no one to practice with). Above all, Elizabeth was a passionate reader who got so absorbed in her books that she stayed up through the night with candles burning, a habit her mother ultimately forbade for fear she would ruin her eyes. Undaunted by her mother's disapproval, Elizabeth bribed her servants at the rate of half a crown per candle to keep her supply going. By her twelfth birthday she had accumulated a debt of 400 crowns (£100), which means she had consumed around eight hundred candles.

If Mary Sidney hailed from the English aristocracy and Aemilia Lanyer from the middling gentry, Elizabeth Cary was born into the

Renaissance equivalent of the wealthy bourgeoisie: her father had neither title nor impressive pedigree, but he had amassed a sizable fortune through his thriving legal career. Having no inheritance from his father, who died when he was a small child, Lawrence enrolled in 1569 at the Inner Temple, one of the four Inns of Court in London, where barristers and judges were trained. Ten years later, at the age of around twenty-eight, he achieved early fame after arguing a case in which the opposing counsel, Edmund Plowden, was one of the best-known jurists of the period. Lawrence lost the case, but Plowden was dazzled by the young lawyer's skills and publicly predicted he would become a "great treasure" for England. Five years later, Lawrence was elected to Parliament as MP for New Woodstock. His election was almost certainly brought about with the help of Sir Henry Lee, the queen's Master of the Armory and lieutenant governor of Woodstock, where he had famously hosted Elizabeth during the summer progresses of 1575. Lee also held the role of Queen's Champion at the Accession Day tilts—the elaborate jousting and theatrical events honoring the date of Elizabeth's coronation—a holiday he had transformed into the greatest public spectacle of the year. Around the time of Lawrence's election, Lee introduced him to his niece, Elizabeth Symonds, whom Lawrence married in 1584 or 1585.

From the perspective of social class, the marriage was a good one for the groom, and less so for the bride. Elizabeth came from a distinguished family: in addition to her famous uncle, her grandfather had been knighted by Henry VIII and her grandmother was the sister of the poet Sir Thomas Wyatt. Lawrence, by contrast, had no inheritance or relations of any distinction: he was entirely a self-made man. But however much the future Lady Tanfield resented marrying someone who worked for a living—and there are hints she resented this a great deal—her husband made a home for her that rivaled those of the high nobility. Around the time of their daughter, Elizabeth's birth, Lawrence acquired the impressive Burford Priory. A former monastic hospital whose medieval ruins Lawrence incorporated into a grand Elizabethan estate, Burford Priory is considered a masterpiece of the stone architecture popular in the Cotswolds. Lawrence also purchased the lordship of the manor of Burford, which was (and is still today) a bustling commercial town due to its prime location on the main road from Oxford to the west of England. Through a series of questionable legal maneuvers, he subsequently stripped the burgesses (the inhabitants of the borough) of their privileges and impoverished the vicarage, earning him the enmity of the entire community. For centuries after his death, legend had it that the ghosts of both Lawrence and his wife swept down the High Street riding in a spectral carriage. The road he had regularly traveled on with his coach, meanwhile, came to be known as "Wicked Lord's Lane."

However heartless Lawrence was to the residents of Burford, he seems to have been a devoted father to Elizabeth, who was the couple's only child. In the absence of a son and with his daughter's gifts so visible, Lawrence pushed her intellectual growth in a manner that Sir Henry Sidney, for example, never dreamed of doing with the talented Mary, whose brothers were always in the limelight. The decision to bring Elizabeth to a witchcraft interrogation was probably Lawrence's most extreme gesture of expanding her horizons, but the curriculum he pursued at home was also far from the standard fare. According to *The Lady Falkland,* he "loved much to have [Elizabeth] read, and she as much to please him," although their tastes didn't always match. When she was twelve, he gave her the weighty tome of Calvin's *Institutes.* No doubt most of her peers would have scoffed at the idea of wading through the French theologian's exposition of Protestant doctrine, but Elizabeth plunged right in. Not only did she read Calvin carefully, but she also surprised—and no doubt disappointed—her fiercely Protestant father by disagreeing with Calvin's central tenets. Indeed, she made so many objections and identified so many supposed contradictions that Lawrence was forced to concede his daughter had "a spirit averse from Calvin." This was the earliest sign of Elizabeth's distaste for England's state religion, a distaste that would become the central theme of her adult life. It was also another sign of the young girl's confidence in speaking her mind.

Around the time Elizabeth was arguing with her father about Calvin, she began working on several projects of her own. Following a path similar to Mary Sidney's, albeit at a much younger age, she started her life as a writer with translations. The first work she translated was Seneca's *Epistles,* a popular book at the time especially among female readers. Given how little control most women had over the major events shaping their lives—from whom they married or where they lived to whether their children survived—the ancient philosopher's stoicism offered a helpful model for endurance. No trace of Elizabeth's translation of Seneca has survived, so there's no way to know how many of the 124 letters she translated. The sheer fact of Elizabeth's acquiring strong enough Latin to do this work—girls, we will recall, were generally discouraged from learning Latin—gives us some sense of her intellectual ambition.

Elizabeth's second translation shows her interests extended far beyond the classics to trends in her contemporary world. Around 1598, she completed an English version of Abraham Ortelius's 1588 *Le Miroir du Monde,* the first modern atlas, as a gift for her great-uncle, Sir Henry Lee. Elizabeth both translated the ninety-four French texts that accompanied Ortelius's maps and wrote out the entire manuscript in her own hand. Her handwriting was in fact unusually beautiful, thanks to Lawrence's having hired John Davies of Hereford as her tutor—the same calligraphy master whom Mary Sidney employed to make the Penshurst copy of her Psalms. In Elizabeth's dedicatory letter to Lee, she described the gift as "the fruits and endeavors of my young and tender years" and expressed her hope that he would amend any errors she made given "the experience of your many years' travels abroad in the world." Of all her relatives, Lee was certainly the best traveled: he had been to France, Italy, Germany, and the Netherlands on multiple occasions, whereas Elizabeth's parents almost certainly never left English shores.

The Ortelius translation was an especially appropriate gift for Lee not only because of his extensive travels but also because of his interest in cartography, a burgeoning field in the late sixteenth century due to the rapid expansion of overseas ventures and international trade. Where Elizabeth would have come across Ortelius's atlas isn't clear—perhaps Lee himself lent the French book to her or to her parents—but she had at least one strong association of her great-uncle with maps. In the early 1590s, Lee commissioned a portrait of the queen standing on top of a map of the world. In this massive painting (nearly eight feet tall and five feet wide) done by the Flemish artist Marcus Gheeraerts the younger, Elizabeth is dressed in a magnificent white gown covered in jewels, with the pointy tips of her delicate shoes strategically placed over Lee's estate at Ditchley in Oxfordshire. Behind her the sky is divided: on one side it's ominously dark and full of clouds, while on the other, the sun shines in all its splendor as if conquered by Elizabeth's will. The map below her feet has been identified as having been published in 1583, just a few years before Ortelius's atlas first appeared.

The Ditchley Portrait, as it came to be known, was made in honor of the queen's visit to Lee during the 1592 progress. Records from Elizabeth's entertainments that summer include her having been taken at Ditchley to a pavilion to see some "enchanted pictures" whose spell she broke with her presence, and it's possible the startling portrait—one of the most iconic images of the queen—was among the bewitched works of art. But whether it was painted before or after the visit, it hung for years in Ditchley's halls, where Lee's young niece would have seen it regularly: Burford was a mere twelve miles away, and her parents and Lee were very close. For a girl with such prodigious talent, this vision of a woman standing on top of the world may in itself have been thrilling. The painting also carried special meaning for the young Elizabeth as a record of her own extraordinary experience that same summer. Records show that, en route to visit Lee, the court stopped for a visit at Burford Priory. On September 16, 1592, the seven-year-old girl may have dined with her queen.

Around the time of her translation of Ortelius, Elizabeth received the first public recognition of her talents. In 1597, the poet and playwright Michael Drayton, whom Lawrence had hired as a tutor for his daughter—supplementing, if not replacing, his own lessons for her—dedicated two poems to the twelve-year-old Elizabeth in his book *Englands Heroicall Epistles*. Addressing her as his "honored Mistress, the sole daughter and heir of that famous and learned lawyer, Lawrence Tanfield, Esquire," Drayton declared himself a "witness of the many rare perfections wherewith nature and education have adorned you." The particular combination of subservience and flattery in Drayton's words wasn't altogether surprising for a poor scholar eager to keep a lucrative post. But more revealing were the specific qualities he praised in his young pupil. First, he admired how well Elizabeth spoke French and Italian: "Sweet is the French tongue," he declared, "more sweet the Italian, but most sweet are they both if spoken by your admired self." Next, he praised her intelligence and "more than womanlike wisdom" that at so "tender an age" made her worthy of "wonder."

Most important for Elizabeth's future career, Drayton drew attention to her gifts as a poet. "The Graces shall have one more sister by yourself," he predicted, "and England by your birth shall add one Muse more to the Muses." It was already unusual for a girl of Elizabeth's age and social class to receive attention in print: the only other female dedicatees in Drayton's book—Lucy Russell, Countess of Bedford, and Lucy's mother, Lady Anne Harington—both belonged to the aristocracy. It was entirely unprecedented for a girl of any class to be publicly praised as a writer. Even if the compliments came from her own impoverished tutor, Elizabeth Cary had been named one of the great female minds of the era.

If Elizabeth had been a man, the next notice of her in the historical records may have been praise for a brilliant work of literature. Instead, her name surfaced five years later in relation to her having made an important marriage. In John Chamberlain's letter to Sir Dudley Carleton written on June 27, 1602, he delivered the latest English news: updates on military expeditions in the Low Countries, privateering ventures in the estuary of the Tagus River near Lisbon, the readying of 6,000 Italians to cross into Ireland from Spain, and his usual smattering of social gossip. "Here is talk of a match," he reported,

> twixt the Lord Keeper's son and the Lady Frances, second daughter of Derby; and twixt Sir Henry Cary and Master Tanfield's daughter with £2000 presently, £2000 at two years, and £3000 at his death, if he chance to have more children, otherwise to be his heir *ex asse* [his sole heir]. Master Philip's son the lawyer shall marry a daughter of Sir Thomas Gorges, and one Poultney, a young gentleman of Norhamptonshire, Mistress Madge Fortescue, and on Wednesday next (twixt June and July when he should keep his mouth wet and somewhat else dry) our Master Trot shall marry one Master Perin's daughter of Hartfordshire, a lusty tall wench able to beat two of him.

There were no magazines or papers at the time that kept track of social events, and the engagements between members of the elite were considered worthy of serious attention. It's no coincidence that of the various matches Chamberlain described, only Sir Henry Cary and Elizabeth's included details of the monetary arrangements (a total of £4,000 in the first two years, and then £3,000 upon Lawrence's death—more than double what Sir Henry Sidney had to give Pembroke for Mary's dowry). As anyone even remotely involved would have perceived, this was a marriage made entirely for financial gain. A cash-poor gentleman from a distinguished family (his father, Sir Edward Cary, was Master of the Jewel House), Henry chose Elizabeth, as their own daughters later put it, "only for being an heir, for he had no acquaintance with her and she was nothing handsome."

On the bride's part, the match was equally unromantic: Lawrence hoped that marrying his daughter into the aristocracy would raise his social position and ideally secure him a knighthood. Both men got what they had bargained for: Henry was largely kept afloat throughout his career at court thanks to Elizabeth's money, and Lawrence was knighted in 1604. How the seventeen-year-old Elizabeth felt about being married off to a stranger interested only in her fortune didn't seem to matter. It's unlikely her father asked for her consent; as her legal guardian, he could arrange the match without involving her at all in the decision. For a girl of such extraordinary intelligence—she was clearly a child prodigy—to be reduced to a monetary sum on the marriage market seems devastating to modern eyes. Nothing about her own talents and passions played any role in determining her future; no one cared if she ever picked up a book or pen again.

Following their wedding in the fall of 1602, the couple lived separately for nearly four years. Initially, Elizabeth remained at Burford Priory with her parents while Henry pursued his career at court. There were certainly occasions when the newlyweds were together—a letter from Chamberlain to Carleton dated December 23, 1602, mentioned Henry and Elizabeth among the guests spending Christmas at Sir John Harington's home in Rutlandshire (the group also included Mary Sidney's son William and Mary's brother Robert). Rumor had it that the marriage was still unconsummated when Henry left England in 1604 to fight in the ongoing Protestant wars against the Spanish in the Netherlands, a continuation of the conflict that had cost Philip Sidney his life almost two decades earlier.

Henry's time on the Continent was hardly what he had hoped for. Captured during the bloody siege of Ostend, a series of Spanish attacks on the Flemish fortress that lasted three years and left tens of thousands dead, he was taken to Spain as a prisoner. His heroism in battle—he apparently continued to charge the enemy while nearly all of his fellow soldiers took flight—won him a reputation for valor recorded in a poem by Ben Jonson:

> *That neither fame, nor love might wanting be,*
> *To greatness, CARY, I sing that and thee . . .*
> *When no foe, that day,*
> *Could conquer thee, but chance, who did betray.*

Jonson's final lines—"He'st valiant'st, that dares fight, and not for pay / That virtuous is, when the reward's away"—put a positive spin on what must have been a very unpleasant ordeal. Due to the exorbitant ransom of £2,500 the Spanish demanded, Henry was left in captivity for a full nine months before his father could raise the sum for his release. It's striking that Lawrence didn't contribute to the effort, but this was perhaps the first hint of what became a lifelong financial conflict between Elizabeth's father and her husband.

Elizabeth spent much of Henry's time abroad in an imprisonment of her own. Soon after his departure, she gave in to her mother-in-law's pressing requests that she move to the Cary household. Who knows why Lady Catherine wanted Elizabeth to live with her, but she was certainly disappointed in her company. As recounted in *The Lady Falkland*, "Her mother-in-law having her, and being one that loved much to be humored, and finding [Elizabeth] not to apply herself to it, used her very hardly, so far, as at last, to confine her to her chamber." Much to Catherine's further dismay, Elizabeth didn't seem to mind being kept in her room: on the contrary, she happily "entertained herself with reading." At this point, Catherine became so enraged that she took away all of Elizabeth's books. Locked up without anything to read, Elizabeth immersed herself in writing.

The first writing Elizabeth seems to have done in the early years of her marriage was to send long letters to her husband. While she was still living at Burford Priory, her mother hadn't trusted her to write to Henry: fearful that Elizabeth's erudition would frighten or repel him, she arranged for someone else to compose her daughter's letters in an appropriately modest style. The idea that husbands didn't want their wives to have too much learning was entirely common at the time. As the writer William Gouge put it in his treatise *Of Domestical Duties:* "If the Lord [God] have endowed [wives] with any gift above the ordinary sort," those women were advised "to note well their own infirmities, and to lay them by their eminent gifts" so that "their proud-peacock-feathers may be cast down."

Once Elizabeth moved to her mother-in-law's home, she wrote to Henry herself. Apparently, he noticed a marked difference in style between the earlier and the more recent letters; to his credit, he preferred the new ones but suspected they'd been written by someone other than his wife. When Henry returned to England in the summer of 1606, he "examined" Elizabeth to see if she had in fact been the sole author. Upon discovering the truth, "he grew better acquainted with her and esteemed her more." This is the first—and nearly only—suggestion in *The Lady Falkland* that Henry admired Elizabeth's intelligence.

In addition to writing her husband lively letters, Elizabeth apparently spent her time at her mother-in-law's composing "many things for her recreation, on several subjects and occasions, [and] all in verse." There are no details as to what the "things" were. But sometime in the early years of her marriage, she wrote her first play. According to her daughters, she was a passionate theatergoer: she loved masques and plays, "especially the last extremely." There's no record of performances she saw, and women of her class very rarely went to the public theaters at this time. Playhouses were considered dangerous for ladies on multiple counts—among them, pickpockets, tobacco fumes, diseases, and lecherous men. In 1594 the Lord Mayor of London condemned theaters for attracting "horse-stealers, whore-mongers, and cozeners." The poet Sir John Davies likewise described the audience at a theater in 1593 as made up of "a thousand townsmen, gentlemen, and whores."

If Elizabeth was unlikely to have gone to the London theaters in the early 1600s, she would certainly have had the chance to see performances at the royal court. These weren't necessarily different plays: the same dramas often made the rounds between the elite courtly audience and the public stage. Thus, we might imagine Elizabeth seated in the Banqueting House at Whitehall Palace with her in-laws, Lady Catherine and Sir Edward Cary, in November 1604 for the first performance of Shakespeare's *Othello*. Other members of the audience were no doubt focused on the tragic downfall of the jealous Moor at the hands of his demonic foe. But Elizabeth may have been struck above all by Desdemona, the young, innocent wife who falls victim to Iago's misogynistic lies without ever thinking she might defend herself. Maybe that was when Elizabeth decided to create her own tragic heroine who would dare to speak back.

CHAPTER SIX

May 17, 1597

Stone House, Billingsgate, London

Aemilia Lanyer

In the spring of 1597, much of England was basking in its recent spate of victories over the Spanish enemy: Robert Devereux, Earl of Essex, had captured the strategic port of Cádiz in June 1596, and a second Armada launched by Philip II the following October had been struck by a storm, sinking 43 Spanish ships and killing some 5,000 of Philip's men. But Aemilia Lanyer was feeling utterly miserable. After roughly five years of marriage to Alfonso without bearing a second child, she decided to consult the astrologer and medical practitioner Simon Forman. Forman cast horoscopes for a wide swath of London society, ranging from members of the aristocracy to the wives of wigmakers. Most of his clients were women. Among the names that stand out from his records were Shakespeare's landlady, Mary Mountjoy, who consulted Forman a few years before taking in the famous playwright as her lodger; and Frances Howard, Countess of Essex (she was married to Robert Devereux's son), who in the early 1600s asked Forman to make for her magical potions that would turn her first husband away and attract the man who became her second husband, Robert Carr, Earl of Somerset.

Forman lived and worked in the former sacristy of the parish church of St. Botolph, Billingsgate, near the northern end of London bridge. As John Stow described it in his 1598 *Survey of London,*

Billingsgate was a large water gate where ships carrying "fish, both fresh and salt, shell-fishes, salt, oranges, onions, and other fruits and roots, wheat, rye, and grain of divers sort" unloaded their goods. The only port for "all such kind of merchandises brought to this city by strangers and foreigners," it was a crowded area that would have allowed Forman's clients to come and go without drawing attention to themselves.

However much some of Forman's clients may have wanted to keep their visits private, consulting an astrologer wasn't a source of embarrassment in Renaissance England. Despite obvious incompatibilities with the Calvinist ideas of predestination and divine providence that dominated the Protestant church at the time, astrology was wildly popular. How the motions of the celestial bodies could possibly exert power over human agency outside of God's will may have troubled English theologians, but the contradictions seem to have posed few problems for the population at large. By no means a fringe science, astrology was part of the university curriculum at Oxford and Cambridge, where it was taught alongside astronomy and mathematics.

Although the queen shied away from officially patronizing astrologers at court, they were nonetheless regularly consulted about how to interpret a comet, when to go to war, or whether to issue a particular decree. In 1558 Elizabeth's favorite courtier (and Mary Sidney's uncle), Robert Dudley, later Earl of Leicester, commissioned the astrologer John Dee to set the best date for the queen's coronation. Several decades later, he likewise asked another of his astrologers, Thomas Allen, to calculate Mary's son William Herbert's "nativity"—a map of the planets' positions at the time of birth—from which Allen predicted William would die at the age of fifty (he did).

Far from the patronage of Leicester and the powerful circles at court, Forman had a workaday practice that combined astrology, medicine, and magic. These areas of expertise were for him entirely compatible: he could read an astrological chart, perform minor surgery, and call spirits from the dead all in a single session. For the English authorities, Forman was nothing but trouble. Over the course of his career he was arrested on multiple occasions both for owning illegal books of magic—his interest in necromancy was considered especially suspect—and for practicing medicine without formal training. In spite of this, Forman became one of the most sought-after healers in London. The College of Physicians, which regulated the practice of medicine in London, deemed him a "magician," "murderer," and "quack" (these were their official verdicts), but his talents were legendary, and his business continued to thrive. Who else could determine whether a disease was a result of natural or demonic forces, prescribe traditional medicines as well as magical potions, and evaluate the effect of the celestial bodies on his patients' health?

Between 1596 and 1603, a rough estimate suggests Forman held around 10,000 consultations. Thanks to the extraordinary records he kept, his "books of judgment" form one of the richest archives about medical health from the period. In large folios written out in a nearly illegible hand, Forman scribbled notes on each of his clients alongside their horoscopes. Six of these massive tomes, filled with biographical sketches, maps of the stars and constellations, and Forman's notes on his meetings, are held today at Oxford's Bodleian Library. Lucky for us, these books contain extensive notes about Aemilia Lanyer.

During May and June 1597, Aemilia met with Forman on at least four occasions. In their first full session on May 17, Forman gathered information about Aemilia's background and discussed her reasons for seeing him (this was more or less the Renaissance equivalent of an appointment with a new therapist). Forman's extensive notations from that day were placed under four different headings: Aemilia's sexual past, her attitude about her sexual past, her financial situation as a child, and her current health. The emphasis on her sexual history almost certainly reflects a prurient interest in his new client rather than any issues Aemilia herself would have raised. As he explained in his "Astrological Judgments of Physic and other Questions" written in the early 1600s, when he wanted to explore a woman's romantic past, he focused his astrological figure directly on sex to see what he might tease out of her. (A man without any obvious medical ethics, Forman fully exploited the intimate access to women that his practice afforded him; he paid the price by suffering for years from venereal disease.)

According to his records from 1597, here's what Forman learned

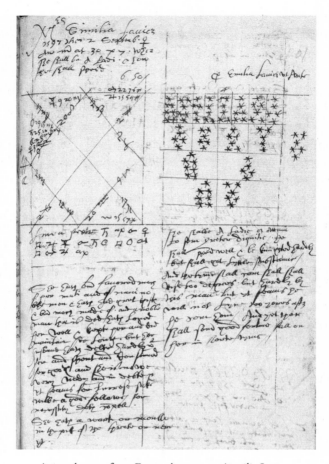

A sample page from Forman's notes on Aemilia Lanyer

about Aemilia. First, "that she hath had a child in fornication"—her son, Henry, presumably named after his father, Henry Carey, Baron Hunsdon—to which piece of information he added the provocative phrase "et sodomita," suggesting Aemilia engaged in unconventional sexual activity. There's no way to know how he came to this conclusion, but it's consistent with what at least today we would regard as his entirely unprofessional, if not actionable, curiosity. Second, that following her pregnancy, she was "for color married to a minstrel." "For color" implies the affair with Hunsdon may have continued after the marriage, possibly until Hunsdon's death in 1596, while

Aemilia's apparent reference to Alfonso as a "minstrel"—a generic term for a singer or musician who entertains for a living—hints at her disappointment in the marriage. Third—and possibly as a way to recover her pride—this was the occasion where she announced that "the old lord chamberlain kept her long and she was maintained in great pomp." Finally, she reported having an income of "forty pounds a year"—possibly left to her by Hunsdon—and boasted of bringing "money and jewels" to her marriage.

In their next meeting on June 3, Aemilia was the one asking the questions, and her reasons for seeing Forman became clear. The most pressing issue was a medical one: she was pregnant and wanted to know if the baby would survive. Henry was now five years old, but she and Alfonso had been unable to have a child of their own, and she'd already suffered several painful miscarriages. In an age before gynecologists, Forman was considered a fertility specialist—around six percent of his patients asked him specifically about their pregnancies, and many more about their gynecological health—and it's likely Aemilia was referred to Forman for this expertise. Forman recorded that Aemilia "seems to be with child of twelve days or twelve weeks" (here it seems he was transcribing word for word what Aemilia said, including her mistakes), and that she had "much pain in the bottom of the belly, womb, stomach & head." He also observed that the fetus "kicks not her body." At the exact moment Aemilia's question was asked, Forman mapped the position of the stars in relation to the twelve astrological houses; he then read the figure according to the elaborate rules laid out in his books. In this case, he predicted, correctly, that Aemilia would soon miscarry.

In addition to concern for her pregnancy, Aemilia had a second reason for consulting Forman that had nothing to do with her health. She wanted to know "whether her husband shall have the suit" and be promoted at court. In his notes to their meeting on June 6, Forman commented that Aemilia was "high minded" and "very brave" ("brave" could mean either courageous or showy in her attire, with the latter more prevalent at the time). He also commented rather mysteriously that "she hath something in the mind she would have done for her." On June 16, Aemilia's question for Forman became more specific: she asked whether Alfonso "shall come to any preferment before he comes home again." Sometime the previous month, Alfonso had volunteered to serve in Essex's latest naval campaign—the so-called Islands Voyage aimed to destroy the Spanish fleet in the northwest harbor of Ferrol and to seize the Azores. This was hardly an ordinary move for a court musician, and it suggests Aemilia and her husband had at least social ambition in common. According to John Chamberlain's June 11 letter to Sir Dudley Carleton, Essex had 4,000 "pressed" (drafted) men, 1,200 musketeers from the English forces in the Netherlands, and nearly 2,000 new "voluntaries" accompanying him.

Essex himself despaired over his men's lack of qualifications, writing in June 1597 that "we are at our wits end to find the fleet so weakly and wretchedly manned," made up of "men of all occupations, some of whom did not know a rope and were never at sea." The recorder player Alfonso probably fit this bill. Chamberlain's description of what motivated one such volunteer—an acquaintance named Hugh Beston—also applied well to Aemilia's husband. "His true errand," Chamberlain declared, "is to be knighted." This wasn't an entirely far-fetched hope. Following his failed siege of Rouen in 1591, Essex had dubbed twenty-one new knights, and he and his fellow commander Lord Howard created an additional sixty-eight knights from their Cádiz expedition in 1596.

Forman's casebooks for July and August didn't include any further visits from Aemilia. When she next saw him on September 2—by this time she was no longer pregnant—her focus had shifted from concern for Alfonso's status to inquiring "whether she shall be a lady." After being the mistress of the queen's first cousin and enjoying the trappings of aristocratic life, Aemilia was clearly desperate to acquire a higher position than what her marriage had so far provided; she wanted to add "Lady" before her name. On this occasion, the stars lined up in her favor. Forman predicted that she "shall be a lady or attain to some greater dignity," although Alfonso "shall get little substance." He then added a further distinction between the two spouses: "The time shall come [when] she shall rise two degrees, but hardly"—that is, with difficulty—"by this man."

Forman was correct about Alfonso, who returned with the exhausted English fleet in October after the total failure of Essex's expedition. After a series of disasters—terrible weather that sent the ships back to England before departing again in much reduced numbers, violent dysentery that weakened many of the men, and a lack of adequate support from the queen—Essex gave up on taking Ferrol and concentrated on intercepting the Spanish treasure ships, but he failed in this venture as well. In the end, no port had been taken, no silver captured, and the Spanish fleet seemed on the verge of attacking the English at Falmouth. Essex's reputation was greatly damaged, and Alfonso enjoyed no change in his rank or fortune. Forman's prediction, however, that Aemilia would rise independent of her husband wasn't entirely unmotivated. During her visit on September 2, their relationship took a personal turn.

The opening for the change seems to have arisen after Aemilia confessed to Forman that she was under serious financial strain. Despite the "money and jewels" she had contributed to the marriage, she told him that Alfonso had "dealt hardly with her, [and] has spent and consumed her goods." "She is now very needy, in debt," Forman recorded, "and it seems for lucre's sake she will be a good fellow for necessity doth compel." Aemilia, that is, seemed to him willing to prostitute herself. Immediately following these notes—as if looking at her now with a newly critical eye—he made his first and only comment about Aemilia's physical appearance: "She hath a wart or mole in the pit of her throat or near it." The entry for that day also included what can best be understood as Aemilia's attempt to prop herself up after the compromising exchange: this is when she told Forman that "she has been favored much of her majesty and of many noblemen, and has great gifts and been made much of." As a supposed favorite of the queen and her courtiers, she would have come at a high price.

By the following week, things had heated up. On September 10, Forman cast his own horoscope on the question, "If I go to Lanier this night or tomorrow, whether she will receive me and whether I shall be welcome [and] halek." "Halek" was Forman's code word for sex, and as a bachelor with a huge sexual appetite, his records were full of both successful and failed escapades. (In 1599, the forty-six-year-old Forman would finally get married for the first time, to a sixteen-year-old girl.) Adding to the drama was the fact that his long-term mistress—a married Catholic woman named Avis Allen who had come to him as a client in 1593—had died in June

1597, leaving him both lonely and on the prowl. Three months later, on September 11, Forman worked through his decision about Aemilia using a different scientific medium. In his manuscript of geomancy—a method of divination based on reading geographic marks or features—he laid out his dilemma under the heading "Best to do a thing or no":

> A certain man longed to see a gentlewoman whom he loved & desired to halek with and because he could not tell how to come to her & whether he should be welcome to her or no, made this question whether it were best to send to her to know how she did and thereby to try whether she would bid the messenger bid his master round to her or no. Thinking thereby he might go the bolder thereby to see her.

Below the geomantic figure he cast was simply the name "Lanier."

Forman's question about whether to visit Aemilia was clearly resolved in the affirmative, and below the September 11 entry he included a postscript on what had happened between them. After his servant returned with the message from Aemilia that "if his master came he should be welcome," Forman went to her house, where he "supped with her and stayed all night." Things didn't go, however, exactly as he had hoped:

> She was familiar and friendly to him in all things, but only she would not halek. Yet he felt all parts of her body willingly and kissed her often. But she would not do [it] in any ways whereupon he took some displeasure & so departed [i.e., stopped being] friends.

In a lighter ink below this entry he added a second postscript: "But yet they were friends again afterward, but he never obtained his purpose & she was a whore and dealt evil with him after." It's impossible to know if this last comment referred to a sequence of events—first they made up, and then she rejected him again (making her, paradoxically, a whore)—or simply reflected a confused set of feelings.

This is the only substantive account of physical contact between

Forman and Aemilia, but the would-be affair seems to have lasted a few months longer. On September 17, Forman drew another geomantic figure to decide how to respond to Aemilia, who had sent for him: "she seemed a friend," he observed, "and is not so." On September 29, she came to see him again, but he didn't write down anything from this visit other than her name and the names of her parents. Then on November 25, he cast his own horoscope to determine "What will be the outcome of Lanier's stories about invoking spirits, trouble or not? And whether I shall end it or no[t] at this time." This is the only reference to Aemilia's practicing divination herself, and it's hard to know what to make of it. As for his second question, he seems to have decided to bring the relationship to an end. For the next two years, there was no mention of Aemilia anywhere in his records. She made a final showing—a cameo appearance of sorts—on January 7, 1600, when Forman consulted the stars in response to the question "why Mrs. Lanier sent for me and what will follow from it [and] whether she intends any more villainy or no."

There's no way to know what actually happened between Aemilia and Forman, nor is there any explanation for why she summoned him in January 1600 so long after their seemingly unpleasant parting. What's missing entirely is Aemilia's version of what happened—who knows what she may have written in her own diary if she kept one, and whether it would have borne any relation to what Forman described. As is so often the case, we're left with only the man's side of the story. What we know about her life in the years around her consultations with Forman is that she gave birth in 1598 to a daughter, Odillya, who died nine months later. We also know that in the spring of 1599, Alfonso left Aemilia, her six-year-old son, and their newborn daughter at home to join another of the Earl of Essex's expeditions, this time in Ireland, where the increasingly reckless courtier was trying to put down a rebellion led by the formidable Earl of Tyrone in Ulster.

Essex had anticipated a short and decisive campaign, but he had horribly miscalculated the level of Irish resistance; instead of launching his attack, he embarked on a much longer expedition that was extravagantly expensive. Much to the queen's further irritation, Essex also created eighty-one new knighthoods to reward his soldiers (Alfonso, alas, was not among them). Relations between Elizabeth and Essex had been faltering for several years, and in 1598, after a disagreement at court over who would be appointed lord deputy in Ireland, Essex blurted out that she was "as crooked in her disposition as in her carcass." Then, upon his return from Ireland in 1599, he committed possibly his worst offense of all. On the morning of September 24, still muddied from his long ride, he burst into Elizabeth's bedchamber at Nonsuch Palace in Surrey uninvited, finding the queen only partially dressed and without either a wig or makeup. He never saw her again.

By the spring of 1600 Essex was a ruined man. Deprived of his office and put under house arrest while under investigation for insubordination in Ireland, his political future was all but finished. In 1601, following an attempted coup d'état that began with his commissioning a performance at the Globe of Shakespeare's *Richard II*—a play that stages the deposition and murder of a lawful king—the former darling of the queen was tried and executed for treason. (Seven months later Elizabeth famously remarked, "I am Richard II, know ye not that?") Alfonso, meanwhile, was far too insignificant a player in Essex's campaigns to have either benefited or lost from his downfall, and he seems to have resumed his day job playing the recorder at court. For her part, Aemilia was left a frustrated woman, unhappy in her marriage and unsatisfied with her place in the world.

A few years after Aemilia's final appearance in Forman's casebooks, her luck finally took a positive turn. In 1604, Anne Clifford's mother, Margaret, Countess of Cumberland, offered Aemilia a place in her household at Cookham. How Aemilia came to know Margaret remains a mystery: there are no traces of their meeting or having mutual friends. But for the second time in Aemilia's life, she was given a chance to leave her ordinary circumstances—she was presumably living with Alfonso and Henry, who would have been eleven or twelve—and enter the household of an aristocratic woman. Very little is known about her experience as a young girl with Susan Bertie, Countess of Kent. Aemilia's time with Margaret Clifford, by contrast, became a central subject in her writing.

Twenty-five miles west of London, Cookham sits above the Thames surrounded by grasslands, meadows, and forest, with views across the river to the gentle Chiltern Hills. The stunning manor house belonged to Margaret Clifford's brother William Russell, 1st Baron Russell of Thornhaugh, who had lent her the estate at a difficult moment when her estranged husband, George, Earl of Cumberland, failed to send her money. Margaret and George weren't officially divorced—this option was available only for kings—but they were formally separated and had a financial agreement for George to support Margaret and Anne, the couple's only child. Margaret was given use of George's mansion in the London parish of Clerkenwell, which he agreed to supply with bedding, linen, and brass and pewter ware; she was also promised an allowance of £1,000 a year. Whatever George's intentions, it took four years before he came through with the household furnishings, and very little of the allowance was ever paid. The move to Cookham was a temporary measure while Margaret waited for her husband to pay up.

In nearly every way, Aemilia's modest childhood and £100 inheritance bore no resemblance to the circumstances of her new mistress. The daughter of the powerful Francis Russell, Earl of Bedford and member of the queen's privy chamber, Margaret had grown up with the greatest privilege and wealth. Her marriage to George Clifford, who became a ward of the Crown at age twelve after his father died and was raised by Margaret's own father, was the envy of many aristocratic parents. There were few bachelors in all of England who could boast a finer pedigree than the young Earl of Cumberland. Unlike the Sidneys and Herberts, who entered the English aristocracy only in the sixteenth century, Clifford lords dated back to the thirteenth century, if not, as some records suggest, to the Norman conquest. After ruling over the Welsh Marches, the family had expanded its base to the north of England, where they possessed vast territories in Westmorland and Yorkshire equivalent to a small kingdom.

The sheer number of castles and manors George stood to inherit was staggering, and Bedford had paid an enormous sum to purchase George's wardship—£2,000 up front, plus an annual allowance of £300 in addition to school and university fees—in order to secure the right to marry the young earl to one of his daughters. Margaret and George's wedding in June 1577 was a sumptuous affair in the grand London cathedral of St. Mary Overy, Southwark, with Queen Elizabeth in attendance; the bride's dress and jewelry alone cost around £1,000. Among the more notable gifts: Bedford gave the newlyweds a mansion on the banks of the Thames in Chiswick and granted them the gift for life of all the swans and cygnets in the river. (This is one of those instances where modern habits have greatly diverged from the Renaissance. In the sixteenth century, swans were considered the rarest of delicacies, and aristocrats could purchase from the Crown the right to own, sell, and eat swans on their property; to identify the swans that were theirs, owners bought an expensive "swan mark" from the monarch, which was used to carve a personal mark into the birds' beaks.)

On the surface of things, George Clifford became one of the most visible figures of the era. In 1590, following the retirement of Elizabeth Cary's uncle, Sir Henry Lee, he became the Queen's Champion at the Accession Day tilts. To commemorate his new status, he commissioned a portrait miniature from Nicholas Hilliard showing him extravagantly dressed with a glove from the queen pinned to his hat. Two years later, Elizabeth named him a Knight of the Garter, the order of chivalry created in 1348 by Edward III in imitation of King Arthur's Knights of the Round Table. George was probably the only Knight of the Garter who could claim a direct link to Arthur's legendary court: one of his ancestral homes in Cumbria, Pendragon Castle, was supposedly founded by Uther Pendragon, King Arthur's father. But despite all this outward glamor, his career was largely marked by failure in ventures at sea. He squandered the better part of his fortune in privateering expeditions aimed at Spanish and Portuguese carracks returning from the Americas, expeditions that he both financed and frequently commanded. His greatest claim to fame was the capture in 1598 of San Juan, Puerto Rico, although an outbreak of dysentery among his men forced him to sail home without either establishing an English settlement on the island or recovering enough booty to compensate him for his costs. As Margaret bitterly put it in a private letter, her husband "ventured many thousands, which we saw come empty home."

However different Margaret's life had been from Aemilia's, the two women thus both had husbands whose careers hadn't lived up to their expectations and who had disappointed them in seemingly every respect. In the summer of 1604, they both also seem to have welcomed the opportunity to live on their own. Some of Margaret's feelings at the time have been recorded by her daughter, Anne, who later wrote that when her parents had occasion to meet "their countenance[s] did show the dislike they had one of the other." By 1603, George had taken as a mistress a woman Anne charitably described as "a lady of quality" ("good natures," she observed, "through human frailty are oftentimes misled"). George had also apparently fathered one or two children with a different woman. Nothing of this kind has been passed down about Alfonso's infidelities, but all signs suggest there was no love lost between him and Aemilia and that she leaped at the chance to get away.

Beyond their shared experience of marital unhappiness, Margaret and Aemilia had something more important in common. They were both well-educated women with a strong interest in religion. This is a side of Aemilia that doesn't surface in Forman's records—he was far less interested in her intellectual life than in her sexual availability—but it comes out powerfully in her account of the time she spent at Cookham. There's no record of what exactly Aemilia was hired to do, but she was likely both a companion to Margaret and a tutor of some sort for the talented young Anne, to whom she might have given lessons in Italian, music (Anne played the viol and the lute), or any number of other subjects that Aemilia seems to have mastered.

Being with a girl of such privilege and wealth, for whom every door in the world was wide open, could easily have created feelings of jealousy or resentment in Aemilia. From her account of the time they spent together, there seems to have been nothing but days of blissful learning and leisure. The women took long walks together during which they sang psalms and meditated on Holy Scripture; they made "sweet music" morning, noon, and night; they sat under a favorite tree where "many a learned book was read and scanned." ("Scanning" is the opposite of skimming—they were clearly hard at work.)

There's no indication that this idyllic period had a lasting impact on either Margaret or Anne; decades later when writing about her education, Anne didn't mention Aemilia, focusing instead entirely on her governess, Mrs. Taylor, and her tutor, Samuel Daniel. Margaret similarly never referred to Aemilia in any of her surviving letters. For Aemilia, however, her time with the Clifford women was transformative. Whether she had ever before tried her hand at writing isn't known—no earlier traces of her work have survived—but it was during this period that she claimed "the muses gave their full consent" to her creative gifts. "The princely palace," Aemilia proclaimed, "willed me to [write]." It's no coincidence that living in a quiet household filled with learned women fostered Aemilia's creative talents in a way that her life as Hunsdon's lover or Alfonso's wife had not. At Cookham, Aemilia became a poet.

The immediate fruits of Aemilia's poetic awakening took the form of an elegiac poem written to Cookham itself. Completed sometime around 1609, "The Description of Cooke-ham" is now generally recognized as the first "country house" poem written in the English language, displacing Ben Jonson's "To Penshurst," which held the honor until Aemilia's poem was rediscovered in the late twentieth century. The English country house poem was an imitation of a classical Roman genre made popular by Horace and Martial in which the poets lavished praise on the rural estates of friends or patrons. The compliments weren't reserved for the house; they branched outward to the great bounty of food and wine, the cheerful servants, and the simple, satisfying lives they were able to live outside of the corrupted city. "Our friend Faustinus' Baian villa," an epigram by Martial begins, "does not hold down unprofitable expanses of broad acreage laid out in idle myrtle plantations, unwed planes, and clipped boxwood, but rejoices in the true, rough countryside."

The fact that Aemilia wrote a poem in this genre confirms her excellent education: she must have read examples of these poems either in Latin or in English translations and had them sufficiently in mind to embark on a version of her own. Thus, "The Description of Cooke-ham" draws upon classical antecedents with praise of the house's gracious surroundings, as in lines like these:

The Walks put on their summer Liveries,
And all things else did hold like similes,
The Trees with leaves, with fruits, with flowers clad,

> *Embraced each other, seeming to be glad,*
> *Turning themselves to beauteous Canopies,*
> *To shade the bright Sun from your [Margaret's] brighter eyes . . .*
> *The little Birds in chirping notes did sing,*
> *To entertain both You and that sweet Spring.*

The poem also shifts the genre's traditional emphasis from the house and gardens to its inhabitants. More than the charms of the rural estate, it was the gift of the women's companionship that engaged Aemilia's attention.

Above all, "The Description of Cooke-ham" is filled with Aemilia's regret over the blissful period of cohabitation, probably no more than a handful of months, coming to an end. The very first word of the poem is none other than "farewell"—"Farewell (sweet Cooke-ham) where I first obtained / Grace"—and Aemilia laments that all of her pleasures are now in the past:

> *Farewell (sweet place) where Virtue then did rest,*
> *And all delights did harbour in her breast:*
> *Never shall my sad eyes again behold*
> *Those pleasures which my thoughts did then unfold.*

Roughly a third of the poem's 210 lines is given over to the sadness that fell upon the house when Margaret and Anne departed, leaving Aemilia—presumably with the rest of the household staff—bidding the aristocratic women farewell at the door. "And you sweet Cooke-ham," she exclaims,

> *whom these Ladies leave,*
> *I now must tell the grief you did conceive*
> *At their departure; when they went away,*
> *How every thing retained a sad dismay.*

In a perfect example of what literary critics call the "pathetic fallacy"—the attribution of human feelings onto the natural world—she imagines that the "grass did weep for woe," the birds could neither "sing nor chirp," the trees "forsook both flowers and fruit" and their leaves withered instantly, "as if they said, Why will ye leave us all?" Aemilia's sense of being abandoned comes out in probably the poem's strangest detail, when she describes Margaret's kissing her favorite tree farewell but not kissing Aemilia. Aemilia then steals the kiss, as it were, from the tree by kissing it in the same spot, jealous that a "senseless creature should possess / So rare a favor, so great happiness."

Had Aemilia become a lady as Forman had predicted, she would likely have had occasion to meet both Margaret and Anne more regularly at court. As it stands, she anticipated the separation would be permanent. "Unconstant Fortune," she bemoans,

> *Cas[t] us down into so low a frame*
> *Where our great friends we cannot daily see*
> *So great a difference is there in degree.*

There's no definite record, in fact, of her ever meeting either of the women again. In a poem she wrote to Anne a few years later, Aemilia challenges the very basis of the class system:

> *What difference was there when the world began,*
> *Was it not Virtue that distinguished all?*
> *All sprang but from one woman and one man,*
> *Then how doth Gentry come to rise and fall?*
> *Or who is he that very rightly can*
> *Distinguish of his birth, or tell at all,*
> *In what mean state his Ancestors have been,*
> *Before someone of worth did honour win?*

How do you know, Aemilia provocatively asks, that the grandmother of your Norman ancestors wasn't a peasant? This was a radical question to pose to a young noblewoman, especially one as obsessed with her heritage as Anne, as we'll soon see. But it's clear Aemilia was suffering once again from having tasted the pleasures of aristocratic life only to have them taken away. She had reached yet another dead end.

Whatever the pain of the loss, Aemilia's experience at Cookham ultimately brought an enormous payoff. In the years after her visit, she embarked on one of the most ambitious literary projects ever

undertaken by an Englishwoman. Given her status outside the ruling elite—she had neither money nor relations to support her—
Aemilia's project was all the more exceptional. In fact, no aristocratic
woman likely had the same strong incentive to write the book
Aemilia had in mind, a book fueled by her longing for a female
utopia. If she couldn't inhabit such a place in person for more than a
few months, the next best thing was to create it through her poems.

CHAPTER SEVEN

June 24, 1603

Dingley Hall, Northamptonshire

Anne Clifford

The summer before her time at Cookham with Aemilia Lanyer, the thirteen-year-old Anne Clifford had an extraordinary adventure of her own. After a mad dash through the English countryside—sleeping one night in the hallway of a friend's palace (all the servants had gone to bed) and killing three horses from heat and exhaustion—she and her mother, Margaret, Countess of Cumberland, arrived at Dingley Hall just in time to receive their new queen. Anna of Denmark, the talented and beautiful younger daughter of King Frederick II, had married James VI of Scotland in 1589 at the age of fourteen. The match was made against the will of Queen Elizabeth, who wanted her Scottish cousin (and eventual heir) to take the Huguenot princess Catherine of Navarre as his bride, thereby consolidating England's Protestant alliance within France. (The Danish kingdom was also Protestant—albeit of the Lutheran variety, which was less theologically rigorous than the Calvinist Huguenots—but Anna's father remained neutral in the ongoing religious wars on the Continent.) Once settled in Scotland, Anna made her mark by becoming an avid patron of theater, dance, architecture, and music, importing as best she could the sophisticated tastes of the Danish court.

Six weeks after James began his long journey from Scotland to his new kingdom following Elizabeth's death, Queen Anna set out with her two eldest children: the nine-year-old Henry, Duke of Cornwall, and the six-year-old Princess Elizabeth. The couple's youngest son, the two-year-old Charles, stayed behind in the care of Lord and Lady Fyvie, who raised him until he was four. Anna was pregnant at the time with a fourth child, and her departure had been delayed to allow for extra arrangements to be made for her safe travel. As it happened, she miscarried in early May. According to some contemporary reports, she took the body of the dead male fetus with her on her trip to disprove malicious rumors that she had feigned his death (and presumably her pregnancy) to gain sympathy from her Scottish enemies. Anna was also kept in Edinburgh longer than expected because the English noblewomen sent to accompany her had been detained in London by their obligations to attend Elizabeth's corpse. She met the first official delegation of her new female courtiers in the northern English town of Berwick-upon-Tweed, just across the Scottish border. The ever-expanding entourage then slowly made its way south, stopping frequently for the queen to meet her subjects.

At Dingley Hall, a stately manor house a hundred miles north of London belonging to Sir Edward Griffin, Anne Clifford was among those eagerly waiting to join the royal progress. As she related in her 1603 memoir, it was "the first time I ever saw the Queen," and "she kissed us all and used us kindly." Anne wrote this memoir sometime after 1609—the exact date of composition is unknown—and it represents her earliest venture in what became a lifetime habit of self-writing. The idea of keeping track of her life in this way was highly unusual, if not unprecedented, for a young woman at the time. As we'll see, Anne wrote a combination of annual chronicles and daily diaries covering the period 1603 until her death in 1676; she also wrote an autobiography in the early 1650s entitled *The Life of Me,* which began with her conception, an event she dated to May 1, 1589. Thanks to the 1603 chronicle, we learn things about Anne's experience of the new king and queen and the shifts in her family's status at court that would be impossible to recover from royal records.

Later the same day that they first met Anna, Anne and her mother set out again "along with the Queen's train, [and] an infinite number of coaches" en route to Lord Spencer's estate at Althorp.

(Centuries later, this would be the childhood home of Princess Diana, daughter of the 8th Earl Spencer.) The Clifford women were among "an infinite company of lords and ladies" who enjoyed a three-day outdoor entertainment Spencer had commissioned from the playwright Ben Jonson. From Althorp they traveled to Sir Hatton Fermor's estate some twenty miles to the south, where King James and his court joined the queen's party. The now unimaginably large group then moved to Grafton Regis, a royal manor house that Queen Elizabeth had given the year before to Anne's father, George Clifford, Earl of Cumberland.

The royal visit to Grafton provided George with a much-sought opportunity to win over the new king. While he had always enjoyed Elizabeth's favor, she never took him seriously as a statesman: the highest recognition he'd ever received was his ceremonial role as the Queen's Champion at the Accession Day jousts. To Elizabeth, George was a model of aristocratic glamor, but not someone she deemed worthy of her inner circle. All of this changed with James, who saw him as a crucial ally in the unsettled north, where the Clifford family was one of the largest landowners; the two men also shared a great passion for hunting. For the first time in his life, the forty-four-year-old earl had a chance for real advancement.

According to Anne, her father spared no expense to treat the new king and queen to the highest level of luxury during their visit, and he "banqueted [them] with great royalty." The entertainments clearly paid off. James named George to the Privy Council and granted him the lucrative wardenship of the west and middle Marches, the lands on the border between England and Scotland. An official position in the governments of both kingdoms, the warden was responsible for the security of the area and for administering local justice. In exchange for George's service, James also agreed to knight no fewer than twenty-three of his followers, significantly raising George's political clout. (James's largesse with George was by no means unique: during Elizabeth's reign the total number of knights in England dropped from around 600 to 500, whereas in the first four months of his rule, James dubbed 906 new knights. Sir Francis Bacon, one of the beneficiaries, nonetheless complained that knighthood had become "a divulged and almost prostituted title.")

The only tinge of sadness in Anne's otherwise ebullient account of the king and queen's time at Grafton had to do with her father's insulting treatment of her mother, who was "not held as mistress of the house, by reason of the difference between my [father] and her, which was grown to a great height." At this time Anne's parents were already effectively separated—as Anne put it, "my father used to come sometimes to us at Clerkenwell [in London], but not often, for he had at this time as it were wholly left my mother." When Aemilia Lanyer joined them at Cookham a year later, we will recall, Margaret was waiting for the allowance George had promised her to arrive. In addition to being treated poorly by George, Margaret was also slighted at Grafton by the queen. Anne reported that Anna "showed no favor to the elderly ladies"—Margaret was forty-three—taking as her immediate favorite the twenty-two-year-old Lucy Russell, Countess of Bedford, who had snuck off to Scotland to serve Anna weeks before any of the other English gentlewomen arrived. Lucy became the first of Anna's new ladies of the bedchamber, joining her inner circle of loyal Scottish attendants.

When the large entourage accompanying James and Anna finally arrived at the royal palace at Hampton Court, they found themselves surrounded by bubonic plague. A contemporary account by the playwright Thomas Dekker grimly entitled *A Wonderful Year* conjured up the horrific scene in London. The city, Dekker wrote, was "a vast, silent charnel-house" with corpses piled high in houses, streets, and churches, emitting a stench so overwhelming that those still able to walk about filled their nostrils with branches of rosemary, "looking like so many boars' heads to be served . . . at Christmas." He also wryly noted that the price of "herbs and garlands rose wonderfully," from twelve pence for an armful to six shillings, or seventy pence, for a handful. Houses were sealed tight with red crosses and the words "Lord have mercy on us" posted on the doors. Far from tending to the sick, clergymen and doctors fled the city as quickly as they could.

As Anne described the scene at Hampton Court, there was no shielding the royal party and its attendants from the ravages of the disease. She slept with her mother "in one of the round towers, round about which were tents where they died two or three in a day" before falling ill herself with a fever "so as my mother was in some [fear] it might turn to the plague." Anne recovered in a few days, but her beloved governess, Mrs. Taylor, was taken away after her husband contracted the plague (he died shortly thereafter). In a scene we would have strained to imagine before our own recent experience of pandemic, Margaret became angry with Anne and ordered the servants to keep her locked up after Anne rode in a coach with a man named Mr. Menerell, who dropped dead the next day. This "put us all in great fear and amazement," Anne admitted; she was then kept in quarantine for nine or ten days before being "allowed to come to the court again."

The "plague was so hot in London," Anne continued, that Margaret forbade her to attend the coronation on July 25. Margaret and George were both present: for people of their status, the social costs of not showing up must have seemed even greater than the risk of contracting the disease. Normally coronations were held in conjunction with the new monarch's "royal entry" into the city, but in this case, the official procession was postponed until the plague died down, making the festivities unusually subdued. (The procession was eventually held the following March.) The ceremony itself followed the ordinary script, but Queen Anna shocked everyone present by refusing to take Protestant communion. This was the first revelation to her English subjects of her Catholicism. Although Anna had been raised in Protestant Denmark, during her time in Scotland she developed a strong distaste for the harsh Calvinist theology of the Scottish Church. At some point during her reign there, she had secretly started to attend Catholic mass. To facilitate this, she kept near her a group of loyal Catholic attendants who quietly coordinated the coming and going of priests disguised as their personal servants. The same practice continued once she came to England, although she regularly showed up at Protestant services, keeping up at least the show of religious obedience. The fact that there was clandestine worship going on inside the royal court was an early sign of the trouble to come when James and Anna's son Charles would take an unapologetically Catholic bride from France as his queen. But this comes much later in our story.

Anne probably wasn't aware of the queen's heretical beliefs at the time of the coronation, or at least whatever gossip there was on the subject didn't catch her attention. She was angry instead about being left out of Anna's new group of maids of honor. "If Queen Elizabeth had lived," Anne bitterly remarked in the first sentence of her 1603 memoir, "she intended to have preferred me to be of the Privy Chamber." Anne even petitioned the queen's favorite, Lucy Russell, Countess of Bedford, to speak on her behalf. A few months after the rejection, Anne changed her mind about wanting to be a member of Anna's inner circle. Judging there to be "such infinite number of ladies sworn of the Queen's Privy Chamber as made the place of no esteem or credit," she claimed to have had "the good fortune to miss it." She was particularly critical of the entertainment—a formal masque—that Anna had arranged in October 1603 to celebrate Prince Henry's arrival at Winchester Castle in Hampshire, where the court had moved due to the ongoing plague in the capital. The performance, Anne wrote, gave the women involved "such ill-names that [the court] was grown a scandalous place, and the queen herself much fallen from her former greatness and reputation she had in the world."

No trace of this masque has survived, so it's hard to know exactly what Anne is responding to; we'll return later to the queen's innovations in masquing, as well as Anne's eventual involvement in several performances. For now, it's worth pausing to reflect on how enormous a change it was for English noblewomen accustomed to serving Elizabeth to make the transition to the new queen. On the surface of things, one might guess their role had diminished: Anna was only James's consort, after all, and not the monarch ruling the country. In fact, Anna's status as the king's wife created greater opportunities for women by virtue of the fact that she established her own largely autonomous court. However much Elizabeth may have shared her private life with her ladies and maids, she turned to her male councilors for matters of state; the men in her Privy Council, not the women in her bedchamber, were ultimately her closest advisers.

Under the new regime, there was a clear separation of male and female spheres, made all the more pronounced by the fact that the king and queen were usually apart. James, who seems to have had intimate relations with other men beginning in adolescence, openly preferred the company of his male courtiers and spent as much time with them as possible (usually on hunting trips). Anna, meanwhile, established her own residence, first at Hampton Court and later at Greenwich Palace. Ambitious women thus had the chance to influence the queen without competing on a daily basis with their male counterparts. While Anna's power was in certain contexts limited—she had little say over political decisions made by James or his privy councilors—she became the de facto arbiter for cultural activity throughout the realm.

Anne Clifford may initially have been left out of Anna's inner circle, but her exclusion by no means compromised her status in society. Unlike the aristocratic but cash-poor Mary Sidney, for example, whose prospects for marriage were greatly enhanced by the exposure she gained as a maid of honor, Anne's birth alone was enough to ensure her position as a highly desirable bride. Her two brothers, Francis and Robert, had died in early childhood, making her the presumed heir to George's roughly 90,000 acres of land in the northern counties of Westmorland and Yorkshire. She was poised to inherit the equivalent of a small kingdom.

The idea that a daughter could inherit her father's estate went against the English practice of primogeniture, whereby all property was to be given to the eldest male child; in cases where there was no male offspring, the next in line was the nearest male relative (any number of Jane Austen's novels may come to mind). But this preference for distant male kin over direct female offspring was relatively new at the time of George Clifford's death. According to English common law, girls without brothers were the rightful heirs over "collateral" males, and this had remained the normative rule until Henry VIII found a way to bypass the precedent and authorize men to name whomever they liked as their heirs. In the case of the Cliffords, the rights of women to inherit had specifically been codified: in 1311, Edward II issued a decree stipulating that the family's massive northern estates were to descend to direct heirs regardless of sex. According to this royal entail, if there were no direct heirs, male or female, the property would be stripped from the family and revert to the Crown. Anne grew up with the greatest of expectations.

The glimpses we have of Anne's childhood suggest an upbringing worthy of a princess. A surviving account book kept by her governess, Mrs. Taylor, lists expenses for her young charge from 1600 to 1602, which included the following items:

A masque for my la[dyship].

Musicians for playing at my la[dyship]'s chamber-door.

Item, to the same who played at my la[dyship] Anne's
masque.

Item, given to Stephens that teacheth my la[dyship] to
dance, for 1 month.

Item, paid for sleave silk.

Item, paid for little silkworms.

Item, for drawing your ladyship in canvas.

Item, for 11 bunches of glass feathers for her ladyship.

Item, two pap[er] books, 1 for account, the other to write
her catechism in.

Item, 2 dozen of glass flowers.

Musicians playing at her door, dance lessons, a masque seemingly put on for her pleasure, sleave silk for her embroidery, silkworms for her to raise (this became a lifetime habit), several books to write in (ditto), eleven bunches of glass feathers, two dozen glass flowers: these were the hobbies and tastes of someone raised for a life of absolute leisure.

What's missing from the list were signs of Anne's excellent education. As a young girl, Anne seems to have been taught primarily by her mother. Unlike Lady Sidney, who was similarly well-educated but whose position at court left her little time for her children, Margaret Clifford never worked a day in her life. Her separation from her husband seems to have made her all the more devoted to her daughter. As Anne later described it in a biographical "summary" she wrote of her mother, Margaret with "singular care and tenderness of affection [did] educate and bring up her said most dear, and only daughter . . . , seasoning her youth with the grounds of true religion and moral virtue and all other qualities befitting her birth."

Margaret's own intellectual gifts were hardly limited to those typically associated with her sex. In addition to being a learned and devout Protestant, she was a passionate student of alchemy, a practiced distiller of medicines, and an enthusiast for mining, investing her own money in experiments to smelt iron with coal. In the portrait of her mother Anne commissioned in 1646—part of a triptych we will return to later—she drew attention to Margaret's impressive range of interests by displaying her favorite books. In Margaret's hand is a book of Psalms, while on the shelf immediately behind her are the works of Seneca, the Bible, and a manuscript entitled "Alchemist Extractions, of Distillations and excellent Medicines," which Margaret apparently compiled herself. Prayer books and Psalters show up frequently in the portraits of Protestant women from this era—Lady Sidney's portrait from around 1550 shows her clutching a small prayer book in one hand, with a glove in another—but it's very rare to see a woman surrounded by secular books of any kind. In choosing to portray her mother this way, Anne clearly wanted to emphasize her intellectual engagement with the world.

Sometime before Anne's tenth birthday, Margaret expanded her daughter's education beyond her own lessons and those of Mrs. Taylor: she hired the poet and historian Samuel Daniel as Anne's tutor. Daniel was one of the star tutors of the era: earlier in the 1590s he was employed by Mary Sidney to teach her own children at Wilton. Privately, Daniel complained about spending so much of his time teaching instead of pursuing his career as a writer. "Such hath been my misery," he wrote to a friend in 1601, "that whilst I should have written the actions of men, I have been constrained to bide with children." To his employers, he was far more gracious. In 1603, he wrote a poem addressed to Anne in which he praised her mother, in effect, for hiring him:

> She, that hath brought forth
> that comely body, [doth] labour to adorn
> that better part, the mansion of your mind
> with all the richest furniture of worth.

Given what would become Anne's lifelong obsession with her property, Daniel's description of her mind as a "mansion" to be filled with "the richest furniture" seems prophetic.

Judging from the portrait Anne commissioned of herself as a fifteen-year-old girl—also part of the 1646 triptych—she received a first-rate education. She shows herself standing next to her lute, which she seems to have just put down as if the painter had interrupted her playing; on the table beside her there's a book of music that she holds open with her hand, and a piece of unfinished embroidery. More than her music or her embroidery, the painting is focused on her reading. The shelves behind her overflow with books, whose titles are displayed on labels placed on the fore-edges of the pages (engraving titles on the spines of books was a practice that began later in the seventeenth century). Anne's library spans the historical periods from antiquity to the Renaissance, and covers the fields of literature, philosophy, history, and religion. In the great humanistic mingling of pagan and Christian learning, Ovid's *Metamorphoses* sits comfortably with Augustine's *City of God.* To show her more contemporary reading, there are copies of Ortelius's *Theater of the Whole World* (a version of the atlas Elizabeth Cary translated for her uncle), Montaigne's *Essays,* Spenser's *Works,* and Sidney's *Arcadia.*

What's missing from the collection are any foreign books in their original languages: though the majority of the works were originally written in French, Italian, or Latin, they are all shown in English translations. An emphasis on reading exclusively in English didn't correspond to the standard recommendations for girls' education—French and Italian were among the most common subjects girls were taught—nor did it reflect the intellectual interests of Anne's tutor: Daniel himself was a translator of French and Italian. The explanation for Anne's English-only library was tied to her father. As Anne later recounted, she "was not admitted to learn any languages because her father would not permit it." "But for all other knowledge fit for her sex," she hastened to add, "none was bred up to greater perfection than herself."

Anne never explained George's prohibition, but it most likely stemmed from his xenophobia. Unlike many of his peers, he never traveled on the Continent, and he had no love for foreigners: his primary dealings with non-Englishmen involved his hostile attacks on their ships. Despite spending his early childhood in a family that continued to practice Catholicism—his Clifford relatives in the north combined loyalty to the queen with rejection of her religion—George's adoption at age twelve by Margaret's staunchly Protestant father and his subsequent studies at Cambridge under the future archbishop of Canterbury John Whitgift turned him strongly against the Roman faith. Giving his daughter access to languages so deeply associated with Catholicism may have seemed risky—better to keep her confined in every sense on English shores. This insularity seems to have stuck: in her eighty-six years, Anne never left the country.

The other aspect of Anne's life over which George tried to assert his will was her marriage. Most of Anne's childhood was spent with her mother, and long stays with George were few and far between. But in July 1605, when Anne was fifteen, he took her from Margaret's care for a monthlong visit at Grafton Regis. During this time, the king and queen came to stay for four days as part of their summer progress, and they were once again entertained "with great magnificence." Anne also noted, without further comment, that her time at Grafton "caused great sorrow to my saint-like mother." In a letter to a friend from this period, Margaret complained that George "goes about to marry [Anne] without my consent." George had in fact begun negotiating a match with William Cavendish, the grandson of the fabulously wealthy Earl of Shrewsbury (William later became Duke of Newcastle). William was especially attractive to George because of the possibility of a double marriage: for reasons that would soon become all too clear, he wanted William's sister, Frances, to marry his brother Francis Clifford's only son, Henry.

As Anne related in a letter to her mother, George broached the topic of her marriage as soon as she arrived. "I have had a great deal of talk with my Lord about that matter you know of for that match," Anne wrote, before quickly reassuring Margaret that "my Lord hath promised me that there should nothing pass, for any marriage whatsoever, but that your consent should be asked as a chief matter." This was an unusual courtesy, as Margaret's approval would by no means have been required. In his role as Anne's official guardian, George was free to arrange whatever match he liked.

It's not clear exactly how much Margaret knew about the scheme at the time of Anne's visit to Grafton, but there were good reasons for her to oppose it. Before things could go any further, however, the forty-seven-year-old George became ill with "bloody flux," or dysentery; less than two months after Anne's return to London, he died. In his last will and testament, he confirmed the devastating news that Margaret and Anne had long been dreading. Already in the will George made in 1598 before leaving on his venture to Puerto Rico, he had provided for Anne in case of his death, but he failed to name her as his heir. In clear violation of the fourteenth-century decree requiring the Clifford lands to pass to the direct heir of either sex, George left his vast northern estates to his brother, Francis. The reasons for George's decision weren't personal: they were dynastic. Since Anne couldn't inherit George's title—titles couldn't be passed to women—there was no way for the earldom and the estates to remain together without handing them over to a male relative. To keep the family line intact, the fifteen-year-old Anne was disinherited.

In light of George's will, the proposed double marriage to the Cavendish siblings took on a more sinister quality. As George had imagined it, William would have been unlikely to sue his own sister and her husband, Henry Clifford—Francis's heir—which would leave Anne without support for any legal proceedings she might undertake. As compensation for the dramatic loss in her inheritance, George left Anne £15,000 as a dowry upon her marriage regardless of who her husband would be. The dowry had one condition: it would be paid out only if Anne chose not to file a lawsuit contesting the will.

By nearly anyone's account, £15,000 was an enormous sum. Sir Henry Sidney, as we saw, was hard-pressed to collect £2,000 for Mary's marriage to the Earl of Pembroke, and the wealthy lawyer Lawrence Tanfield paid what was widely regarded as an extravagant £4,000 to Sir Henry Cary for his daughter Elizabeth's portion. In Margaret's eyes, however, Anne's £15,000 dowry was woefully inadequate. As she remarked with chilling hauteur, it was "a portion that many merchants' daughters have had." According to her estimate, Anne's "ancient inheritance," reflecting centuries of wealth in the Clifford family, was worth more than six times the figure George had provided. She calculated Anne should receive at least £100,000 (equivalent to around £14 million today).

When Anne reflected on this period some forty years later in *The Life of Me,* she described her disinheritance without any hint of bitterness or resentment:

> My father, for the love he bore to his brother and the advancement of the heirs male of his house by his last will did leave to his brother Francis, who succeeded him in the

Earldom of Cumberland, and to the heirs male of his body all his castles, land, and honors, with a proviso that they should all return to me, his only daughter and heir, if the heirs male failed.

From this account, it might seem she had peacefully accepted George's decision. Nothing could be further from the truth. Although there are no records of Anne's immediate reaction to the news of her disinheritance—no diary or memoir for 1605 has survived—she and Margaret were well aware this was coming and were ready for a fight. In his last letter before his death, George begged Margaret to "take as I have meant in kindness the course I have set down for disposing of my estate."

Within a year of George's death, Margaret Clifford filed on Anne's behalf the first of a series of lawsuits that Anne would continue to pursue for nearly four decades. This would become one of the most impressive challenges to patriarchy that England had ever seen. As a widow, Margaret enjoyed legal rights that she didn't have as a married woman, when she was bound by the rules of coverture: wives couldn't sign contracts, initiate lawsuits, or make their own wills without their husband's involvement. But widows could do all of these things on their own. In addition to hiring lawyers and archivists to prepare the lawsuit, Margaret personally got involved in searching the family's records for historical precedents she could find to support Anne's claims. What emerged was something George almost certainly knew nothing about: nearly all of the most valuable properties the Cliffords possessed had come to them through women.

In the late thirteenth century, Anne's ancestor Roger de Clifford married the heiress Isabella de Veteripont, who had inherited the castles of Brougham and Appleby as well as the sheriffwick of Westmorland from her father. When Isabella's childless sister, Idonea, died, Isabella inherited Idonea's castles of Brough and Pendragon. As Margaret proudly declared in a letter to one of James's privy councilors, Anne's claims to the Clifford lands came from "women heretofore and [are] now going to women again." In bringing to light the entirely forgotten role women had played in the Cliffords' accumulation of their wealth—and there were several other women besides Isabella and Idonea who had contributed property over the centuries—Margaret launched what would become one of the central projects of Anne's life. When Anne took on the monumental task of writing the Clifford family's history much later in her life, she would proudly affirm her own role in the long female dynastic line.

After filing the initial lawsuit challenging George's will, Margaret and Anne set out in the spring of 1607 to visit the contested lands. This was the first time Anne had been to her father's northern estates since infancy. Who knows if George deliberately kept her from seeing the extraordinary castles and manors that he had decided not to give her; it may simply have been a result of his busy life at court and on the seas. There was certainly no way for George to imagine how attached Anne would become to the Clifford lands. The trip in 1607, however, was anything but sentimental in its purpose. "By reason of these great suits in law," Anne explained, "my mother and I were in a manner forced for our own good to go together from London down into Westmorland."

Presumably Margaret's lawyers had encouraged the women to visit the properties as a way of asserting Anne's rights. Margaret also wanted to establish her role at those estates where George had given her life control in her jointure properties. This settlement, which produced over £1,000 a year in rent collected from the various tenants, was no doubt intended as a peace offering to keep her from fighting the rest of his will. Margaret turned out to be a much more attentive—and demanding—landlord than her husband had ever been, appointing eleven commissioners to manage the estates while also making decisions of her own. Starting in 1606, she required her tenants to carry a load of coal apiece each year from the mines at nearby Stainmore to Appleby, where she and Anne arrived on July 22, 1607.

It's hard to imagine how Anne felt when she first laid eyes on Appleby Castle. A twelfth-century Norman fortress that had belonged to Richard the Lionheart (one of the heroes of Sir Walter Scott's *Ivanhoe*), the property was given in 1203 by Richard's successor—his brother, King John—to his henchman Robert de Veteripont, the grandfather of the heiress Isabella. Strategically positioned with a sweeping view over the Eden valley, Appleby was built to guard the nearby ford crossing the river. Its most impressive structure, which today houses a museum of Norman history, is a square stone keep known as Caesar's Tower, a three-story structure whose walls are nearly six feet thick. In times of siege, the lord of the castle and his retainers used the keep as a stronghold, with the ground floor stocked with provisions and a well to ensure a steady water supply. Anne and Margaret didn't live in Caesar's Tower—however hostile George's relatives may have been, things hadn't reached this level of aggression yet—and their rooms in the mansion house would have likely been fitted for their comfort and ease. But from the moment they arrived at the high curtain wall and entered the imposing stone gates of the castle, there could be no mistaking Appleby for a luxurious Renaissance palace.

After several months at Appleby, the Clifford women moved north to Brougham, a thirteenth-century castle with a striking double gatehouse and great keep where Anne recorded sleeping in the very "chamber where my father was born." Like Appleby, Brougham was part of Margaret's jointure, and the women seem to have been received with what Shakespeare describes as "ceremonious affection." This was not the case when they traveled south to Yorkshire in early October to arrive at Anne's birthplace of Skipton Castle, which was under Francis's possession. There, they found the impressive twin-towered Norman gatehouse "shut against us by my uncle of Cumberland's officers in an uncivil and disdainful manner." As Anne would later learn, among the ancient parchments kept in Skipton's Muniment Room—a storehouse for family records secured by heavy locks on a strong door—were several manuscripts that supported her claims to the Clifford lands. There's no way to be sure if this was why Francis instructed his household servants to keep Anne and Margaret out. But it was Anne's first taste of the acrimony that would now characterize nearly all of her interactions with her father's family.

Despite her well-known status as the disinherited daughter of the Earl of Cumberland, Anne's stock on the marriage market remained high. The two likely outcomes of the lawsuit—a dowry of £15,000 or an inheritance of 90,000 acres—were both sufficiently attractive to keep the suitors coming, and Margaret was actively pursuing what she regarded as Anne's ideal match. Her first move was to extricate her from all negotiations with George's choice, William Cavendish. In a March 1606 letter to Robert Cecil, Earl of Salisbury and King James's secretary of state—marriages at this level of society were of interest to the highest officials—Margaret declared that she "never gave consent nor [did] my daughter so far to treat of marriage [with Cavendish]." She then articulated her policy going forward: "never any match should be hearkened unto by my consent, but those that will maintain the rights belonging to [Anne's] birth from her ancestors." Anyone interested in marrying Anne would need to take her side in the inheritance battle.

The other requirement for Anne's future husband was less explicitly stated, but no less critical: anticipating that James would play a crucial role in determining the lawsuit's outcome, Margaret wanted a son-in-law who would have real sway with the king. This had become all the more important because of the strong dislike James seems to have taken to Margaret, whom he had treated from the start as the adversary of his well-loved courtier George. Among the many gifts the king gave to his new ally was to ignore Margaret's official request that George pay her promised support. This is how she ended up with Aemilia Lanyer at Cookham in 1604, living off her brother's hospitality.

Even after George's death, the king's feelings for Margaret didn't soften. In July 1606 she bitterly complained to Ludovic Stuart, Duke of Lennox, that she knew "some ladies that were suspected to be acquainted with the gunpowder treason that had more grace at the court than I now had." In the fall of 1605, a group of Catholic conspirators unhappy with James's refusal to grant them more religious freedoms plotted to blow up Parliament during its opening session on November 5. Their aim was to kill everyone present—members of Parliament, government ministers, and most importantly James, Anna, and Prince Henry—in what would have been the most violent act of domestic terrorism in English history. The plot was discovered some ten days before the planned attack; on the evening of November 4, one of the conspirators, Guy Fawkes, was arrested while preparing to detonate thirty-six barrels (roughly 1,400 kilograms) of gunpowder. However much Margaret was exaggerating her state of disfavor, likening herself to women who secretly knew about this horrific plan captures her sense of total alienation from

James's court. It also helps to explain her desperation to find Anne a husband who might have James's ear.

Several promising candidates came and went, including Grey Brydges, Baron Chandos, who had recently inherited Sudeley Castle in the Cotswolds, where he became famous for throwing lavish parties; and William Cecil, Lord Ros, son of Lord Burghley and nephew of Robert Cecil. By early 1607, Margaret had pushed these possibilities aside in favor of an untitled courtier named Richard Sackville. This may have seemed like a less compelling match than Brydges or Cecil, but Richard's deep appeal lay in his grandfather. Thomas Sackville, Earl of Dorset, was a widely respected and powerful statesman who had amassed a large fortune while serving as lord treasurer under both Elizabeth and James. (A true Renaissance man, he was also the co-author of *Gorboduc,* a tragedy about divided succession that was one of Shakespeare's sources for *King Lear.*) In a letter Dorset wrote to George More, treasurer to Prince Henry, he asked More to speak to Margaret on his grandson's behalf and "put this error out of my lady's conceit, namely that mine opinion is that women are not capable of inheritance of honor." As Dorset had well understood, the key to winning Anne's hand was the outspoken support of her right to her father's land.

If what drew Margaret to Richard's eligibility as a son-in-law depended on his grandfather, what drew Anne to her new suitor was far more personal. Although her feelings in the matter weren't necessarily a high priority to Margaret—as we've seen, marriage choices were almost always made by parents without much say from their children—Anne and Richard met frequently both at court and at her mother's house. According to contemporary reports, she "did conceive an affection, and inclination" to him, and he "had taken liking" to her. Despite the happy coincidence of its being a love match, there was a final wrinkle in the story before the marriage could take place. When Dorset died in April 1608, leaving Richard's largely ineffective father, Robert Sackville, as the new earl, Margaret lost some of her enthusiasm. Within months she was pursuing a match with James's new favorite at court, Sir Robert Carr. This negotiation didn't get very far, however, and by early 1609 the agreement with Richard was settled.

Anne and Richard were married in London on February 25,

1609, in her mother's chambers in Austin Friars, the luxurious palace built by Henry VIII's notorious chief minister, Thomas Cromwell, on the grounds of a former Augustinian monastery. Margaret's lawyer, John Greenwood, described the event in seemingly unremarkable terms: the couple "joined their hands together and by words of the present time plighted their faith and troth each to other in matrimony and used the ring and the other usual ceremonies of marriage." He also mentioned that the chamber, which had once been a chapel, was "sumptuously adorned." Greenwood's attention to both the "usual ceremonies" and the adornment of the chapel was in fact a response to certain irregularities surrounding the marriage. Beginning in the thirteenth century, English law required that all marriages be announced from the pulpit of a parish church on three consecutive Sundays, to allow time for any objections—evidence of a prior betrothal, for example—to be raised. The only way to receive an exception to this practice of "calling the banns" was to purchase a license from the church, but even with a license couples were required to wait a month before taking their vows. In the case of Anne and Richard's marriage, no banns had been read nor was a license obtained, and there had been nothing comparable to the festive celebration that would normally accompany so prominent a match. The whole thing felt suspiciously rushed.

As it happened, the seemingly improvised wedding was driven by an urgent development. In the summer of 1608, Richard's father became gravely ill. By early February 1609, he was dying. If Robert died before Richard turned twenty-one—he was not quite twenty at the time—Richard would by law become a ward of the Crown. There were a number of courtiers eager to purchase his wardship and thereby secure the rights to marry the wealthy young heir to a bride of their own choice—precisely what happened when Anne's maternal grandfather, the Earl of Bedford, became the guardian of George Clifford and married him to his daughter Margaret. The only way to avoid this situation for Richard was for him already to be married to Anne at the time of his father's death. Although boys had to be twenty-one before coming into their inheritance, they could marry at the age of fourteen (for girls, the legal age for marriage was twelve). The imminent death of Richard's father combined with the equally imminent rise in his own fortune—he stood to become Earl of Dorset—convinced Margaret to move as quickly as possible.

Anne and Richard were married two days before Robert died, but the unusual circumstances surrounding the wedding came at a cost. The archbishop of Canterbury refused to allow the marriage to be registered, explaining to Margaret that he could do nothing "without the King's majesty's knowledge." Shortly thereafter, two of Richard's siblings—Edward and Anne Sackville—brought a case before the archbishop's court of appeals (the Court of Arches) to establish the marriage's validity. Later in life Anne Clifford came to despise her brother-in-law, but in this instance, he and his sister were genuinely trying to help resolve the legal questions surrounding the match. The depositions that have survived from the witnesses, including that of Margaret's lawyer, Greenwood, affirmed the existence of a precontract between the spouses, the presence at the ceremony of an authorized minister who followed the Prayer Book service, and the consent of both the bride's and groom's legal guardians (Margaret Clifford and Robert Sackville, respectively). After weighing the evidence, the court ruled the union was legitimate.

Following her father-in-law's death on February 27, the nineteen-year-old Anne became the Countess of Dorset and moved to Knole House, the Sackville family's magnificent estate in Kent. Generally ranked in the top five of England's largest houses—it's known as a "calendar" house with 365 rooms, 52 staircases, 12 entrances, and 7 courtyards, although in fact these numbers aren't exactly right—Knole was built as a palace for the fifteenth-century archbishops of Canterbury before becoming a royal possession under Henry VIII. When Thomas Sackville acquired the home in 1603, he began massive renovations, employing roughly two hundred workmen, including craftsmen from Italy, to create the opulent rooms that Richard and Anne would make their new home.

Home, perhaps, isn't quite the right word: there is nothing homey or comfortable about Knole, which sits on a sprawling thousand-acre deer park and has the feeling of a state museum. (It belongs today to the National Trust.) To reach the house from the main road, visitors travel down a curvy drive nearly a mile in length before arriving at Bourchier's Tower, an impressive gatehouse that hides from view the vast structures within. Passing through a grassy courtyard to the inner Stone Court, Anne and Richard's guests would have entered the Great Hall, the largest space in the palace, where feasts and entertainments were held. Thomas Sackville had commissioned a two-story, carved oak screen just inside the entrance, decorated with leopards and other symbols of his family; on special occasions, musicians would be tucked away behind the windows at the top of the screen to play for guests below. After one exited the hall and descended the Great Staircase, which only family members and distinguished guests were allowed to use, the first floor opened into a maze of rooms, with private apartments tucked behind the public galleries and show rooms. Elegant "grotesque" carvings surrounded the marble and alabaster mantelpieces, beautiful plasterwork covered the ceilings, and stained glass bearing the Sackville arms and mottos filled the arched windows. In the early seventeenth century, there were hundreds of servants on the regular staff, who were apparently very well trained: one of Thomas Sackville's contemporaries praised them as "a very rare example in this present age of ours, when housekeeping is so decayed." Among other examples of his extravagance, Thomas designed a grand bedroom to be used by King James, who never ended up visiting.

Centuries later Knole would be the birthplace of the writer Vita Sackville-West, who, as an only daughter to her parents, was unable to inherit the palatial estate. What she lost as an inheritance she preserved in literature: Knole was the setting of both Sackville-West's novel *The Heir* and her lover Virginia Woolf's much more famous *Orlando* (Woolf famously quipped that Knole "looked a town rather than a house"). It's to Sackville-West, we might recall, that we owe the first edition of her distant relative's diaries: in 1923, she published *The Diary of Anne Clifford, with a Long Preface,* which contained the memoir from 1603 and the diaries of 1616, 1617, and 1619 (no diary for 1618 has survived).

In her "Long Preface" to *The Diary,* Sackville-West conjured up what Anne may have felt three hundred years earlier: "Knole I have seen as Anne Clifford saw it," she wrote, "quietly magnificent, down there in Kent, with its grey towers and wide lawns and glinting windows, and the flag floating high up in the cool empty blue." However splendid Knole may be, she also intuited Anne's preference for the "barbarous castles" and "wild heaths and moors" of her ancestral lands in the north. Indeed, Knole may have belonged for some years to Anne, but Anne never belonged to Knole. Her living within the "gay harbors of anguish" no doubt drove her to turn more fully within herself. "I gave myself wholly to retiredness as much as I could," she wrote, "and made good books and virtuous thoughts my companions."

What Anne omitted from this description of her "retiredness" was the activity that would preserve her thoughts and experiences for posterity: her extensive autobiographical writing. Soon after her marriage, she began chronicling her past, beginning (as far as we know) with her memoir of 1603, a particularly momentous year. By 1616, if not sooner, she had established the habit of recording her daily life in a diary. There, she kept track not only of her trials and tribulations in her ongoing inheritance battle, but also of her inner life: "I kept my chamber, being very troubled & sad in mind"; "I [worked] very much within doors and strived to set as merry a face as I could upon a discontented heart"; "I sat still thinking the time to be very tedious."

Anne's use of her diary as a repository for her personal feelings and experiences may seem ordinary to modern eyes, but it was far from the norm at the time. Largely kept by men, diaries were used to record both their public lives—there were military or naval logs, travel journals, doctors' and astrologers' casebooks (such as Simon Forman's)—and their private activities. Ben Jonson mocks the latter practice in his play *Volpone*, where Sir Politic Would Be describes his diary as "wherein I note my actions of the day":

> *Notandum,*
> *A rat had gnawn my spur-leathers; notwithstanding,*
> *I put on new, and did go forth; but first*
> *I threw three beans over the threshold. Item,*
> *I went and bought two tooth-picks, whereof one*
> *I burst immediately, in a discourse*
> *With a Dutch merchant, 'bout ragion del stato.*
> *From him I went and paid a moccenigo [a small coin]*
> *For piecing my silk stockings; by the way*
> *I cheapened sprats, and at St. Mark's I urined.*

Many fewer Renaissance women's diaries have survived, and those that have tend to be rather dry records of household chores and prayers. One of the best known, a diary kept by Lady Margaret Hoby between 1599 and 1605, is made up almost entirely of mind-numbing entries like these: "After private prayers I went about the house and then I read of the Bible till dinnertime"; "After private prayer I went to the church"; "After, I prayed, dined, and then kept company with a kinswoman of mine, then I took order for supper, dispatched some business, and after went to private prayer." What's extraordinary about Anne's diaries in comparison to Hoby's—or nearly anyone's in the period—is just how much she lets in. Treating herself as a historical subject living an important life, Anne became the most important female diarist of the era.

CHAPTER EIGHT

February 2, 1609

Banqueting House, Whitehall Palace

Aemilia Lanyer

At the end of the long Christmas entertainments at court in the winter of 1609, Aemilia Lanyer may have attended what from a feminist perspective was certainly the most provocative masque of the era. Commissioned by Queen Anna, Ben Jonson's *Masque of Queens* centered on twelve queens drawn from history and literature who appeared onstage in a "magnificent building" representing the House of Fame (inspired by Chaucer's poem of the same name). Built by the great architect Inigo Jones, who would earn lasting fame for designing the new Banqueting House following its destruction by fire in January 1619, the impressive *machina versatilis* (changing machine) was topped by a triumphal throne where the masquers posed as if they were statues in a classical monument. The "queens" then descended one by one to climb into small chariots that rode around the stage before dismounting to begin a formal dance. All of this was accompanied by music written by Alfonso Ferrabosco the younger, whom Aemilia would have known well. The son of an Italian immigrant musician who played for Queen Elizabeth at the same time as Aemilia's father, Ferrabosco was himself employed as one of James's court musicians alongside Aemilia's husband, Alfonso. Further consolidating the ties between the families, sometime around 1609 or 1610 Ferrabosco married Aemilia's sister-in-law, Ellen Lanyer.

The Masque of Queens was performed at Whitehall Palace on Candlemas, the festival celebrating Mary's presentation of Jesus at the temple forty days after his birth. Besides the guest of honor—on this occasion, the French ambassador, Antoine Le Fèvre de la Boderie, who wrote a detailed account of the evening—there's no record of the audience, which may have ranged anywhere from several hundred to several thousand people. Male and female courtiers were seated according to their rank in boxed seats, on benches, or in the galleries, while throngs of ordinary people like Aemilia would have been admitted without attention to their social position and found places where they could. The Banqueting House was typically packed to its absolute limits; a special order was issued in 1613 that women were prohibited from wearing farthingales, or hooped petticoats, to save space among the audience. If Aemilia was present, she would likely have caught a glimpse of her former mistress, Margaret Clifford, Dowager Countess of Cumberland, who would have been seated comfortably among the noblewomen. She would certainly have seen from a distance her former charge, Anne Clifford, who had an official role onstage.

There's no good equivalent today to the Renaissance masque. Like bearbaiting, it has disappeared from our ordinary cultural offerings, but it can best be understood as a combination of dance and theater with the official masquers performing non-speaking roles while a short script was read by professional actors. The key difference from other theatrical performances at the time—a Shakespeare play, for example—is that the masquers were all members of the nobility. Dressed in elaborate costumes that corresponded to the theme of the masque, they performed a highly choreographed dance before "taking out" chosen members of the audience (fellow aristocrats or honored foreign guests) onto the floor. These newly recruited dancers in turn chose partners to join them, ultimately leading to an enormous dance party. Each masque was created for a particular occasion and meant to be performed only once, with production costs that ranged from £2,000 to £4,000 apiece. When we think of the Renaissance court at its most extravagantly wasteful, the masque should be front of mind.

During Elizabeth's reign, Aemilia would have had occasion to see various entertainments at court through her ties to Baron Hunsdon and others, but she would rarely have seen a masque. Elizabeth had preferred other forms of spectacle, and her general stinginess made her reluctant to open her coffers for so fleeting a pleasure. Under James, the masque became the royal court's defining cultural event, due largely to the influence of Queen Anna. Anna had already taken an interest in masques during her time in Scotland, but her own role there didn't extend beyond her privileged place in the audience. In England, she made the masque her own. In the course of her first decade as queen, Anna commissioned a series of masques from Jonson and Samuel Daniel, which—unlike any of the masques the court was accustomed to—were written for exclusively female casts. Shocking the English court even more, Anna abandoned her seat next to the king and took a leading role herself. In a world in which all professional actors were male and all female roles were played by cross-dressed boys, the spectacle of aristocratic women performing onstage could be seen as revolutionary, if not obscene.

The Masque of Queens pushed the limits of courtly decorum further by presenting the masquers in costumes that violated all standards for female chastity. Many of the women were dressed as warriors, but far from being covered with armor as their male counterparts would have been, their breastplates were made of a transparent gauze that revealed their torsos. A few of the women had one breast fully exposed with the other lightly covered by a sash in a style associated with the Amazons. This was how Anne Clifford, cast in the role of the ancient Egyptian queen, Berenice, was dressed, as was Lucy Russell, Countess of Bedford, playing the Amazon queen Penthesilea. Who knows how these noblewomen, whose ordinary dress at its most risqué may have shown some cleavage, would have felt about displaying their bodies to an audience that included the king. It's almost certainly the case that Queen Anna, who ran daily rehearsals for a month before the event and was involved in nearly every aspect of the performance, knew she was pushing the boundaries. For Aemilia, who was busy at the time writing poems about patriarchy and the oppression of women, the vision of these women proudly displaying their bodies but not speaking a word may have been at once thrilling and maddening.

Inigo Jones's drawing of Anne Clifford's costume,
with notes about its colors ("Green," "Carnation,"
"White," with "Sky" crossed out)

Aemilia's reaction to the aristocratic female masquers would
also have been complicated by what had preceded them onstage:
The Masque of Queens began with an opposing group of twelve
actors in what Jonson called the "antimasque." The idea to have
an antimasque came from Anna, who, as Jonson explained in his
preface, "commanded me to think on some dance or show that
might precede hers and have the place of a foil or false masque."
To fulfill Anna's vision, Jonson imagined the creatures most unlike
the splendid and powerful queens at the masque's center, scripting
parts for "twelve women in the habit of hags or witches, sustaining

the persons of Ignorance, Suspicion, Credulity, etc., the opposite to good Fame." This little shop of horrors in which one "hag" after another appeared before the audience and gleefully recited her evil charms and spells didn't actually involve women performers: Jonson's "twelve women" actors were boys or men in drag. It would take more than fifty years and a civil war before women were allowed to perform spoken roles onstage: the audience who attended the December 1660 performance of *Othello* would have been the first to see a real woman playing Desdemona. This was the first known appearance by a female actor in an English theater; to prepare those present for the shock, the 1660 production included a warning in the form of a spoken prologue:

> *I come unknown to any of the rest*
> *To tell you news: I saw the Lady dressed;*
> *The woman plays to day, mistake me not,*
> *No man in gown, or page in pettycoat.*

There was no such announcement clarifying the gender identity of the hags in *The Masque of Queens*. According to the elaborate stage directions Jonson laid out in the script, the male actors dressed as women came out from behind a curtain designed as an "ugly hell" with flames that cast smoke up to the roof. Each was "differently attired, some with rats on their head, some on their shoulders; others with ointment pots at their girdles; all with spindles, timbrels, rattles or other venefical [poisonous] instruments, making a confused noise with strange gesture." Presumably this was unlike any other theatrical performance Aemilia had ever witnessed, unless she happened by chance to have seen Shakespeare's *Macbeth* when it was performed at court in 1606. (It didn't come to the London theaters until 1611, when Aemilia's astrologer, Simon Forman, recorded having been in the audience at the Globe.)

Both Shakespeare and Jonson were no doubt inspired by the new king's fascination, if not obsession, with the topic of witchcraft—James, as we've seen, had even published a book, *The Demonology*, on the subject in 1597. If Shakespeare had James in mind in writing *Macbeth*, Jonson's witches in his antimasque were designed to please

James's queen. Maybe Anna wanted to set her aristocratic fellow masquers in the strongest relief possible by first parading onstage a group of women at their most degraded and loathsome. Or maybe she was interested in putting before her audience two very different kinds of femininity that were both nonetheless threatening to men: on the one hand, demonic witches, on the other, formidable and sexy queens.

If Aemilia didn't see *The Masque of Queens* in person, she would have been able to read it in print: later in 1609, Jonson's masque was published by the London bookseller Richard Bonian. Seeing the glamorous list of the women masquers who had performed—Jonson included a list of their names in order of rank, from "the Queen's Majesty" through the six countesses to the five ladies, concluding with the soon-to-be-married Lady Anne Clifford—Aemilia may have felt the desire to be connected to such a group herself. It's hard not to see that a longing for female community played a role in the book of poems she was writing, a book that included but went far beyond "The Description of Cooke-ham" written after her idyllic time with Anne and her mother.

Aemilia's *Salve Deus Rex Judaeorum,* named for its long central poem, was entered in the Stationers' Company in October 1610—the first official step toward publication—and appeared in print in 1611. Thus, the daughter of an immigrant father and a mother unable to sign her name made English history by becoming the first woman in the seventeenth century to publish a book of original poetry. Of the Latin title, which translates as "Hail, God, King of the Jews," Aemilia explained that "it was delivered unto me in sleep many years before I had any intent to write in this manner." (This suggests she was dreaming in Latin: another sign of her erudition.) Published by the same Richard Bonian who had brought out Jonson's *Masque of Queens* two years earlier, Aemilia's *Salve Deus* was a landmark publication not only by virtue of its female author. It was also arguably England's first book of feminist poetry. Written for women and about women, *Salve Deus* had as its central theme a defense of women's rights.

In the same year the King James Bible first appeared in print, establishing the most influential English translation of scripture ever produced, Aemilia dared to tell a different story. Over the

SALVE DEVS

REX IVDÆORVM.

Containing,

1 The Paſsion of Chriſt.
2 Eues Apologie in defence of Women.
3 The Teares of the Daughters of Ieruſalem.
4 The Salutation and Sorrow of the Virgine
    Marie.

With diuers other things not vnfit to be read.

Written by Miſtris *Æmilia Lanyer,* Wife to Captaine
Alfonſo Lanyer Seruant to the
Kings Majeſtie.

AT LONDON
Printed by *Valentine Simmes* for *Richard Bonian,* and are
to be ſold at his Shop in Paules Churchyard, at the
Signe of the Floure de Luce and
Crowne. 1 6 1 1.

Aemilia's title page proudly declared her authorship,
even if it also described her as "Wife to Captain
Alfonso Lanyer."

course of 230 rhyming stanzas of eight lines each, "Salve Deus Rex
Judaeorum" lays out the story of Christ's Passion from a distinctly
female perspective. The formal challenge of writing the poem was
itself daunting: it's no easy feat to compose over 1,800 lines of *ottava
rima* (iambic pentameter stanzas written in an *abababcc* rhyme
scheme). But Aemilia's greater audacity was in tackling the subject
of Christ's crucifixion. To justify this, she makes the same claim for
divine inspiration that the great Protestant poet John Milton would
make sixty or so years later in writing *Paradise Lost.* Describing her
own "poor barren brain" as "far too weak" for the task, she asks God
to "give me power and strength to write":

Yet if he please to illuminate my spirit,
And give me wisdom from his holy hill,
That I may write part of his glorious merit,
If he vouchsafe to guide my hand and quill
Then will I tell of that sad blackfaced night,
Whose mourning Mantle covered Heavenly Light.

Given the fact that the poem proceeds to do exactly what she petitions for, Aemilia shows her reader that her prayer has been answered: she's not so much writing as channeling the divine word. It's hard to believe this is the same woman who only a decade earlier desperately sought the advice of an astrologer and boasted of her many male admirers at court. Now around forty, Aemilia seems to have found God—or rather, God seems to have found Aemilia.

Aemilia's narrative of Christ's Passion begins on the "very night our Savior was betrayed." As part of her overall strategy in "Salve Deus" of celebrating female virtue, the poem draws attention both to the wicked acts of men (Caiaphas, Judas) and to the compassionate acts of women (the daughters of Jerusalem, the Virgin Mary) in the days leading up to Christ's arrest. None of this comes as a surprise. But when Aemilia arrives at the moment that Pontius Pilate considers Christ's fate, she does something totally unanticipated. Relinquishing her own role as narrator, she hands the poem over to Pilate's wife. Among the most minor figures in the New Testament, Pilate's wife has a single line of verse in only one of the four gospels. In Matthew 27:19, a woman who is never named urges her husband, the Roman governor in Judaea, to disregard the will of the people calling for Christ to be crucified: "Have nothing to do with that just man," she warns Pilate, "for I have suffered many things this day in a dream because of him."

In early Christian commentaries and apocryphal writings, this woman was often called Procula Claudia, or simply Procula. In medieval England, Procula was paraded onstage in the mystery plays as an evil woman who almost prevented Christ's saving humankind; in the York Cycle's play named for her—*The Dream of Pilate's Wife*—Percula, as she's called there, receives her dream from the Devil himself. There's no way to know if Aemilia knew this or other medieval dramas; it's more likely she would have noticed the more positive treatment Pilate's wife was given in the Geneva Bible, the popular translation done by English Protestants in the 1550s. Consistent with the Protestant belief that everyone should have access to the Bible directly, the translation was heavily glossed with marginal notes. Next to the verse from Matthew regarding Pilate's wife was a single gloss suggesting that Pilate should have taken the "counsel of others to defend Christ's innocence." But whether the treatment of this woman was negative or positive, she had never been asked to perform the role Aemilia gave her in "Salve Deus," where she delivers one of the strongest defenses for women's rights that Christianity had ever seen.

In Pilate's wife, Aemilia found her perfect heroine: a woman whose intervention at the crucial moment could have changed the course of history, if only her husband had listened. With the scriptural verse from Matthew before her, Aemilia made two crucial additions to the story. First, she transformed Pilate's wife into a faithful believer who already regarded Christ as her Lord. "Hear the words of thy most worthy wife," she begs her husband, "who sends to thee, to beg her Savior's life." Far from simply reporting that she's had an ominous dream, as she does in Matthew, Pilate's wife explicitly warns Pilate that he will be killing the son of God.

Second, Aemilia turned Pilate's wife into a proto-feminist. After urging Pilate to let Christ go on religious grounds, she comes up with a new reason for why he should be pardoned: "Let not us women glory in men's fall / Who had power given to over-rule us all." If men are sinful enough to crucify their savior, then women should be liberated from men's rule. "Your indiscretion sets us free," she declares, "And makes our former fault much less appear." In these four short lines, Aemilia's character anticipates the killing of Christ as the basis for women's freedom from patriarchy.

As if this weren't radical enough, Pilate's wife moves in "Salve Deus" from making her argument about the Crucifixion to reconsidering the reason for Christ's sacrifice in the first place. "Our mother Eve," she exclaims,

> . . . who tasted of the Tree
> Giving to Adam what she held most dear,

Was simply good, and had no power to see,
The after-coming harm did not appear.

If Eve had no way to know the damage she might do, Adam was only too aware: it was he who received the command directly "from God's mouth." Eve was simply a victim of misinformation and "too much love," whereas Adam, not betrayed by the "subtle Serpent's falsehood," knew exactly what he was doing.

Aemilia was certainly not the first person to defend Eve on grounds of her innocence or to propose that Adam be held responsible for the Fall. She was possibly the first to argue that the crime of killing Christ so overwhelmed any fault of Eve's that women's subordination should come to an immediate end. "If unjustly you condemn [Christ] to die," Pilate's wife concludes,

> . . . *Then let us have our Liberty again,*
> *And challenge [attribute] to your selves no Sovereignty;*
> *You came not in the world without our pain,*
> *Make that a bar against your cruelty;*
> *Your fault being greater, why should you disdain*
> *Our being your equals, free from tyranny?*
> *If one weak woman simply did offend,*
> *This sin of yours, hath no excuse, nor end.*

Hundreds of years before the women's liberation movement, Aemilia used the figure of Pilate's wife to argue that the sexes should be equal. In doing so, she also rescued a voice from history, giving full personhood and agency to a woman whom the Bible didn't regard as worthy of a name.

In daring to interpret Christ's sacrifice in her own terms, Aemilia was taking the Protestant encouragement of women to study scripture to an entirely new level. It was one thing to incorporate subtle changes to the way women's experiences are described, as Mary Sidney had done with her translation of the Psalms. It was another thing to change the history of the Crucifixion so that a new woman had a starring role. To support her project, Aemilia conjured up a community of powerful women readers. Casting as wide a net as possible—seemingly without regard to rivalries or enmities among those she chose—she wrote no fewer than nine dedications that prefaced "Salve Deus" in the book, with not a single man included among the dedicatees. It's not clear why Bonian allowed Aemilia this costly rollout of pages: paper was extremely expensive, and most books of poems had a single dedication or none at all. Maybe he hoped the dazzling cast of characters Aemilia addressed would help the book to sell. It wasn't every day, after all, that a reader could imagine herself in the company of Queen Anna, Princess Elizabeth, and a sweeping array of countesses: the book doubled as an Englishwoman's hall of fame.

Besides showing off her aristocratic connections—some fabricated, some real, as we'll see—Aemilia had a set of practical motives. She almost certainly needed money, as she nearly always did, but dedications rarely generated significant income: the average gift that poets received from a dedicatee at the time was a decent but hardly life-sustaining payment of £2. In her poem "To the Lady Susan, Countess Dowager of Kent," the woman who took her in as a young child decades earlier, Aemilia denies any interest in a monetary reward: "No former gain hath made me write / nor any future profit is expected." Her dedication to Anne Clifford ("To the Lady Anne, Countess of Dorset") is more solicitous. Addressing Anne as "God's steward," she urges her to follow in the path of her noble family:

> And as your Ancestors at first possessed
> Their honors, for their honorable deeds,
> Let their fair virtues never be transgressed,
> Bind up the broken, stop the wounds that bleeds [sic],
> Succor the poor, comfort the comfortless.

In the very same poem in which Aemilia rants against the class system—this was the occasion for her defiantly asking why "gentry come to rise and fall" since "all sprang but from one woman and one man"—she leans on Anne's secure position of privilege to beg for her largesse.

More likely than receiving a gift of a pound or two, Aemilia may have hoped Anne would offer her a position in her household—a more permanent arrangement to what she briefly enjoyed with Anne's mother, Margaret, at Cookham. Around the time *Salve*

Deus appeared in print, Anne's husband, Richard Sackville, Earl of Dorset, departed with his own entourage for a long trip to the Continent (a version of the grand tour), leaving Anne in need of appropriate company and staff. In a 1611 letter, Anne's mother advised Richard on what kind of people Anne should have around her during his long absence. Margaret was specifically concerned that "no friend or ally of hers or yours shall resort to her to dissuade her against the religion wherein she was brought up"; she also wanted to make sure no one attempted to convince Anne to drop her lawsuit. Without mentioning it explicitly, Aemilia goes out of her way to convey both her awareness of the inheritance battle and her sympathy for Anne's position:

> *You are the Heir apparent of this Crown*
> *Of goodness, bounty, grace, love, piety,*
> *By birth it's yours, then keep it as your own,*
> *Defend it from all base indignity.*

Combined with the strong Protestant theology that runs through "Salve Deus" itself, Aemilia may have imagined herself perfectly suited for the job.

Anne's household may have been the most obvious fit, but Aemilia's dedications include several other bids for employment. In at least one case, she petitioned someone she had never met. "Although great Lady, it may seem right strange," she begins her poem to Katherine Howard, Countess of Suffolk, "that I a stranger should presume thus far / To write to you," she imagines her poems might pave the way for her:

> *Vouchsafe sweet Lady, to accept these lines*
> *Writ by a hand that doth desire to do*
> *All services to you whose worth combines*
> *The worthiest minds to love and honour you.*

Drawing special attention to Katherine's young daughters—"And let your noble daughters likewise read / This little Book that I present to you"—Aemilia might in this case have been aiming for a position as a tutor or governess.

Aemilia's ambition to find a place extended to the royal house-hold. Her dedication to Queen Anna, which opens the book, laments her current distance from the court and her subsequent lack of all earthly pleasures:

> *So I that live closed up in Sorrow's Cell*
> *Since great Eliza's favor blest my youth,*
> *And in the confines of all cares do dwell,*
> *Whose grieved eyes no pleasure ever vieweth.*

Despite her claim that "great Eliza's favor blest my youth," there's no evidence Aemilia ever received anything from the former queen; whatever ties she had to Elizabeth were likely indirect, coming either through her father (as court musician) or her lover (as lord chamberlain). When she makes her petition to Anna, she presents herself in an entirely independent role: "Vouchsafe to view that which is seldom seen," she declares, "A woman's writing of divinest things." Aemilia wanted to be recognized as a female devotional poet.

As Aemilia would certainly have known, there were no women writers who received patronage at the English court: the position someone like Jonson enjoyed, with multiple commissions and eventually a royal pension of roughly £65 a year, was beyond anything she could reasonably have imagined for herself. But the queen's interest in promoting women in her entertainments may have encouraged Aemilia to imagine a role inside Anna's court, with *Salve Deus* as the poetic equivalent of the all-female masque. Hoping to enlist the queen's support in the most exalted manner possible, she asks that Anna shine her heavenly "beams" upon her poems: "I humbly wish that yours may light on me / That so these rude unpolished lines of mine / Graced by you, may seem the more divine."

If the purpose of many of Aemilia's dedications was to improve her current circumstances, one of her poems—not coincidentally, written to Mary Sidney—reveals a goal at once less practical and more ambitious. In "The Author's Dream to the Lady Mary, the Countess Dowager of Pembroke," she seeks Mary's blessing to replace her as England's leading woman poet. The idea that such a position even existed was by no means obvious: again, there were no women recognized at the time as professional writers, nor was there an obvious audience for women's literature. Aemilia's aim in the poem was to create the idea of a female legacy—a mantle that could be passed from one woman to the next—with herself as its most recent laureate.

"The Author's Dream" is the longest of all *Salve Deus*'s dedications, and it's also the most poetically creative. Written as an elaborate vision that came to Aemilia in her sleep, the poem sets out first to celebrate Mary's accomplishment as a divine poet, and then to anticipate her approval of *Salve Deus* itself. This second aim risked seeming presumptuous, and Aemilia's decision to frame her poem as a dream was likely strategic: it granted her a form of self-protection. For whatever Aemilia imagines in the poem, there's no trace of her ever having met Mary Sidney; the two women may have been at some of the same events at court in the 1580s and 1590s, but they didn't have a personal relationship. As we'll see, however, Aemilia certainly knew Mary's achievements as a writer, and she regarded Mary's Psalms as having paved the way for her own more audacious project.

Aemilia's poem to Mary begins with extravagant praise. The great female poet is seated in a throne in the "Edalyan groves," an obscure reference to the city of Idalion in Cyprus linked to the goddess Aphrodite; while the nine Muses strum on harps and viols, Mary is crowned by "Eternal Fame." After rising to stroll through beautiful woods and bowers, Mary then joins a group of nymphs and goddesses to sing "those rare sweet songs" of David, which waft over Aemilia in her sleep. In the margins, Aemilia notes that the "heavenliest music" she heard was none other than "The Psalms written newly by the Countess Dowager of Pembroke." Where Aemilia would have encountered Mary's translation of the Psalms isn't clear; it's tempting to think Margaret Clifford had a copy at Cookham and that these were the very Psalms the women read and sang in the woods. But unlike the group of courtly women who performed in *The Masque of Queens,* all of whom had links to one another and might have shared their manuscripts or books, Aemilia had no obvious ties to other educated women outside of the network she was trying to create in *Salve Deus* itself.

In attributing the Psalms to Mary alone—"written newly by the Countess Dowager of Pembroke"—Aemilia departed from the trend among her contemporaries to credit Philip as their primary author. Although she generously describes Philip as "valiant Sidney, whose clear light / Gives light to all that tread true paths of Fame," her compliments are ultimately a vehicle for heaping more praise on Mary:

> So that a Sister well she may be deemed,
> To him that lived and died so nobly;
> And far before him is to be esteemed
> For virtue, wisdom, learning, dignity.

This insistence on Mary's preeminence as a poet is not an end in itself: it's part of the poem's larger design. For when Aemilia awakes from her dream, she rushes to Mary to present her with *Salve Deus*:

> For to this Lady now I will repair,
> Presenting her the fruits of idle hours;
> Though many Books she writes that are more rare,
> Yet there is honey in the meanest flowers.

Calling her poems "the meanest flowers" hardly masks her ambition: after spending most of the poem praising Mary's accomplishments, Aemilia now proposes herself as the great poet's successor. "And Madame," she declares, "if you will vouchsafe that grace / To grace those flowers that spring from virtue's ground"—if you will spread your grace, in other words, on my humble poems—may it not offend you "to see your Savior in a Shepherd's weed / Unworthily presented in your view / Whose worthiness will grace each line you read." Aemilia's "Salve Deus" might be a modest depiction of Christ, but Mary's sheer act of reading will elevate its worth. In the absence of a female canon, Aemilia sought to invent one.

Following her slew of dedications to individual noblewomen, the long prefatory section of *Salve Deus* ends with a letter "To the Virtuous Reader." There, Aemilia makes a bold announcement: "I have written this small volume, or little book, for the general use of all virtuous ladies and gentlewomen of this kingdom." She wanted, in short, only female readers. Discouraging the greater part of the literate public from picking up her book could hardly have helped with sales, and it's not surprising that when *Salve Deus* was issued for a second time later that year the letter was nowhere to be seen. As for what she imagines as her book's "general use," Aemilia explains her goal of teaching women to stick together:

> This have I done to make known to the world, that all women deserve not to be blamed though some forgetting they are women themselves, and in danger to be condemned by the words of their own mouths, fall into so great an error, as to speak unadvisedly against the rest of their sex.

However concerned she may have been with women's "speak[ing] unadvisedly against the rest of their sex," she quickly shifts the letter's focus toward women's treatment at the hands of men. The only positive example of a man she comes up with is Jesus Christ, whose goodness derives entirely from women: not only was he "begotten of a woman, born of a woman, nourished of a woman," but he also "healed wom[e]n, pardoned women, comforted women," and after his resurrection "appeared first to a woman." The letter ends with an appeal to both men and women to "speak reverently of our sex." Before she even launches into the book's long polemical poem, Aemilia throws down the gauntlet to misogyny.

Whether anyone in early-seventeenth-century England was ready for Aemilia's challenge was another question entirely. Unlike Mary Sidney's Psalms, which received praise at the time from all quarters, no one publicly complimented Aemilia's eloquence or devotional wisdom. After the book's two printings in 1611 (due to a change in the partnership of the printers, not marked demand), *Salve Deus* wasn't reissued for another 360 years. There's no way to know what Aemilia's early readers may have made of it. But what can be gleaned is how Aemilia tried to shape the experience of her book for a few people in particular. Of the nine copies of *Salve Deus* that have survived, two were specially made as gifts. Since books were usually sold unbound as loose pages, the contents of any single volume were much more flexible than they are today, making it possible to add or subtract materials as the author, printer, or purchaser saw fit. In the case of *Salve Deus,* the interesting clues lie in Aemilia's changes to the contents of her dedications.

The first of these "presentation copies" was done for Thomas Jones, Lord Chancellor of Ireland and Archbishop of Dublin. Given the date on the book's title page—8 November 1610—it was received at least several months before *Salve Deus*'s official publication. In addition to the date, the inscription states that the book was a "gift of Mr. Alfonso Lanyer," and includes the signature "Tho: Jones." Missing from the prefatory pages that follow are the poems to Lady Arbella Stuart, Susan Bertie, Katherine Howard, Lucy Russell, and Mary Sidney, as well as the letter "To the Virtuous Reader." The omission of the letter is easy to explain: Jones was hardly the target (all-female) audience Aemilia describes. The shuffling of dedications is less transparent, but it likely reflects Jones's alliances at court. Alfonso seems to have known Jones from his time in Ireland serving under Essex, and he must have been hoping to gain something—patronage, money—for himself or Aemilia in response to the gift. This is the only occasion in Aemilia's surviving history that there's any hint of collaboration between her and Alfonso. It's also an extremely rare example of a Renaissance husband using the intellectual achievements of his wife to pursue either his own or their joint ends.

The second surviving personalized copy of *Salve Deus* reflects an even greater gesture of social ambition. Bound in expensive vellum with gilt borders and figures on all four corners, the book was made as a gift for Prince Henry. On the cover is Henry's coat of arms; on the front and back bindings, his personal emblem of three ostrich feathers inside a gold coronet. Whether the book reached Henry isn't known, but at the top of the first page in very small print is the name "Cumberland." This could either refer to Anne Clifford's uncle, Francis, the current Earl of Cumberland, or more likely to her mother, Margaret.

Given how central a figure Margaret is in *Salve Deus*—in addition to "The Description of Cooke-ham" and a separate dedication, "To the Lady Margaret, Countess Dowager of Cumberland," Aemilia begins and ends "Salve Deus" with elaborate praise of her former mistress—Aemilia may well have leaned on her connections at court to help get the book into Prince Henry's hands. Henry was a friend of Anne's husband, Richard Sackville; at the investiture celebrations for Henry's creation as Prince of Wales in 1610, Anne had performed in Daniel's masque *Tethys' Festival*—she played the role of the river nymph Aire—and Richard participated in the celebratory tilts. As with the book for Jones, Henry's copy was clearly curated for his particular circle: the dedications to his mother and sister— Queen Anna and Princess Elizabeth—were both included, as well as those to Anne, Margaret, and the queen's favorite, Lucy, Countess of Bedford. The dedication to his cousin Lady Arbella Stuart, whom James had imprisoned in 1610 after her secret marriage to another claimant to the throne, William Seymour, was judiciously left out.

Whatever hopes Aemilia had from getting *Salve Deus* into the hands of the heir to the throne were dashed with the eighteen-year-old prince's sudden death from typhoid fever in 1612. The next year Aemilia suffered a more immediate loss: Alfonso died from unknown causes at the age of around forty. There's no record of Aemilia's response to his death; even if all indications suggest the marriage wasn't a happy one, Aemilia would have lost both Alfonso's regular income as a court musician and any possible advantages that might have come to her through his promotion of her work. As with Mary Sidney, if under very different circumstances, widowhood seems to have brought a sudden end to Aemilia's career as a writer. After *Salve Deus*'s publication, there are no further traces of her poems.

By any conventional metrics, Aemilia's literary career had been a flop. *Salve Deus* was never reprinted in her lifetime, she never received offers of patronage or employment from any of the women to whom she dedicated her poems, and her book disappeared for centuries from England's literary annals. What can't be measured, however, is what it meant for educated women with some money to spare to find *Salve Deus* for sale at Bonian's shop in St. Paul's Churchyard—the unbound pages probably cost around five pennies—and to be immersed in Aemilia's brilliant account of Christ's crucifixion and the fall of humankind. What can't be measured is what Anne Clifford may have felt if she read her former tutor's daring book of poems challenging the patriarchal system in a manner far beyond what she and her fellow aristocratic women had done in their silent performance in *The Masque of Queens*. What can't be measured, finally, is what impact both the contents of *Salve Deus* and the sheer fact of its publication may have had on Elizabeth Cary, who was busy finishing a play set in the same world of ancient Judaea that Aemilia conjured up, starring a new feminist heroine of her own.

CHAPTER NINE

December 17, 1612

Stationers' Hall, Ave Maria Lane, London

Elizabeth Cary

Roughly a week before Christmas in 1612, the clerk at the Stationers' Company in London entered in his register, "A book called Mariamne, The Tragedy of the fair Mariamne Queen of Jewry." No author was named, and after collecting the usual fee (between four and seven pennies), he probably never gave the title another thought. The Stationers' clerk certainly couldn't have imagined that the "book called Mariamne" would be a significant event in the history of English literature. When it appeared in print the following year, Elizabeth Cary's *The Tragedy of Mariam* became the first original play by a woman ever published in England. Alongside Aemilia Lanyer, whose *Salve Deus* had appeared two years before, Elizabeth found a way to express her frustration with the conditions of women's lives through writing creative literature.

For an independent woman like Elizabeth, who had taught herself several foreign languages, fought with her father on questions of religion, and loved nothing more than to be left alone with her books, the idea of being a submissive wife posed an unusual challenge. At church services throughout her childhood, she would have heard repeated the conventional tripartite formula: a married woman should be chaste, silent, and obedient. This message was broadcast in the Church of England's official "Homily on the state of matrimony," read both at weddings and at some ordinary services during the year. Women might order their children and servants around, but "as for their husbands, them must they obey, and cease from commanding, and perform subjection." "When the wives be stubborn, froward, and malapert," the sermon warns, "their husbands are compelled thereby to abhor and flee from their own houses, even as they should have battle with their enemies." Recalcitrant wives were not only at risk of upsetting their marital harmony: they might lose their husbands altogether.

The advice to wives given by the English Church echoed through the many Renaissance books published on the topic of marriage, the vast majority of which targeted male readers. There's no easy explanation for why men seem to have become so self-conscious—and presumably so anxious—about their marital relations at this time, but one possible answer lies in the mixed message of Protestantism. On the one hand, the Protestant church placed more emphasis than Catholics previously had on the importance of marital companionship. As John Milton would describe it in his 1643 *Doctrine and Discipline of Divorce*, there was nothing worse than the loneliness of a bad marriage. Procreation without compatibility, he exclaimed, was nothing more than "two carcasses chained unnaturally together." (Milton was speaking from experience: his marriage to Mary Powell in 1642 lasted only a few weeks before his young bride returned home to her parents; the couple was reunited a few years later, but only after Milton threatened to divorce her.)

On the other hand, Protestants insisted on strict hierarchy in the household, frequently comparing marriages to small kingdoms in which husbands needed to assert their rule. This was King James's argument in his 1599 treatise *Basilikon Doron, or His Majesties Instructions to His Dearest Sonne, Henry the Prince,* in which he advised the five-year-old Henry to "treat [your wife] as your own flesh, command her as her lord, cherish her as your helper, rule her as your pupil." "Ye are the head," James reminded the boy, "she is your body. It is your office to command, and hers to obey."

The emphasis on wifely obedience in Renaissance marital treatises wasn't unusual: nothing was more threatening to patriarchal norms than women behaving independently. But perhaps more surprising was the insistence on silence in nearly all aspects of a woman's life. The idea that women should be quiet in the public sphere—a position maintained even when women appeared onstage in courtly entertainments, as in *The Masque of Queens*—was routinely traced to the epistles of St. Paul. In his instructions to the Corinthians, Paul ordered the men to "let your women keep silence in the churches, for it is not permitted unto them to speak."

English domestic treatises routinely extended this concern about women's speaking in churches to their private homes. In his 1617 *A Bride-Bush, or A Wedding Sermon compendiously describing the duties of married persons,* William Whately advised that a wife's speech and gestures toward her husband "must carry the stamp of fear upon them, and not be cutted, sullen, passionate, tetchy, but meek, quiet, submissive." The wife's tongue "must be neither keen, nor loose, her countenance neither swelling nor deriding, her behavior not singing, not puffing, not discontented, but favoring all lowliness and quietness of affection." There are some women, Whately continued, who "chafe and scold with their husbands, and rail upon them, and revile them, and shake them together with such terms and carriage, as were unsufferable toward a servant." Such wives were "blemishes of their sex, monsters in nature, botches of human society."

The simplest advice male authors like Whately offered to women was to keep their mouths shut whenever possible. "If the wife would keep silent when her husband begins to chide," Robert Cleaver suggested in his 1598 treatise, *A godly form of household government,* "she should not have [such] unquiet dinners." To communicate with the outside world, wives should rely on their husbands as their spokesmen. According to Cleaver, the ideal dynamic in a marriage was like that between trumpeter and trumpet: "As the voice of him that sounds a trumpet is not so loud as the sound it yields, so is the wisdom and word of a woman, of great virtue and efficacy, when all that she knows, and can do, is, as if it were said and done by her husband." In *A Preparative to Marriage* (1591), Henry Smith put it even more plainly: "the ornament of a woman is silence, and therefore the law was given to the man rather than to the woman, to show that he should be the teacher and she the hearer."

Insubordination could be spotted even in the way wives addressed their husbands. "Contrary are those [names] which argue equality or inferiority rather than superiority," William Gouge argued in *Of Domestical Duties,* published in 1622:

Remember the fearful issue that had like to have fallen out by reason of such appellations given by Sarah (Gen 12:19; 20:2) and Rebekah (Gen 26:9) to their husbands. Not unlike to those are such as these, Sweet, Sweeting, Heart, Sweet-heart, Love, Joy, Dear, &c. and such as these Duck, Chick, Pigsnie, &c.

"Sweetheart," "duck," and "chick" were out, but so were Jack, Tom, or Will—such nicknames were unseemly and to be used only for servants. The best solution, Gouge proposed, was for the wife to add the title "Master" to her husband's surname. Or even better: just call him "Lord."

According to her daughters, Elizabeth tried her best to adapt to the repressive norms of wifely behavior. As they related in *The Lady Falkland,* Henry Cary was "very absolute, and though [Elizabeth] had a strong will, she had learnt to make it obey his." She had a deep fear of riding horses, but because Henry "lov[ed] hunting and desir[ed] to have her a good horse woman," she "for many years rode so much, and so desperately, as if she had no fear, but much delight in it, and so she had, to see him pleased." Getting dressed up "was all her life a torture to her," they reported, "yet because he would have it so, she willingly supported it, all the while she lived with him in her younger days, even to tediousness." The tediousness extended to her maids, who complained they had to "walk round the room after her (which was her custom) while she was seriously thinking on some other business, and pin on her things and braid her hair." But "the desire to please him," her daughters concluded, "had power to make her do that, that others would have scarce believed possible for her." The vision of the marriage that emerges is certainly not one of mutual love and respect. Elizabeth seems to have craved Henry's approval and conformed to his tastes as best she could, while Henry showed no sign of reciprocation. "Where his interest was concerned," *The Lady Falkland* concluded, "she seemed not able to have any consideration of her own."

The notion that Elizabeth should always put her husband's interest ahead of her own turned out to be entirely unsustainable for her later in the marriage. But in the early years, her outlet for exploring the idea of marital rebellion was channeled through her writing. *The Tragedy of Mariam* tells the story of the death of the Hasmonean princess Mariam at the hands of her tyrannical husband, Herod the Great. A close ally of Mark Antony, Herod was named king of Judaea in 37 BCE. A ruthless politician, he murdered anyone who got in his way, including Mariam's grandfather Hircanus, high priest of Jerusalem, and her brother, Aristobolus. To marry Mariam, Herod had repudiated his first wife, Doris, and their children. Although it brought him the kingdom, the union with Mariam was not simply strategic: Herod fell passionately in love. The match was initially a good one—at least from Herod's perspective—but after some years his treacherous sister, Salome, began to plant false rumors of Mariam's infidelity. In the second round of these rumors, which included the entirely unfounded accusation that Mariam was trying to poison him, Herod ordered his wife to be killed. The innocent and loyal Mariam went to her death without great protest, preferring to die with her dignity intact rather than attempt to win back a husband she had come to despise.

This is the outline of the story Elizabeth inherited, passed down to posterity in two separate works, *The Antiquities* and *The Wars of the Jews,* by the first century CE Jewish historian known as Flavius Josephus (originally named Joseph Ben Matthias, he boasted of being a descendant of the Hasmonean dynasty on his mother's side). Originally written in Greek, Josephus's histories were translated into Latin, French, German, and Italian during the fifteenth and sixteenth centuries. In 1602 the first English translation, Thomas Lodge's *The famous and memorable works of Josephus,* appeared in print. There were also several European plays written about Herod and Mariam in the sixteenth century: Lodovico Dolce's Italian *Marianna,* which—despite its title—focuses heavily on Herod; and Hans Sachs's German *Tragedia der Wütrich König Herodes,* in which Mariam dies at the end of the second act (there are five acts in all). Close study of these works alongside Elizabeth's hasn't revealed many parallels, and it seems Josephus was her primary source. Wherever she first encountered the story, she was drawn above all to the tragic figure of Mariam.

Around the time Elizabeth wrote her play—likely sometime before the birth of her first child in 1609—there was another ancient woman dominating the English stage. In 1606 or 1607 Shakespeare's

Antony and Cleopatra was performed in London, giving audiences the most complex and seductive vision of the queen imaginable. In choosing to write about Mariam, Elizabeth may have been looking for a second figure from this fascinating historical moment to put in the limelight, someone on the margins of Cleopatra's drama with a compelling story of her own. There's no question that Elizabeth had Cleopatra in mind: on multiple occasions in the play Mariam draws attention to her Egyptian contemporary as a rival, comparing herself (favorably) to the "wanton queen" who tried to steal Herod for herself. "All her allurements, all her courtly guile," Mariam boasts, "[c]ould not my face from Herod's mind exile." If Mary Sidney found a way to celebrate the morally complicated Cleopatra for her stoicism in her translation of Garnier's *Marc Antoine,* Elizabeth pulled from the archives a woman who not only shared Cleopatra's courage in confronting her own death, but who was also unequivocally virtuous.

In creating a heroine whose fate was sealed by her refusal to bow to a despotic and irrational husband, Elizabeth may also have had another recent play of Shakespeare's in mind. The parallels between *Othello* and *The Tragedy of Mariam* are striking: both Desdemona and Mariam are victims of vicious rumors; both have husbands who choose to murder rather than trust their wives. But if Elizabeth was thinking about *Othello*—and as we've seen, she would have had a chance to see it performed at court in 1604—she decided to give it a feminist twist. As the title suggests, *The Tragedy of Mariam* was almost entirely focused on its female protagonist: Herod doesn't even appear in the play until act 4. What interested Elizabeth wasn't the psychological unraveling of the jealous husband, but the heroic struggle of his wife. In Mariam, Elizabeth saw a woman who, like Desdemona, was subjected to an outrageous injustice; she then transformed her character from a passive victim to an active heroine. The result was the most powerful exploration English literature had yet to see of a wife's right to follow her own conscience over the will of her husband.

In the very first line of the play, Mariam announces having violated one of the three cardinal rules for the ideal wife: "How oft have I with public voice run on." The idea of Mariam's speaking with a "public voice" was already shocking: there were no female preachers or politicians in Renaissance England, and a respectable woman would not have dared to speak on her own behalf in the public sphere. Elizabeth makes Mariam's infraction all the stronger by having her reveal that not only has she spoken aloud without the protection of her husband, but she has also compared herself to none other than Julius Caesar. The comparison isn't meant to be flattering to either of them: Mariam has just received news of Herod's supposed death, and she likens her reaction to Caesar's when he wept for the death of his rival Pompey. "One object yields both grief and joy," she exclaims, chastising herself for her seeming hypocrisy: "you wept indeed, when on his worth you thought / But joy'd that slaughter did your foe destroy." As it happens, the struggle over how to respond to Herod's death turns out to be an exercise in vain: later the same day, Mariam learns the rumors were false and Herod is very much alive. But the experience of imagining his death helps to clarify her feelings toward him, feelings in no way compatible with either ancient Judaean or Renaissance definitions of a wife's duty to her husband.

No sooner does Herod return to Jerusalem than Mariam makes clear she has no intention of submitting to his will. Far from keeping her thoughts to herself, she shares with him both her anger over his killing of her relatives and the hardening of her prior love for him into hate. She also violates her oath of marriage by swearing never to have sex with him again. When Herod's counselor, the decent and loyal Sohemus, tells Mariam that Herod is on his way home, she bluntly responds: "I will not to his love be reconciled / With solemn vows I have forsworn his bed." For Protestants, wifely chastity was defined by having sexual relations only with one's husband: refraining from sex altogether, especially if you were of childbearing age, didn't count. From a seventeenth-century English perspective, by refusing to sleep with Herod Mariam could be charged not only with disobedience but also, paradoxically, with unchastity.

Thus, Sohemus's unequivocal reaction—"But you must break those vows"—echoes what any priest in the Church of England might have said. There are no vows a married woman could rightly take that would override those she made to her husband. This message is reinforced by the Chorus, which throughout the play expresses the most conservative positions available. "When to their husbands they themselves do bind," the Chorus declares,

Do they not wholly give themselves away?
Or give they but their body, not their mind,
Reserving that, though best, for others' prey?
No sure, their thoughts no more can be their own,
And therefore should to none but one be known.

From the strict perspective of patriarchy, Mariam has a right neither to her own body nor to her freedom of thought. More than the false accusation of her adultery or her attempt to poison Herod, it's Mariam's refusal to play the role of a submissive wife that leads to her murder. Once she has behaved in such a conspicuously independent fashion, it's easy for Herod to believe the worst.

There's no way to know exactly where Elizabeth stood in relation to Mariam's conduct. Unlike other rebellious wives in the theater of the period—Katerina in Shakespeare's *Taming of the Shrew* comes readily to mind—Mariam is never "tamed." As the play's sympathetic protagonist, she's also given the chance to speak for herself without ever being silenced. Possibly the strongest proof that Elizabeth was actively exploring how far women might go in pursuit of their liberty lay in her conception of Mariam's enemy, Salome. As related by Josephus, Salome was a dishonest, conniving woman who not only slandered Mariam but also betrayed a series of husbands. Her first husband, Joseph, was executed after Salome made up accusations of his adultery with Mariam. She got rid of Joseph to marry Constabarus, a decent man who was governor of Idumea and Gaza, but she soon tired of him as well. This time, she showed some clemency: instead of arranging to have him murdered, she sent him a bill of divorce. The divorce wasn't granted, but Salome ultimately got what she wanted: her brother Herod ordered Constabarus to be killed. Some twenty years later, Salome pursued a third marriage with the prince of Arabia, Silleus, whom she had taken as a lover. Silleus, however, refused Herod's prenuptial condition that he convert to Judaism—maybe he just got nervous about Salome's marital history—and the two never wed.

Given these historical materials, Elizabeth would have had no trouble depicting Salome as an exclusively unsympathetic villain. Instead, she also gives her the chance to shine. When we first meet Salome alone onstage, she's in the midst of plotting how to replace Constabarus with Silleus. The temporal linking of these two events that were historically separated by several decades is part of Elizabeth's general adherence to the so-called classical unities of drama—the idea introduced by Aristotle in his *Poetics* that the action in a play should unfold in a single place over the course of a single day. The compression of time also serves to intensify Salome's motivation to get rid of her current husband: she has another man waiting in the wings.

From the moral abyss of Salome's marital scheming, Elizabeth takes an unexpected turn: she has her villain deliver an eloquent defense of a woman's right to divorce her husband. In a long soliloquy that reveals Elizabeth's impressive gifts in the arts of rhetoric, Salome begins by imagining what would happen if the tables were turned and Constabarus wanted to leave her: "A separating bill might free his fate / From such a yoke that did so much displease." "Why," she then asks,

> *should such privilege to man be given?*
> *Or given to them, why barred from women then?*
> *Are men than we in greater grace with Heaven?*

Having spoken out loud what women weren't supposed to think even privately, she concludes by announcing her new role as a feminist pioneer:

> *I'll be the custom-breaker, and begin*
> *To show my sex the way to freedom's door.*
> *And with an offering will I purge my sin,*
> *The law was made for none but who are poor.*

On the surface of things, it's not surprising that Elizabeth put her greatest challenge to tradition in the mouth of her heroine's enemy: any accusation of her sympathy for Salome could easily be dismissed on the grounds of her obvious wickedness. Salome is, after all, the source of nearly everything that goes wrong in the play, and her aristocratic disdain for law and order—"the law was made for none but who are poor"—puts her in dramatic opposition to everything the Chorus, for example, strives to uphold.

Elizabeth's caution about what she'd written is borne out by her

decision to have Constabarus condemn Salome in terms that would
have resonated to Protestant English husbands:

> *Are Hebrew women now transformed to men?*
> *Why do you not as well our battles fight,*
> *And wear our armor? Suffer this, and then*
> *Let all the world be topsy-turved quite.*
> *Let fishes graze, beasts swim, and birds descend,*
> *Let fire burn downwards whilst the earth aspires,*
> *Let winters heat and summer's cold offend.*

And yet: however forceful these and other critiques of Salome's
actions, her words are never retracted nor is she punished for them.
In Salome's determination to "show my sex the way to freedom's
door," combined with Mariam's refusal to bend her will to her
husband's—"Yet had I rather much a milkmaid be," she declares,
"[t]han be the monarch of Judea's queen"—Elizabeth revealed a gift
for radical thinking.

Between 1611 and 1613, two works written by women that fundamentally challenged the status quo appeared from the London
press. Using figures from the ancient world to work through some
of the intractable problems women faced in seventeenth-century
England—misogyny, male domination, control over one's body
and speech, the right to divorce—both *Salve Deus* and *The Tragedy of Mariam* had the potential to change the conversation about
women's role in the world. As with Aemilia's poems, however, Elizabeth's play had very little obvious success. She received one strong
endorsement of her literary talents roughly a year before the play
appeared in print. In 1612, her former writing tutor, John Davies of
Hereford, dedicated his book of poems, *The Muses' Sacrifice,* to three
women of letters: Mary Sidney, Countess of Pembroke; Lucy Russell, Countess of Bedford; and Elizabeth herself. About Elizabeth,
Davies declares:

> *Thou makest Melpomen proud, and my heart great*
> *Of such a pupil, who, in buskin fine,*
> *With feet of state, doth make thy muse to meet*
> *the scenes of Syracuse and Palestine.*

"Buskin" refers specifically to the boot worn by actors in ancient Greece, and more broadly to the spirit of tragic drama; Melpomene is the muse of tragedy. The play Elizabeth set in Syracuse has sadly been lost, but the "scene" of Palestine clearly refers to *The Tragedy of Mariam,* which Davies must have read in manuscript. After praising her in a typically backhanded compliment regarding female talent—"Such nervy limbs of art and strains of wit / Times past never knew the weaker sex to have"—he ends his dedication by warning against the oblivion that might follow were she not to publish her work: "And times to come, will hardly credit it / if thus thou give thy works both birth and grave."

The irony was that, despite its publication, *The Tragedy of Mariam* did meet "both birth and grave" for several hundred years. As a closet drama meant to be read privately, it was never performed in the London theaters, and it wasn't reissued after its 1613 printing. Whether Elizabeth even authorized its publication in the first place remains unclear. *The Lady Falkland* refers to a work "stolen out of that sister in-law's (her friend's) chamber, and printed," adding that it subsequently "by her own procurement was called in." It's possible that this "stolen" work was only the dedicatory sonnet Elizabeth wrote to her sister-in-law, who was also named Elizabeth Cary; the sonnet in question appears in only two of the twenty or so surviving copies of the play. But given that *The Tragedy of Mariam* delved deeply into female disobedience, divorce, and spousal murder—topics that would hardly have been popular among her husband's circle at court—it seems more likely the work in question was the play itself.

Unlike *Salve Deus,* which openly credited "Mistris Aemilia Lanyer, Wife to Captaine Alfonso Lanyer" as its author, the title page for *The Tragedy of Mariam* stated that the play was written by "that learned, virtuous, and truly noble lady, E.C." For those who knew Elizabeth personally, the initials would have identified her, but it suggests she wanted to remain unknown to the public at large. It's also striking that the sister-in-law to whom Elizabeth wrote the only dedicatory poem in the book was also named Elizabeth Cary—and in this case, her full name was included. By removing the sonnet from the printed copies, Elizabeth thus eliminated another obvious indication of her own identity. Maybe

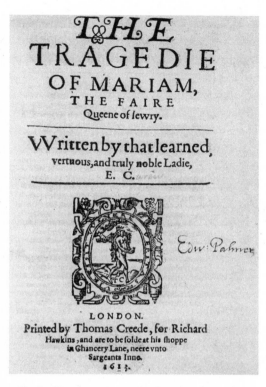

Elizabeth's title page touts her learning, but at least
partially obscures her identity.

Henry forced her to do this: it's unlikely he would have supported
either her publishing the work or her using his sister's name for all
to see. Given that *The Tragedy of Mariam* is never mentioned in
The Lady Falkland, it may have disappeared from the family records
altogether. But even if the play was buried, its expression of wifely
outrage continued to simmer in Elizabeth until it would ultimately
reach a boiling point.

Meanwhile, Elizabeth focused on her ever-growing family.
Indeed, in the decade or so after writing *Mariam,* her life was fully
consumed by motherhood. For the first seven years of their marriage, Elizabeth and Henry had been childless. This wasn't altogether surprising, given how little time they'd spent together. After
their wedding in 1602 Elizabeth had remained with her parents

while Henry pursued his career at court; when he went to the Continent to serve as a soldier in the Protestant wars, she had moved in with her mother-in-law (this is when she was locked up in her room without her books).

When Elizabeth finally got pregnant in 1608, the news made its way into the letters of John Chamberlain, who wrote to Sir Dudley Carleton on December 9, 1608, that "Sir Henry Cary brought his lady to town the last week in great pomp accompanied with five coaches besides many horsemen and herself in a litter because she is with child." Whatever delays there may have been in starting a family were now more than compensated by one successful pregnancy after another. Katherine's birth in 1609 was followed by Lucius in 1610, Lorenzo in 1613, Anne in 1614, and then seven more children between 1615 and 1624, all but one of whom lived past infancy. Given the high rates of infant mortality during the period—historians estimate that in early-seventeenth-century England roughly one out of every six children died in their first year of life—Elizabeth's family was something of a miracle.

However blessed Elizabeth was with the health of her children, the demands of childbirth and mothering took an enormous toll on her well-being. In addition to growing obese—her daughters noted she was "a long time very fat"—she suffered from what today would almost certainly be diagnosed as postpartum depression. After both her second and fourth children were born, she fell into a "deep melancholy," losing "the perfect use of her reason, and was much in danger of her life." In lines subsequently struck through in the manuscript copy of *The Lady Falkland*—at least one of her children didn't want their mother's psychological struggles included—Elizabeth is described as being in a state of "plain distractedness," a diagnosis that might include verbal and mental incoherence, fits of laughter and raving, and moments of delusion. During one of these dark periods, "for fourteen days together she ate nor drank nothing in the world, but only a little beer with a toast, yet without touching the toast."

Elizabeth's daughters stopped short of saying their mother exaggerated her symptoms, but they suggested she was "giving full way to them" in order to gain Henry's sympathy, "thinking her husband would then be most sensible of her trouble, knowing he was

extraordinary careful of her when she was with child or gave suck."
(Unlike nearly all women of her class, Elizabeth insisted on nursing
her own children.) Later in *The Lady Falkland*—in lines also struck
through—Elizabeth is described as having been "transported with
her own thoughts . . . [so that she] would forget herself, where she
was and how attended." On these occasions, she was "seldom able
for the earnestness of her thoughts to distinguish her own necessi-
ties, not discerning whether she was cold or hungry."

Despite her struggles with both her physical and mental health,
Elizabeth remained fully committed to what had become her absolute priority: to settle her religious faith outside of the Protestant
church. According to *The Lady Falkland,* Elizabeth's "first care" as a
mother was to make sure her children were "instructed in the princi-
ples of Christianity," but not "in the particular Protestant doctrines,
of the truth of which she was little satisfied." Dating back to her
childhood aversion to Calvin, Elizabeth had been skeptical about
Protestant theology. When she was around twenty, her daughters
reported "she grew into much doubt of her religion." Contribut-
ing to her doubt was her growing fascination with Catholicism,
brought on in part by her brother-in-law Adolphus Cary's enthusiasm following a trip to Italy from which he returned with a "good
opinion of Catholic religion." Although Adolphus seems to have
remained solidly Protestant until his death in 1609, he became an
avid reader of the Catholic church fathers, especially St. Augustine,
and he persuaded Elizabeth—no doubt the most bookish member
of the family—to join him in his reading.

Elizabeth was soon hooked. For some time she refused to
attend the mandatory services in the Church of England, ultimately returning to Protestant worship only after meeting with several learned bishops who convinced her that she could reconcile
her private beliefs with the church's practices. But the issue was far
from resolved. Indeed, as her daughters noted, "she seemed to prefer
nothing but religion and her duty to God before [Henry's] will." In
other words, religion was the one area in which Elizabeth had the
courage to defy her husband.

There's no way to know how seriously Henry took his wife's
deviant religious proclivities in the early years of their marriage: he
was too busy pursuing his career at court. In 1617, he became comp-

troller of the royal household, a position that made him a member of the Privy Council; three years later, he was created Viscount Falkland, a new title in the Scottish peerage. (The fourth rank in the British peerage, viscount is above baron and below duke, marquess, and earl.) For someone who began his life as a gentleman of no distinction, these were significant achievements. We might recall that Mary Sidney's father, Sir Henry Sidney, served Elizabeth for decades without ever becoming a privy councilor or being able to afford the queen's offer of a barony. But the costs of the promotions weren't easy for Henry Cary either. To become comptroller he apparently paid £5,000, an enormous sum that likely included "gratuities" or bribes for his supporters, clothes and food for the celebrations, and a fee for assuming the position.

At this point, Henry was already stretched well beyond his means. When in 1621 the king offered him the post of lord deputy of Ireland, he persuaded Elizabeth to mortgage her jointure—the money put aside by her father, Lawrence Tanfield, for her use in case Henry predeceased her. This pushed Lawrence over the edge. Unlike George Clifford, he seems to have had no earlier intention of finding a male relative to inherit his wealth instead of his daughter; he also had no fancy title to pass down. But after seething for years over Henry's squandering of Elizabeth's fortune, he altered his will to replace his daughter with her eldest son, Lucius, who was thirteen or fourteen years old at the time. When Lawrence died in 1625, Elizabeth was officially disinherited.

Henry and Elizabeth's move to Ireland was not only a disaster financially: it also greatly exacerbated their long-simmering religious differences. One of Henry's chief responsibilities as lord deputy was to enforce Irish conformity to the Protestant church. Ireland had posed a serious challenge to the idea of a national church since the early days of the Protestant Reformation, when Henry VIII first broke with Rome and required all his subjects to practice the new religion. Irish revolts against the Protestant church raged throughout the sixteenth century; in the 1590s, they came to a head in Tyrone's rebellion, which Essex failed to put down in 1599 and which lasted a total of nine years. From England's perspective, the problem was not only within Ireland, but also involved the Irish alliance with Catholic forces on the Continent, including ties to the pope and the Spanish king. When the English finally defeated the Catholic Irish lords in 1603, James forced them to abandon their titles, their armies, and their rule over their subjects. They were also made to swear loyalty to the English Crown. The result was a major exodus of Irishmen to Catholic Europe, and a provisional peace in the British Isles.

It was against this backdrop that Henry took the helm as James's lord deputy. As a member of a staunchly Protestant family and a former soldier in the Protestant wars on the Continent, he seemed the right man for the job. In many ways, he was: Henry zealously persecuted Catholic priests, expelling them from the country in a 1623 proclamation, and he served heavy penalties upon men and women still practicing the forbidden faith. This second group, however, now included Elizabeth. With the move to Ireland, Elizabeth finally had the chance to attend Catholic services and put an end to the charade of her Protestantism; ever an eager linguist, she apparently even learned Gaelic so that she could use the Irish Bible. When Henry discovered what she was up to, he was beside himself with rage. The last thing he needed was for his own wife to break the very rules he was trying to enforce.

Whatever Henry's frustrations, nothing prepared him for what Elizabeth was planning to do next. In the summer of 1625, she left Dublin with her children Anne, Mary, Patrick, and Henry for a visit to London. The official purpose of the trip was to further her husband's interests at court—his financial position had become more desperate than ever—but it turned out to be focused instead on her own religious activities. Upon her arrival, London was experiencing a horrible wave of plague, and she and her children escaped to her mother's home in Oxfordshire. They were joined there by her eldest daughter, Katherine, who was already married and pregnant with her first child. Within a week, Katherine became gravely ill and went into labor three months early; she and the infant both died. Elizabeth comforted herself in her grief by insisting that she'd seen next to Katherine's deathbed "a bright woman clothed in white having a crown on her head," whom she "assuredly believed to be our Blessed Lady." While Protestants still recognized the Virgin Mary as the mother of God, her role in Protestant worship had been dramatically scaled back, and the cult of Mary had been eliminated. For

Elizabeth to claim to see a vision of this kind smacked of Catholicism.

Once the plague had passed, Elizabeth returned to London, where she began to meet on a regular basis with a group of scholars and priests known as Arminians, a new faction within the English Church. Named for the late-sixteenth-century Dutch theologian Jacobus Arminius, who rejected Calvin's theory of predestination, the Arminians seemed to straddle the line between Protestantism and Catholicism. Elizabeth was clearly testing whether she could find an acceptable branch of English Protestantism before making a more radical leap. Despite major efforts on their part to lure her, she remained unconvinced.

In a November 30, 1626, letter to James Ussher, Protestant archbishop of the Church in Ireland, the renowned anti-Catholic clergyman Alexander Cooke wrote "to acquaint you with an accident lately fallen out" that "concerneth my Lady Falkland." (The use of the word "accident" seems particularly comical, as if she had fallen from a horse.) As the leader of the Irish Protestants, Ussher worked closely alongside Elizabeth's husband—he had delivered the sermon at Henry's inauguration as lord deputy in 1622—and he had a strong personal stake in keeping Elizabeth within the fold. (Ussher was also a learned theologian who became famous for trying to establish an exact date for God's creation of the world; working backward through the chronology of the Bible, he concluded the event occurred on October 23, 4004 BCE.)

Cooke's news to Ussher about Elizabeth was predictable if unwelcome: "She, within this fortnight, hath declared herself to be a Papist." No one, it seems, took Elizabeth's conversion lightly. Puritans like Cooke weren't happy to see the wife of Ireland's lord deputy convert, while the more Catholic-leaning but still Protestant Arminians regarded Elizabeth's decision as a "disgrace" for their cause. Indeed, their leader, John Cosin, bishop of Durham, blasted her for having "sinned damnably in departing from that church wherein she was born and baptized"; another influential member of the group, Richard Montagu, former chaplain to James I and archdeacon of Hereford, warned her that as "an English papist," she would "di[e] in the state of damnation." Elizabeth was remarkably untroubled. To the powerful men's threats of eternal damnation,

The "Procession Picture" of Queen Elizabeth I, painted by an unattributed artist, circa 1601. Despite her nearly seventy years, she appears as a young woman.

Miniature of Mary Sidney, painted by
Nicholas Hilliard, circa 1590

Portrait of Lady Mary Sidney,
mother of Mary Sidney, painted
in the circle of Hans Eworth,
circa 1550–1560. This likeness
dates from before Lady Sidney
was disfigured from smallpox in
1562 after caring for the queen.

The Ditchley Portrait of Queen Elizabeth I, painted by Marcus Gheeraerts the younger. The portrait was commissioned by Sir Henry Lee, Elizabeth Cary's great-uncle, circa 1592.

Portrait of Elizabeth Cary, Viscountess Falkland, painted by Paul van Somer I in 1620. According to her daughters, Elizabeth was "very low," or short, in stature.

Jan van Belcamp, Attr., the "Great Picture," triptych, 1646, oil on canvas, reproduced by courtesy of Abbot Hall, Lakeland Arts Trust, England. The monumental painting was commissioned by Anne Clifford after she finally came into her inheritance.

Miniature of George Clifford, Earl of Cumberland, painted by Nicholas Hilliard, circa 1590. Clifford commissioned this portrait himself to celebrate his status as the Queen's Champion.

Portrait of Elizabeth Cary's husband, Sir Henry Cary, the future Viscount Falkland, painted by Marcus Gheeraerts the younger in 1603. The couple was married the year before.

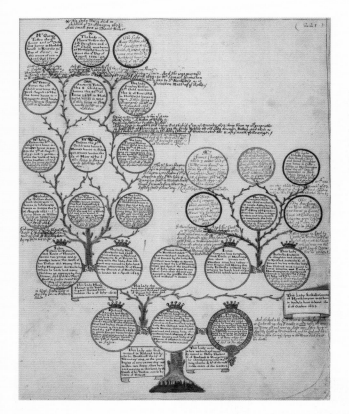

Illustrated genealogical tree from Anne Clifford's *Great Books of Record,* showing her own personal history (she is the tree holding up the rest of the structure at the very bottom of the page)

Miniature painted by Nicholas Hilliard in 1593, possibly depicting Aemilia Lanyer

A pair of chopines, high-heeled footwear favored by Elizabeth Cary, made in Italy circa 1550–1650

Anthony van Dyck, portrait of Philip Herbert, 4th Earl of Pembroke (c. 1634), Anne Clifford's second husband

Philip Herbert, 4th Earl of Pembroke, and his family, painted by Anthony van Dyck between 1634 and 1635. Anne Clifford sits awkwardly at her husband's side, looking melancholic and out of place.

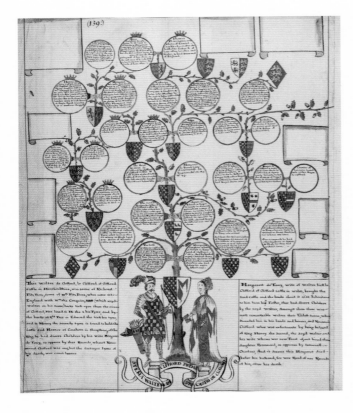

A genealogical tree from Anne Clifford's *Great Books of Record* showing her illustrious ancestry

she replied that "if ever she turned again, she will turn Puritan, not moderate Protestant, as she phraseth it; for moderate Protestants, vis. Mr. Cosin, etc. are farther from Catholics than Puritans."

It was one thing to infuriate a group of bishops and priests. It was another thing altogether to act so brazenly against the wishes of her husband. Nearly twenty years after writing *The Tragedy of Mariam,* Elizabeth followed her heroine in putting her own conscience above her marital vows. In Elizabeth's case, the price of disobedience may have fallen short of being murdered, but it was the social equivalent. In a letter written to the king on December 8, 1626, Henry referred to Elizabeth as the woman "whom, now I may say, I have long unhappily called wife." After offering the fleeting hope that "if she shall no more hear the charms of those [Catholic] enchanters, she may recover out of those distractions whereinto they have put her," he soon gave up hope. "For a last refuge," he exclaimed in a letter to the secretary of state Sir John Coke dated December 29, "I must resort to a separation *a mensa et thoro* [from board and bed]." This was the closest he could come to filing for divorce.

As it happened, Elizabeth's conversion came at an awkward time in English history. On March 27, 1625, King James died at the age of fifty-eight following a stroke and a bout of severe dysentery, leaving the throne to his twenty-four-year-old son, Charles. In the years preceding his death, a new religious war had broken out in central Europe between the Holy Roman Emperor Ferdinand II and the Protestant Elector Palatine of the Rhine, Frederick V. Frederick, who had married James's daughter, Elizabeth, in 1613, was offered the crown of Bohemia in 1618 following Bohemia's rebellion against the emperor Ferdinand, triggering what came to be known as the Thirty Years' War.

Despite his concern for his daughter, James refused to support Frederick with either money or military aid. Instead, he was focused on keeping the peace with Ferdinand by trying to marry Charles to a Catholic princess. His first choice was the Spanish Infanta, Maria Anna, daughter of King Philip III; for several long years, Charles was sent back and forth to Spain while James's councilors negotiated the match. Charles apparently complained to his father that the marriage was "continually prostituted in the lower house" of Parliament, where there was fierce opposition to having a Spanish queen. In the end, the negotiations failed, and a new alliance was quickly made with Princess Henrietta Maria, the youngest daughter of the deceased French king Henry IV and the Italian-born Marie de' Medici. The couple was married several weeks after James's death.

A fervent Catholic whose marriage agreement stipulated, among other things, that Catholic chapels be built in every royal palace, Henrietta Maria caused an immediate stir at court by refusing to be crowned by a Protestant priest (she skipped the coronation). Even more than her mother-in-law, Queen Anna, had done when she came to the throne in 1603, Henrietta Maria filled her household with Catholic maids, priests, and even musicians, all imported from France. Very soon, her court was also overflowing with aristocratic Englishwomen drawn to the forbidden faith. Among them was Elizabeth Cary, who, as early as November 17, 1626, was reported to have been "newly banished [from] the court for lately going to Mass with the queen." According to *The Lady Falkland*, the king put her under house arrest.

After six weeks, Charles released Elizabeth, claiming he hadn't meant for her to be locked up for so long. Henry was much less forgiving. He refused to give her any money and pressed the king to send her to her mother, a staunch Protestant who regarded Elizabeth's behavior as treasonous. Elizabeth understandably refused to go, declaring in a March 1627 letter to Charles's privy councilor Lord Conway that she would live at her mother's home at Burford Priory "in the nature of a prisoner," given that her mother "hath expressed to me that if ever I come down to her . . . she will never give me the least relief." "I have no meat, drink, nor clothes, nor money," she complained, begging Conway that Henry be forced to "give me necessary means to feed and clothe me."

Two months later, Elizabeth had still received nothing. At this point, she took her case directly to the king. In a lengthy petition written on May 18, 1627, that reviewed her father's disinheriting her, her mother's cruelty, and her own desire for nothing "but a quiet life and to reobtain my lord's favor, which I have done nothing to lose, but what I could not with a safe conscience leave undone," she begged Charles to command Henry "to supply me weekly with so much, as may be, (by your majesty or any that you please to appoint) thought necessary to support me for victuals, house rent, and apparel." The king agreed, and a letter sent to Henry by the Privy Council ordered him to pay Elizabeth £500 a year (around £60,000 today). Henry stubbornly refused, insisting that her poverty was greatly exaggerated: "I care not to have such an imposture," he wrote, "prodigal as I know her to be." Invoking the parable of the prodigal son from the gospel of Luke, in which, after squandering all of his portion the younger son is beset with hunger, Henry declared it unlikely Elizabeth was "constrained to eat husks with hogs."

There's no way to know exactly how severe Elizabeth's situation was, or how her contemporaries perceived it. On the outside of a letter that she sent to Conway in June 1627 further pleading her case, Conway scribbled: "Doubteth much she is neglected." The verb "to doubt" in this period could mean either what it does today, or (as in Queen Elizabeth's poem, "The Doubt of Future Foes") "to fear." There's no question, however, that she was cut off from any obvious income—neither her husband nor her mother was providing for her—and that her comforts were greatly reduced. According to *The Lady Falkland,* Elizabeth lived alone with a single maid, Besse Poulter (who also converted to Catholicism), in a humble cottage outside of London, spending weeks eating scraps of pie crust or bread until a wealthy friend began to send her deliveries of meat. During Lent, she supposedly consumed only the water used to boil the fish, giving the fish itself to Besse.

These are details that could have come only from Elizabeth, and she may well have been exaggerating things to gain her daughters' sympathy. For whatever was happening with her husband, her relations with her children were also horribly strained. The younger children who had come with her to London were sent back to Dublin to live with their father, who had remained there with their older siblings Lorenzo, Lucy, and Elizabeth. In one of the most critical passages in the entire biography, her daughters observe that "having been left young by her and not been a good while in her hands (especially three daughters) and now seeing her but when they would, as they had the while had from their father the care of both father and mother, so they paid to him the love and respect due to both, leaving her but a small part."

Sentiments of this kind are very rare in the heavily patriarchal world of Renaissance England, where men weren't known to take up the role of primary caregiver. But in throwing off the English Church, Elizabeth had in effect lost custody of her children. This was a battle she would go on to fight, but in 1627 she found herself unusually alone. However much she may have suffered, the situation also suited her. There were no babies to be nursed, no servants demanding she get dressed, no horses she was forced to ride, no sermons or services she had to attend. For the first time since the early years of her marriage, when Henry was fighting in the Protestant wars, Elizabeth could devote her time to whatever she chose. She took up her pen with new passion.

CHAPTER TEN

January 5, 1617

Presence Chamber, Whitehall Palace

Anne Clifford

In the morning of January 5, 1617, at Dorset House in London, Anne Clifford prepared for an eventful day at court. Wearing her "new black wrought taffeta gown" or another of the fancy dresses she'd ordered to be made, the twenty-six-year-old Countess of Dorset arrived at Whitehall to attend the ceremony in King James's Presence Chamber for the "creation" of his favorite courtier, George Villiers, as first Duke of Buckingham. Later that day, she dined with Alethea Talbot, Countess of Arundel, and her husband, Thomas Howard, before attending a new play by Shakespeare's sometime collaborator John Fletcher. (Shakespeare had died the previous year, but his former acting company, the King's Men, carried on and performed Fletcher's work.) The next day, on the holiday of Twelfth Night (also known as Epiphany), Anne had a "scrambling supper"—the Renaissance term for a buffet—with Lady Arundel and Mary Sidney's daughter-in-law, Mary Talbot, Countess of Pembroke, before attending Ben Jonson's *Christmas, His Mask*.

Anne made no comment in her diary about the masque, but in a letter John Chamberlain wrote to Sir Dudley Carleton following the performance he remarked that it earned "no great speech nor commendations"; the evening was memorable, he noted, only for the fact that Buckingham danced with the queen. On the surface of things this seems unremarkable, but because nearly everyone at court suspected that Buckingham and James were lovers, Anna's willingness to dance with him was seen as a major concession. James even declared before his Privy Council that "he loved the Earl of Buckingham more than any other man," and in private letters he referred to him as both his "sweet heart" and his "wife." Archeological excavations undertaken in the early 2000s at one of James's smaller residences, Apethorpe Hall, revealed a secret passageway between James's and Buckingham's private chambers. How much Anne knew about any of this isn't clear, but her attention was focused elsewhere. As the Christmas entertainments at court came to an end, she was about to confront the greatest challenge to her lawsuit since it had begun ten years before. Thanks to the survival of her diaries for both 1616 and 1617, we are able to follow all of these events in minute detail.

On January 8, Anne and her husband, Richard Sackville, Earl of Dorset, returned to Knole from London. That same night, she reported, "My Lord and I had a falling out about the land." (Following the custom of the period, she always referred to Richard as "my Lord.") She gave no further details about the marital squabble, but her next diary entry reflected its consequences. "Upon the 9th I went up to see the things in the closet [her private chamber]," she noted, while "my Lord [was] sitting the most part of the day reading in his closet." After they'd avoided each other that day, Richard left for London "upon the sudden, we not knowing it till the afternoon."

The next time Anne heard from Richard was nearly a week later, when she received a letter that must have filled her with dread. In her diary entry on January 16, she recorded the news without comment: "my Lord [wrote] that I should come up to London the next day because I was to go before the King on Monday next." Given the "falling out" they'd had about her lawsuit, there would have been no question in Anne's mind that this summons before the king wasn't good news. As she prepared to leave Knole to return to court, she was bracing for a fight.

In the six months before the events of January 1617, Anne had been involved in intense negotiations over the fate of the Clifford estates. This was provoked by the death of her beloved mother, Margaret, on May 24, 1616, which fundamentally changed Anne's relationship to her father's lands. During her widowhood, Margaret maintained control over a number of castles and manors in Westmorland that George had left her in her jointure settlement. He had mistakenly hoped, as we've seen, that his generosity might keep her from fighting the rest of his will. With Margaret's death, the vast jointure properties legally reverted to George's brother, Francis Clifford, Earl of Cumberland, who had been living at Skipton Castle in Yorkshire (this was the castle Anne and Margaret had been physically barred from entering in 1607).

In the four days it took for the sad news of her mother's death to reach Anne at Knole, Francis quickly began to take possession of Margaret's estates. In at least one instance, he staged an outright siege. According to a letter sent on June 7 by the Privy Council to the deputy lieutenant in Westmorland, Francis's men had "forcibly broke up the doors and windows of the Castle of Appleby, where diverse servants and goods of the late countess were," and "with strong hand have put [out] all the said earl of Dorset's agents." There are no details of the actual skirmish, but the letter's insistence that "the castles and houses where the goods of the late countess are or were at her death should be kept from violence" suggests the situation had devolved to clan warfare.

For a little over a month, Anne remained far from the conflict. But even hundreds of miles to the south, there was no real peace to be had. At Knole, she received a steady stream of friends who awkwardly mixed their condolences for her mother's death with strong urgings that she settle her case. During a visit to Queen Anna at Greenwich, Lady Knollys spoke to her with "some unkind words," prompting Anne to "take my leave of the queen and all my friends there." The loss of support from her female allies at court, combined with the unrelenting pressure from nearly all of the men around her, could easily have broken her resolve. But there was no stopping Anne's determination to make Westmorland her own.

On July 1, 1616, Anne set out for the north. Her first and most urgent task was to bury her mother. In her will, Margaret stated her desire to be buried in Northumberland next to her favorite brother, Sir Francis Russell, who had died thirty years earlier (Margaret understandably wanted to spend eternity with her own family, and not with George). Upon learning this, Anne was distraught, interpreting her mother's relinquishing her claims to be counted as a Clifford as a "sign that I should be disinherited of the inheritance of my forefathers." A few days after the will reached her, she received a letter informing her of Margaret's deathbed change of heart. In her last hours, she had changed her will, giving Anne the right to bury her wherever she pleased.

Margaret had died at Brougham Castle, where her corpse was being kept and her officers were still in place. This was where Anne and her entourage were staying, and the simplest thing would have been to bury her mother there. But Anne wanted her to lie at St. Lawrence's Church at Appleby, whose castle Francis had hostilely seized. Her reason for this was almost certainly strategic rather than sentimental: she wanted to strengthen her own right to the estate. Not surprisingly, Francis tried to block her, but Anne's agents ultimately secured permission for the burial from the Appleby borough authorities. Seven weeks after Margaret's death, on July 11, 1616, Anne arrived with her mother's corpse at the stone church that was badly in need of repairs (Anne would see to this herself some forty years later) but boasted a beautiful tower whose lower part dated to the thirteenth century and a fourteenth-century porch with impressive ornamental molding. She was accompanied by around forty men and women on horseback. At midnight, she recorded, "the body was put into the ground," and at "about 3 o'clock in the morning we came home [to Brougham]."

Anne's trip to Westmorland turned into a prolonged stay of nearly five months. By early August 1616, she had managed to obtain a letter from the king ordering that she "should not be molested in Brougham Castle," allowing her to establish a base from which to conduct her business. Two weeks later, she was joined by her husband, who had kept his "faithful promise that he would come after me into the North as soon as he could." She also proudly noted in passing that her cousin Henry Clifford—Francis's heir—arrived in the north with "far less train than my Lord," who had "a great company of horse." Once Richard was with her, Anne performed a symbolic act of "dressing" the room where her mother had died, presumably removing the black hangings and "set[ting] up the green velvet bed where," she noted, "the same night we went to lie."

Meanwhile, Anne had already begun her efforts to disrupt Francis's claims on the estates. As she related in her diary, she obstructed his collecting rent by personally ordering the tenants at Whinfell Park near Brougham to "keep the money in their own hands till it were known who had a right to it." She also signed a warrant for a stag to be killed on Francis's southern estate of Stainmore. After Anne sent her own workers to gather hay on land Francis believed to be his, things took a violent turn: she reported that "two of my uncle's people were hurt by Mr. Kidd [her mother's loyal servant, now serving Anne], one in the leg, the other in the foot." Francis responded by having the authorities issue a warrant "for the apprehending of all my folks" involved in the event. War was being waged not only in the courts, but also in the fields.

Anne left Brougham Castle in early December 1616, riding twenty-nine miles on horseback to Roos in southern Westmorland where her coach awaited her to bring her to London in time for the Christmas festivities. There, she quickly understood that her legal battle had become a topic of interest at court, involving even James: "Everybody," she wrote, "was persuading me to hear and to make an end since the King had taken the matter in hand." How Anne felt about the constant pestering isn't clear, but she seems at some level to have enjoyed the attention. It was certainly unusual for a woman to find herself at the center of a major legal dispute, and she noted her new status with pride. On December 23 she declared, "Now I had a new part to play upon the stage of this world." For someone like Anne, who regularly attended plays at court and had performed in several masques, the idea of understanding her experience through the prism of the theater is striking. Compared to her role, for example, as the Egyptian queen Berenice in Jonson's *Masque of Queens*, Anne's "new part" gave her both a public voice and a much larger platform: she was no longer a silent masquer at Banqueting House, but a real player on the "stage of the world."

The drama between James and Anne began on January 18, two days before the scheduled meeting, when she was invited to the king's Drawing Chamber (a private gallery next to his bedchamber) for a conversation along with her husband. Anne described kneeling with Richard before the king, who asked them "to put the matter wholly into his hands." Richard promptly agreed—he had no doubt arranged for the meeting in the first place—but Anne refused to budge. As she recounted in her diary, "I beseeched His Majesty to pardon me for that I would never part with Westmorland while I lived under any condition whatsoever."

There probably weren't too many people in the kingdom, male or female, who would have dared to reject the king's offer to take charge of their affairs. But in addition to her own formidable determination, Anne had been buoyed by a private conversation with the queen. Before seeing James, Anne had visited Anna in her own chambers in the palace, where she also met her friend Elizabeth de Vere, Countess of Derby. Anne noted that Lady Derby explained to the queen "how my business stood and that I was to go to the king," to which Anna responded by "warning [me] to take heed of putting my matters absolutely to the king lest he should deceive me." Anna and James had long been living separate lives, and it was no secret that they often had competing interests at court. But for the queen to urge Anne not to trust the king was an extraordinary act of female solidarity (possibly verging on treason). This is the kind of moment Aemilia Lanyer dreamed of in her preface to *Salve Deus:* powerful women protecting one another from the hostile acts of men.

On Monday January 20, Anne arrived at Whitehall after dinner (the meal eaten at midday) and spent the first few hours of the afternoon in the private chambers of Lucy Russell, Countess of Bedford, who had her own lodging at court. Around eight o'clock, Anne was called to her meeting with James, where she found herself in very different circumstances from two days before. The scene that followed is one of the most dramatic in all of Anne's diaries:

> I was sent for up to the King in his Drawing Chamber, when the door was locked and nobody suffered [allowed] to stay here by my Lord and I, my Uncle Cumberland, my Coz. Clifford, my Lords Arundel, Pembroke, Montgomery, and Sir John Digby. For lawyers there were my Lord Chief Justice Montague and Hobart Yelverton, the King's solicitor Sir Randal Crewe that was to speak for my Lord & I. The King asked us all if we would submit to his judgement in this case. My Uncle Cumberland, my Coz Clifford & my Lord answered they would, but I would never agree to

it without Westmorland, at which the king grew in a great chafe, my Lord of Pembroke and the King's solicitor speaking much against me. At last when they saw there was no remedy, my Lord fearing the king would do me some public disgrace, desired Sir John Digby would open the door, who went out with me.

However intimidated she may have been—she was the only woman in a room filled with powerful men—Anne had stood her ground. Under the doctrine of coverture, Richard had the right to accept the terms of the king's settlement, but he couldn't force Anne either to give her consent or to drop her claims to the land. Since by the traditions of common law—which the king was attempting to override—Anne should have been the legal heir, she had the right to continue her suit. It was for this reason that James bothered to include her in the meetings, and that he found her resistance so infuriating. Anne's diary entry ends with her pronouncing the day a great victory, thanks to both divine and marital support: "This Day I may say I was led miraculously by God's providence, & next to that I trust all my good to the worth & nobleness of my Lord's disposition, for neither I nor anybody else thought that I should have passed over this day so well."

Anne's triumphant mood was short-lived. She may have left the negotiating room at Whitehall without giving her consent, but the men proceeded to make a deal without her. By March, the so-called King's Award was signed and sealed by both Francis and Richard. According to its terms, Francis and his direct male heirs had the right to keep the Clifford lands; should Francis's male line fail, however—and Henry was his only son—the inheritance would revert to Anne. To compensate Anne, Francis was obliged to pay her the sum of £17,000 with a gift of an additional £3,000 if she agreed to drop all litigation. Since Anne's marriage portion of £15,000 had been stipulated on her not challenging the terms of her father's will, none of this had been paid. Thus Francis was effectively paying off the promised dowry, with an additional bonus of either £2,000 or £5,000.

These were truly enormous sums of money (remember, the average shoemaker made £4 a year)—and a cash payment of either

£17,000 or £20,000 was infinitely more appealing to Richard than the income that would be generated by the Clifford lands. In the words of the late seventeenth-century John Aubrey, "the earl of Dorset lived in the greatest splendor of any nobleman of England." A man of expensive habits—sumptuous clothes, extravagant hunts, and reckless gambling, among others—Richard was also constantly in debt. Anne's diary is full of references to Richard's losses: in June 1616, "my Lord lost 200 twenty-shilling pieces" to Lord Salisbury in a race between their footmen; in February 1617, "my Lord's cocks did fight against the king's," a "business" she described as "chargeable to my Lord"; in January 1619 during the Twelfth Night festivities, "my Lord lost 400 pound pieces playing with the king," and the list goes on.

While Anne spent most of her time at Knole, Richard lived the life of a wealthy bachelor. "All this week," Anne complained in September 1617,

> I being left at home and was sad to see how ill things went with me, my Lord being in the midst of his merry progress far out of Sussex where he had hunted in many gentlemen's parks, then went to Woodstock to meet the King, and he stayed up and down at several gentlemen's houses a good while.

It would be hard not to hear Anne's bitterness in describing Richard's "merry progress." While he was gallivanting through Sussex with "two or three hundred horse[men] in his company," she was left behind playing cards in her closet with her cousin and making quince marmalade.

As it happened, Richard wasn't occupied only with hunting, checking on his tenants, and paying court to the king. He was also involved in several long-term and costly extramarital affairs. According to Aubrey, he kept Elizabeth Broughton, an "exquisite beauty" who had run away from her father, as his mistress in London—her "price," Aubrey noted, "was very dear"—and he also fathered one or two children with the "celebrated beauty and courtesan" Venetia Stanley, to whom he gave a hefty annuity of £500. These details may not be true, and it's possible Aubrey confused Richard with his brother Edward Sackville, who may have been Venetia's lover. But there's no question that Richard strayed from the marriage, and that Anne suffered both publicly and privately from his infidelities.

In her diaries, Anne described in particular Richard's relationship with Martha Temple, the wife of his gentleman servant, Thomas Penyston. On August 24, 1619, she recorded that "after supper came Sir Thomas Penyston and his lady," and then added: "This coming hither of my Lady Penyston's was much talked of abroad in the world and my Lord was much condemned for it." Anne didn't comment on how it felt to entertain her husband's mistress in her own home, with everyone around them aware of the affair. A few months later, she noted in her diary's margins that "the 29th of November Richard was the last time my Lord saw Lady Penyston at her mother's lodging in the Strand." How she knew the location of the illicit rendezvous isn't clear, but the idea that the couple was meeting at the home of Martha's mother, Lady Stowe, suggests very little was done to keep things secret. The affair seems to have ended only with Martha's death from smallpox the following year.

In addition to his affairs with other women, Richard had suspiciously close ties to one of his male retainers, Matthew Caldicott, who was listed in the catalogue of the Knole household as "my Lord's favourite." Whether the two men were lovers can't be verified, but Matthew surfaced regularly in Anne's accounts of her marital woes. At one point Richard and Matthew spent a full week alone together at one of the Sackville estates in the country, about which Anne drily recorded: "my Lord lived privately at Buckhurst having no company with him but only Matthew." On other occasions, she allowed herself to express the level of anguish she felt about Matthew's interference in her marriage more directly. "Upon the 8th being Whitsunday we all went to church," she wrote in June 1617, "but my eyes were so blubbered with weeping that I could scarce look up and in the afternoon we fell out about Matthew." "On the 9th," she continued, "I wrote a letter to the Bishop of London against Matthew." The letter hasn't survived, so there's no way to know the exact terms of her complaint. But in addition to whatever private grievances she had against him, Anne recognized Matthew as an adversary in her legal battle. A highly ranked member of the household, he was present for many of the conversations she and

Richard had on the subject, always interjecting on Richard's side. At one point Matthew personally sent Anne an ultimatum from London, where he was staying with Richard, urging her "to yield to my Lord's desire in this business at this time or else I was undone forever."

There's no question that Anne and Richard's marriage was strained by her refusal to drop her claims to her inheritance. Unlike Elizabeth Cary, whom her daughters described (at least for the first twenty years of her marriage) as unable "to have any consideration of her own" where her husband's interests were concerned, Anne made no concessions to Richard's desire for her to accept the King's Award and receive the extra £3,000. "The 5th, my Lord went up to his closet," Anne wrote in April 1617,

> and said how little money I had left contrary to all they had told him. Sometimes I had fair words from him and some-times foul, but I took all patiently and did strive to give him as much content and assurance of my love as I could possibly, yet I always told him that I would never part with Westmorland upon any condition whatever.

That Richard found Anne's position both maddening and incomprehensible can be seen in a letter he sent her on October 6, 1617, roughly six months after he had signed and sealed the Award without her consent. "I commend my love to yourself whom in all things I love and hold a sober woman," he wrote, "your land only excepted, which transports you beyond yourself and makes you devoid of all reason." Anne felt something similar about Richard, as she explained in a December 1615 letter to her mother. Referring to her first child, Lady Margaret Sackville, who was born in July 1614, Anne declared, "My Lord is a very kind, loving and dear father, and in everything will I commend him, saving in this business of my land, wherein I think some malign spirit works, for in this he is as violent as is possible."

Anne's claim about Richard's kindness to young Marga-ret was true to a point. In his October 6, 1617 letter, he spoke of their daughter with palpable warmth. "First, sweet heart," Richard began, "you must remember me to the little lady with the hot foot who dreamed her lord father was stolen away with bullbeggars, and cried so sweetly with her little warm tears." ("Bullbeggar" was a variant of "bull-bear" or "bugbear," all obsolete terms for a frightening specter.) His concern about Margaret's nightmare in which he was carried off by demons—a nightmare likely provoked by his own long absence from home during his "merry progress"—as well as his referring to her as "the little lady with the hot foot" suggests a level of parental care and playfulness hard to conjure up from Anne's diary.

What emerges above all from those pages is Richard's manipulative use of Margaret as a weapon in the couple's ongoing legal dispute. In May 1616, he took Margaret away from Knole, no doubt hoping Anne would miss her enough to relent. "At night was brought me a letter from my Lord," she wrote, "to let me know that his determination was the Child should go live at Horsley [one of Richard's estates in Surrey] and not come hither anymore, so this was a grievous and sorrowful day to me." Margaret was kept from Anne in the care of servants and her two aunts, while Richard continued his glamorous life at court. "All this time," Anne noted,

> my lord was at London where he had infinite and great resort coming to him. He went much abroad to cocking, to bowling alleys, to plays and horse races and was commended by all the world. I stayed in the country having many times a sorrowful and heavy heart, and being condemned by most folks because I would not consent to the agreements, so as I may truly say I am like an owl in the desert.

The evocative final image of "an owl in the desert" was a quotation from Psalm 102. Like so many educated Protestant women, Anne knew her Bible well, and she regularly drew upon its vast resources to frame her own experiences. In this case, the psalm's expression of sorrow and isolation must have felt like a perfect fit:

My heart is smitten, and withered like grass,
So that I forget to eat my bread.
By reason of the voice of my groaning my bones cleave to my skin.
I am like a pelican of the wilderness: I am like an owl of the desert.

I watch, and am as a sparrow alone upon the house top.
Mine enemies reproach me all the day, and they that are mad against
me are sworn against me.

In her experience of extreme loneliness at Knole, Anne found common ground with the voice of the Hebrew prophet.

Between his long absences, his squandering of money, and his infidelities, Richard was far from the husband Anne could have hoped for. Despite all of this, she seems to have loved him, and she suffered when he withdrew his affection. Her feelings of rejection were most acute when he refused to share her bed, which she kept close track of in her diaries: "Upon the 7th my lord lay in my chamber"; "This night my lord should have lain with me in my chamber, but he and I fell out about Matthew," and so on.

Anne's desire to share a bed with Richard wasn't only romantic or sexual. After Margaret, who was born in 1614, four years passed without the birth of a second child. However preoccupied Anne was with gaining her own inheritance, she also wanted Richard to have a son to inherit the substantial Sackville estates. Given her own experience, her greatest fear was that Richard would pass over Margaret in favor of his brother, Edward, in order to keep his title and lands securely in the male line. Viewing this possibility not as a predictable form of patriarchy at work—this is how she came to understand her father's decision to disinherit her—but instead as an act of overt aggression, she recorded in her diary on June 25, 1617, that Richard and Edward were plotting "to do me and my child a great deal of hurt." Five days later, she noted feeling "extremely melancholy and sad to see things go so ill with me, and fearing my Lord would give all his land away from the child."

In 1618, Anne was pregnant again. As with Elizabeth Cary's first pregnancy in 1608, the news made it into Chamberlain's letters to Carleton. Or rather, on January 2, 1619, he reported the sad outcome: "The countess of Dorset the last week miscarried of a son that was born dead." Since the 1618 diary hasn't survived, there's no record of how Anne took the loss, which must have happened right around Christmas. Her diary for January 1619 begins with announcing her convalescence: "The first of this month I began to have the curtain drawn in my chamber and to see light." Tragically, this stillbirth wasn't her only experience of losing a child during these years. In a genealogical table she made later in life, she recorded having borne three sons to Richard, only one of whom lived long enough to be named: Thomas Sackville was born at Knole in February 1620 and died there five months later. Between the entries for Margaret and Thomas—each in its own discrete little circle—she had inserted this additional text: "This Lady Anne had also two sons more by the said Richard Earl of Dorset, but they died in their infancy."

In October 1622, Anne gave birth to a second daughter, Isabella, who was named after her thirteenth-century Clifford relative, Isabella de Veteripont, the wealthy heiress who brought the castles and estates of Westmorland into the family. Isabella Sackville, like her older sister Margaret, was a healthy child who would live well into adulthood. A letter from Richard that has survived from May 1622 shows that he was at least no Henry VIII in his insistence on male offspring. "Sweet life," he wrote to Anne, "God bless you and my lady Margaret, and the little sweet thing in thy belly be it a Richard or an Isabella." (It's touching to see the couple had picked out names.)

There were seemingly moments of tenderness between Richard and Anne: he routinely called her "sweet life" or "sweet heart" in his letters, although this could have been a performance of affection—a way of reassuring her (and maybe even himself) that the marriage wasn't without love. The terms of endearment may also have simply been conventional: surviving letters between Anne's parents, who by all accounts couldn't stand one another, begin, "To my most beloved Lord," and "To my loving wife, the countess of Cumberland," or even more intimately, "My sweet Meg." Whatever the feelings were between them, Anne's years with Richard were on the whole very difficult. Between the constant demands of her lawsuit, the loss of multiple children, the tension over their daughter Margaret, the sadness about Richard's decision not to back her cause and the insult of his infidelities: all of this took an enormous physical and emotional toll. Once Anne lost her mother in 1616, her loneliness intensified. The queen and other female friends at court might have supported her on particular occasions, but they were no substitute for Margaret's abiding presence. Most of the time, she seems to have felt completely alone in the world.

In this vacuum of sympathy, Anne had several sources of consolation. Throughout her life, she was an avid reader with wide-ranging interests. As John Donne, who knew her in his capacity as rector of a small parish near Knole, remarked, Anne could "discourse of all things, from predestination to slea-silk" (the latter was a kind of floss silk easily separated for embroidery). Reading for Anne was typically a social experience, and she enjoyed being read to by friends and servants. In January 1617, she "began to have Mr. Sandys's book read to me about the government of the Turks"; a few weeks later, she noted that "Rivers used to read to me in Montaigne's *Essays,* and Moll Neville in the *Faerie Queene.*" "I spent most of the time," she wrote that August, "in playing at glecko and hearing Moll Neville read [Sir Philip Sidney's] *Arcadia.*" (Rivers was a friend and agent of Richard's; Moll was Richard's niece and retained as a gentlewoman in Anne's service; glecko was a popular card game played with three people.)

Anne also spent time studying the Old Testament with Richard Rands, the rector of a local church whose living was controlled by the Sackville family (they paid for his income and home). In the winter of 1617, she and Rands met privately to read the Bible together, with Rands presumably explicating difficult or obscure passages as Anne sat with her needlework beside him. After working their way through at least Exodus and Leviticus (these are the two books she mentioned), Richard abruptly put an end to their sessions. "My Lord found me reading with Mr. Rands," Anne wrote on March 27, "and told me that it would hinder his study very much so as I must leave off reading the Old Testament until I can get somebody to read it with me." At least in this context, Anne played the role of the obedient wife and "made an end of reading Deuteronomy" that same day. But in the winter of 1619, she proudly reported having completed the Bible in its entirety: "The 20th I made an end of reading the Bible over which was my Lady my mother's [copy]. I began to read it the 1st of February, so as I read all over the whole Bible in less than two months." At this point Anne was clearly reading on her own. Or she may have felt as if she was reading alongside her pious and learned mother.

An even more fundamental source of comfort to Anne than reading was writing in her diaries. Even this was in part a shared experience, and not simply something she did in private. According to her secretary George Sedgwick, Anne "kept in a large folio paper book a diary or journal, wherein she caused to be entered the occurrences of the day, and all the strangers that came to her house, whether upon visits or business." "Caused to be entered" means someone else was doing the physical writing, at least when it came to noting the comings and goings in the house. The pages of her diaries were themselves divided between the main text in the center, which seems to have been used to record daily events in real time, and a smaller column for marginal insertions on the left. There, we find reflections on what had already been described in the main section as well as information or events left out from the original entries.

Besides the 1603 memoir and the diaries from 1616, 1617, and 1619, all of which were preserved in a copy made in the late eighteenth century, the only surviving diary—and the only original manuscript to survive—is from 1676. There's reason to believe, however, that Anne kept diaries for most if not all of the intervening years, and that they were destroyed either during her own lifetime or shortly thereafter. The perception of the diaries as not worthy of preservation surprisingly comes up in Anne's funeral sermon, preached by her friend Edward Rainbow, bishop of Carlisle. Rainbow began his discussion of Anne's diary-keeping by invoking St. Bernard's advice that one's "actions in passing might not pass away." He also spoke admiringly of her "judging her time to be better spent thus, than in the ordinary tattle, which custom has taught many (of her sex especially)." All of this praise is then set against his acknowledging the "censures others may pass on this exactness of diary as too minute and trivial," and he ended by declaring that "after some reviews, [the diaries] were laid aside." There's no way to know what exactly "laid aside" meant. Anne's early-twentieth-century biographer George Williamson claimed her grandson, Thomas Tufton, Earl of Thanet, had the diaries destroyed, but the recent discovery of an inventory drawn up in 1684 of Clifford's books in Appleby Castle suggests Tufton preserved "all my Lady Pembr[oke's] Books of her own Writing" in a trunk.

Beyond the handful of surviving diaries, our detailed knowledge of Anne's life comes from the annual memoirs she kept from 1650 through 1675 and her 1649 *The Life of Me*. There's reason to believe Anne used the diaries to write these more comprehensive

autobiographical works (the annual memoirs are in effect summaries of the diaries) and then left the diaries behind. It's tantalizing,
however, to think that hidden somewhere in Appleby Castle there
might be a stash of books with Anne's scribbling from at least some
of the missing years. It would be particularly interesting to hear her
relate the series of events beginning in the summer of 1623, when
Richard fell seriously ill, through his untimely death at the age of
thirty-five the following spring.

Anne wasn't with Richard on his deathbed, "being then very
sick," as she later wrote, "and ill myself at Knole." In a letter he sent
her two days before he died, he claimed to be on the mend. "Sweet
heart," he wrote,

> I had resolved to come down to Knole, and to have received
> the Blessed Sacrament, but God hath prevented it with sick-
> ness, for on Wednesday night I fell into a fit of [vomiting]
> which held me long, then last night I had a fit of a fever . . .
> I thank God I am now at good ease, having rested well this
> morning. I would not have you trouble yourself till I have
> occasion to send for you.

In his will, dated that same day—and therefore indicating he might
have known he was closer to death than he let on—he left Anne,
whom he called his "dearly beloved wife," a range of gifts from
practical to sentimental: all of the rings and jewels given to her at
her wedding, six silver candlesticks, half of the linen at Knole, a
sumptuous coach lined with green cloth and silk lace, six bay coach
horses, and a single cash sum of £500. In a codicil, he added a specific cloak that she must have particularly liked.

More significantly, Richard confirmed the legal arrangements
for Anne to receive her jointure lands in Sussex, lands he had threatened to take away from her on several occasions during their disputes over her inheritance battle. These properties were far from
trivial: they generated roughly £2,000 of annual income. To his
daughters, Margaret and Isabella, he gave generous marriage por-
tions of £6,000 and £4,000, respectively, as well as £200 in "old
gold" to be divided between them. His brother Edward inherited
his title and estates, but also his enormous debts.

In *The Life of Me*, Anne described Richard with great affection:

"This first lord of mine," she wrote, "was in his own nature of a just mind, of sweet disposition, and very valiant in his own person." She added that she was "happy in many respects being his wife." If the 1624 diary had survived, we would certainly know more about how Anne took the news of his death and what her mourning was like. In *The Life of Me,* written twenty-five years later, she reported only that shortly thereafter she had the "smallpox so extremely and violently that I was at death's door and [had] little hope of life in me." She soon recovered, but like Lady Sidney sixty years earlier, she was left horribly scarred. The disease, she declared, "did so martyr my face that it confirmed more and more my mind never to marry again." The thirty-four-year-old Anne was determined to remain a widow.

Anne's resolution held a mere six years. In 1630, she married Mary Sidney's younger son, Philip Herbert, Earl of Pembroke and Montgomery, and lord chamberlain of James's household. Anne had known Philip for much of her adult life, if not since childhood: their mothers were friends who had marched together as countesses at Queen Elizabeth's funeral; Anne and Philip's first wife, Lady Susan de Vere, had danced together in *The Masque of Queens;* and Richard and Philip were fellow favorites of the king.

Unlike her first match, Anne's relationship with Philip was loveless. The marriage was made, she unabashedly put it, to help her in "crossing and disappointing the envy, malice and sinister practices of my enemies." Among this group she counted as her "extreme enemy" her brother-in-law Edward. As Anne related it, Edward's efforts to wrest what he could from her and her daughters extended to outright burglary: while she was staying at Bolebroke Castle (her principal jointure property in Sussex), his men tried to steal money she'd received from her tenants there—a plot that was "timely discovered and prevented by one who accidentally saw them enter in at the window." In marrying Philip, one of the most powerful men in the kingdom, Anne was gaining an ally not only against Edward, but also against Francis and Henry Clifford. In the summer of 1632, "by commission under my said Lord's and mine hand and seal," Anne renewed her claims to "vindicate my right and interest in the lands of my inheritance." At least in this respect, Philip would bring her better luck.

CHAPTER ELEVEN

May 13, 1619

Henry VII Chapel, Westminster Abbey

Mary Sidney

On May 13, 1619, Mary Sidney put on her mourning clothes to participate in her second funeral for an English queen. When Elizabeth had died in 1603, Mary was recently widowed, and the event was one of her first formal appearances as Dowager Countess of Pembroke. By the time of Anna's death in 1619, Mary had become one of the grande dames in the kingdom. In Anne Clifford's diary for that year, she reported her own role as one of the official mourners at the funeral, where she met "my old Lady of Pembroke & diverse others of my acquaintance with who I had much talk." "My old Lady of Pembroke": the fifty-seven-year-old Mary must have seemed ancient to the twenty-nine-year-old Anne, whose own mother had died at fifty-five and who was attending the funeral of her forty-four-year-old queen.

Despite her relative youth, the death of Queen Anna on March 2, 1619, hadn't come as a surprise. After years of declining health in which she suffered from gout, an ulcerated leg, and serious gynecological problems, she spent her last six months confined to her bed with consumption and dropsy. Although Anna never achieved widespread popularity—both a foreigner and a Catholic convert, she was viewed by many with suspicion—she'd had a major influence on England's cultural life. In addition to the court masque, which, thanks to her involvement, became the signature dramatic form of the era, the queen kept her own musicians and composers (many of whom were sent over from Europe by her brother, the Danish king Christian VI) as well as companies of both adult and child actors to perform plays for her wherever she went. She was also an avid patron of art, and especially of religious paintings, some of which traveled with her from palace to palace. With James's leisure focused almost obsessively on hunting, Anna kept the English court fully civilized.

James hadn't been able to reach Anna on her deathbed at Hampton Court Palace, where she'd been living since September 1618: he himself was bedridden a hundred miles away at Newmarket. At the queen's side during her final days was her eighteen-year-old son and the heir to the kingdom, Prince Charles, but as Anne Clifford related in her diary, rumor had it that "the prince was there when the pangs of death came upon her but went into another chamber some half an hour before she died." (Ever the historian connecting the dots, Anne also noted that the queen passed away in the same room as Henry VIII's third wife, Jane Seymour.)

Despite having been ill for some time, Anna didn't leave behind a written will. In his letter to Sir Dudley Carleton on March 27, 1619, giving a detailed account of her death, John Chamberlain estimated the queen's jewels alone were valued at £400,000, and her plate at £90,000. He also described her collection of silks, linens, and "all other kinds of hangings, bedding and furniture" as "for quantity and quality beyond any prince in Europe." Those with her at Hampton Court in her last days reported that she had verbally indicated her intention to give everything to Charles, with James serving as her executor.

After the king's commissioners completed their audit of her estate—discovering, along the way, that two of her servants had embezzled £30,000 in gems—James gave instructions for her most valuable stones, jewelry, and ornaments to be kept either at his Secret Jewel House in the Tower of London or in the custody of his Master of the Jewel House, Sir Henry Mildmay. He also arranged for his favorite courtier (and probably his lover) Buckingham to receive "some reasonable portion" of all the queen's inventory, as well as a gift of more land, to thank him for "his good service and tender care of the king in his last [i.e., latest] sickness." He even tried, but failed, to give him the "keeping" of Denmark House, Anna's primary London residence. (Traditionally called Somerset House, the name was temporarily changed during Anna's reign as queen.)

By September 1619, Anna's estate was fully settled, with the bulk of the inheritance, including Denmark House, passed to Charles; James received a yearly income of £60,000 as well as £24,000 from her jointure. It's hard to convey how staggering these sums are—the queen was the equivalent of our richest billionaires today. Even more shocking was that in spite of Anna's wealth, she left James at least temporarily short on cash, forcing him to delay her funeral. According to a letter written by Thomas Lorkin, one of James's courtiers close to the scene, "the queen's funeral is like[ly] to be deferred for want of money to buy the blacks (for Sir Lionel Cranfield saith, he will not take them up upon credit), till the latter end of May." As was the tradition, the royal household bore the cost of supplying the official mourners with cloth for their mourning livery. Cranfield, a wealthy merchant who had become Master of the Wardrobe the previous year, wanted to pay for all expenses up front to avoid exorbitant fees. It turns out this decision was shortsighted: whatever money was saved by not taking the cloth on credit paled in comparison to the other costs produced by the funeral's delay. As Lorkin put it, Cranfield would have done well to consider "that expense his majesty is like to be at, all the interim, in maintaining the Queen's household, which wants nothing of its full allowance 'til the Funeral be celebrated."

Following the tradition of the English monarchy, Anna's coffin was treated with nearly the same pomp and ceremony she was accustomed to while alive. (The Venetian ambassador Giovanni Scaramelli, we might recall, was taken aback by Queen Elizabeth's courtiers treating her remains "as though she were not wrapped in a fold of cerecloth, and hid in such a heap of lead, of coffin, of pall, but was walking as she used to do at this season, about the alleys of her garden.") There's no record of whether Mary Sidney came to Denmark House to pay her respects—given her status and the prominence of her two sons in James's court, it's very likely she did—but we have an account of such a visit from Anne Clifford. On April 19, Anne recorded in her diary that she sat with the corpse "a good while" before strolling with a cousin through the palace's privy galleries filled with "fine delicate things"—the visit was a combination of paying respects to the dead and a museum outing. Four days later, Anne returned for a longer stay: "Then I went to Denmark House and heard prayers there and this night I watched all night with the queen's corpse." In addition to Anne on that occasion, "there watched with me my Lady Elizabeth Gorges and diverse other ladies and gentlewomen, besides there sat up my brother Compton, my cousin Gorges, my cousin Thatcher, and Mr. Reynolds." This was only the overnight crowd: another group of courtiers, male and female, had stayed until midnight.

On May 13, 1619, Anna was finally buried in Westminster Abbey. The funeral was of an extravagant grandeur: 280 poor women led the enormous procession of civil servants, members of the royal household, priests and bishops, male and female courtiers, and seemingly endless heraldic flags and banners through the city. According to Chamberlain's account of the preparations to Carleton in his April 24 letter, "the number of mourners and the whole charge spoken of is beyond proportion, above three times more than was bestowed upon Queen Elizabeth." In a subsequent letter, written the day after the funeral, he described the procession as "a drawling tedious sight, more remarkable for number than for any other singularity." "Though the number of Lord and Ladies was very great," he confided to Carleton, "yet methought all together they made but a poor show, which perhaps was because they were appareled all alike or that they came laggering all along even tired with the length of the way and weight of their cloths, every Lady having twelve yards of broad-cloth about her, and the countesses sixteen."

It's among this group of countesses, burdened by the sheer quantity of their black cloth, that we can conjure up Mary Sidney. How she bore the long day of marching and standing isn't clear, but her health had certainly been failing in recent years, so much so that in 1614 she had left England for medical treatments. Her destination was the fashionable resort town of Spa in Belgium, whose hot mineral springs had been used as cures since ancient times. (Hence the origin of the term "spa" for wellness centers worldwide.) This was the first time Mary had traveled outside of the British Isles, making her an unusually provincial member of her cosmopolitan family. Her brother Philip had been on several diplomatic missions to the Continent and spent the last year of his life as governor of the Dutch city of Flushing; and her younger brother Robert, who was given the governorship of Flushing in 1589 (two years after Philip's death), remained in that post until King James returned the city to the Dutch in 1616.

Details of Mary's travel have survived, thanks to the correspondence between Robert Sidney and his deputy in Flushing, Sir John Throckmorton, who oversaw the logistics of Mary's journey (Robert was back in England at the time). Throckmorton reported her arrival on June 25, 1614, where she was met in the port by his son, who asked "to know her pleasure whether she would come ashore or from her ship embark into another that might carry her for Antwerp." She chose to continue the journey, boarding a smaller ship to travel down the narrow Westerschelde estuary. There's no record of how long she stayed in Antwerp before making the roughly hundred-mile trip by land to Spa, but by August 1 Robert received a letter from her, reporting that she felt "very well with the use of those waters." No details were given about her specific course of treatment, but a contemporary report described the regular practice at Spa of drinking "fifteen cups of water, each of a wine pint" to begin each day. The waters must have continued to do Mary some good, or at least she had hopes they would: she returned to the therapeutic springs for the summers of 1615 and 1616, spending the winter moving between Utrecht, Amiens, Antwerp, and possibly Breda.

The best account of Mary's life at Spa comes in a letter written by one of her fellow travelers in August 1616. For once, Sir Dudley Carleton was sending news to John Chamberlain, and not the other way around. Having arrived at Spa in late July, Carleton described with some surprise the large international crowds at the resort, of whom the English made up a large part:

> Here we found the town full of men, women, and children of all ages, of all conditions, of all nations in Europe . . . and at our arrival the English did equal in number all other strangers, who were of three ranks, some which came for diseases of the body, others of the mind, the rest for good fellowship.

Among the English guests worthy of attention, the very first Carleton mentioned was none other than Mary: "The countess of Pembroke we found here, who complains chiefly of a common disease and much troublesome to fair women, *Senectus,* otherwise we see nothing amiss in her." ("Senectus" is the Latin term for extreme age.) Carleton continued with details about Mary's activities, which belie any sense of her decrepitude:

> She hath met with a fit companion, the Countess of Barlemont, whose husband is governor of Luxembourg, and they are so like of disposition and humor that whilst the men entertain themselves at pick-staff (a game proper to this place) they shoot at mark with pistols.

Not much is known about Lady Barlemont outside of her marriage to Florent, Count of Barlemont, and her parentage: her father, Philip, was Count of Lailang and ruler of territory that belonged to the Holy Roman Empire on the border between Belgium and France; her mother was the daughter of the Duke of Arenberg, who ruled over several Dutch provinces. She was, in short, of a pedigree very much worthy of the Dowager Countess of Pembroke, and the two seem to have become fast friends.

According to Carleton, the women lodged together with Lady Barlemont's two daughters at what he described as Spa's "court of the English." In addition to doing target practice and playing local games, they were seen dancing, attending plays and entertainments, and smoking tobacco. This last habit—which came into vogue at the English court after Sir Walter Raleigh returned with the crop from Roanoke Island in 1586—was regarded as good for your health. A Spanish treatise on the subject translated into English in 1577 claimed that tobacco was useful to relieve, among other ailments, toothache, worms, and bad breath. By 1610, Sir Francis Bacon noted it was a habit difficult to quit. According to Carleton, Mary seems to have become a regular user. "It seemed strange unto her," he observed, "that all our company forbore it, as if in her conceit all English had drawn no other breath."

In his August 1616 letter to Chamberlain, Carleton didn't mention Mary's other frequent companion at the resort besides Lady

Barlemont. The following spring, however, Chamberlain wrote to Carleton about a rumor circulating in London: "Here is a suspicion that the old Countess of Pembroke is married to Doctor Lister that was with her at the Spa." Sir Matthew Lister was Mary's personal physician, who had accompanied her on her travels in 1614. Born in 1571, and hence ten years Mary's junior, Lister had taken his medical degree at the prestigious University of Basel (there were no equivalent medical schools in England, so aspiring doctors either did lengthy apprenticeships at home or went abroad). In 1607 he was elected to England's College of Physicians, quickly becoming one of the most popular doctors at court: he counted among his patients both James and Anna.

Lister's willingness to leave this illustrious practice to travel to Spa with Mary may in itself have raised eyebrows. It's highly unlikely a secret marriage took place, but it's possible the two were lovers. The idea was not so subtly suggested in Robert Sidney's daughter Lady Mary Wroth's unpublished play, *Love's Victory*, where the character Simeana, sister of Philisses, is in love with Lissius, who initially swears off love but ultimately falls in love with someone else. Whatever happened between Mary and Lister, Mary's gratitude for his service is confirmed by her generous provision for him upon her death. According to Chamberlain, she left him "six or seven score [120 to 140] pounds a year during his life," which, in Chamberlain's eyes, Lister had certainly earned. He's "well-worn [out] in her service," he commented to Carleton, "for they say he looks old."

Gossip about Mary's adventures with the English physician and the Belgian countess may have filled drawing rooms across London, but in a handful of Mary's letters from these years a different side of her life at Spa comes into view. After more than a decade in which there are no signs of her writing, she seems to have resumed her vocation. Maybe she needed the distance from her responsibilities managing her jointure estates to reawaken her intellectual ambitions; maybe the cures of the water were also therapeutic for her creative talents. Whatever the reason, in a series of letters attributed to Mary as part of an exchange with a fellow Englishman, Sir Tobie Matthew, she made clear she was once again fully engaged in her literary work.

A wealthy courtier who converted to Catholicism in the early

1600s and lived for decades on the Continent, Matthew was born in Salisbury to a Welsh family with close ties to the Herberts. Whether he and Mary met before he left England isn't clear, but he was part of the large English circle Carleton found at Spa; in his August 1616 letter to Chamberlain, he described Matthew as having been "deep in the waters before our coming." In 1650, John Donne's eldest son, John Donne the younger, published Matthew's correspondence in a book entitled *A Collection of Letters Made by Sir Tobie Matthew, Knight,* which is where the letters Mary sent to her friend first appeared. Because Donne Jr. was a sloppy editor who paid no attention to chronology in putting together the collection, it's hard to know exactly when anything was written. But Mary's letters refer directly to her time at Spa, dating them to sometime between 1614 and 1616.

In the first of Mary's letters included in the collection, she began with an account of her improved health. "Now I will tell you somewhat, which I know will please you, and it is this," she wrote,

> That whereas you thought and told me, that the Spa would do no body good this last season, I owe too much both to it and you to let you go away with that error. For if you saw me now, you would say, it had created a new creature. Therefore, let all pictures now hide themselves, for, believe me, I am not now as I was then.

After boasting of her newly improved appearance—an apparent cure of her "Senectus"—she shifted her focus from body to mind and referred intriguingly to an exchange of manuscripts. "My translation," she declared, "shall be very shortly with you, and you shall have better matter for your thoughts to work upon, if this mind of mine could fit itself with power enough for your service." The letter ended with an affirmation of her commitment to their friendship: "But nothing shall take me from being a friend as perfect to you, as you can have any in the whole world."

The mention of Mary's translation is at once tantalizing and frustrating; who knows how much work she may have done over the years that wasn't preserved. Despite having been at the very center of English literary life decades earlier, Mary was now oddly in the position of so many women writers who never found an audience outside of their immediate circle, and whose works were therefore lost forever. Mary's lack of public recognition for whatever she wrote during her widowhood may have been her choice. She still enjoyed an exalted reputation—Aemilia Lanyer's praise of her in *Salve Deus* had been written only a few years before the trip to Spa—and she continued to see literary works dedicated to her, if not nearly at the pace of the 1590s. Her sons were now both major literary patrons themselves, which meant she was also often mentioned in dedications to them. (Their fame as patrons would reach its apex in 1623 as joint dedicatees of Shakespeare's First Folio.) Whether she was a countess or a dowager, in England or on the Continent, it's hard to believe she wouldn't have had ample support should she have wanted to publish anything she'd written.

But no translation of Mary's from her time at Spa has survived in manuscript or print, so there's no way to know what exactly it was that she wanted to share with Matthew. Since he himself was a translator of English to Italian—in 1618 he published an Italian translation of thirty-eight of his friend Sir Francis Bacon's essays, a book he dedicated to Cosimo II de' Medici, Grand Duke of Tuscany—she may have sent him an Italian translation of her own. There's precedent for her working in this language as well as in French: in the late 1590s she had translated one of Petrarch's *Trionfi*, a set of six poems cycling through the "triumph" of love, chastity, death, fame, time, and eternity. Written in the mid-fourteenth century and first published in Italy in 1470, the *Trionfi* had become immensely popular in England at the time of Henry VIII: an inventory of Henry's tapestries includes eleven depictions from these poems, and his last wife, Queen Katherine Parr, owned a printed copy that was passed down to Mary Tudor.

Mary Sidney's choice to translate Petrarch's *Trionfo della Morte* (*The Triumph of Death*) fit with her general preoccupation with mortality in the 1590s. As with the two French works she translated (Mornay's *Excellent discours de la vie et de la mort* and Garnier's *Marc Antoine*), the Italian poem gave her a chance to work through in a different context the tragic losses—of her daughter, her parents, and her brother—that she had endured in the space of a few years. Unlike her translations of Mornay and Garnier, however, which

Mary published soon after their completion, *The Triumph of Death* never saw print in her lifetime. It survived only because it happened to be included in a manuscript that Sir John Harington—the same person who claimed that Mary, as a woman, couldn't possibly have done the Psalms translations herself—sent in 1600 to Lucy Russell, Countess of Bedford. Despite his having questioned her authorship, the manuscript included three of Mary's Psalms, as well as his own collection of epigrams. Harington joked to Lucy, in fact, that his works followed Mary's "as a wanton page is admitted to bear a torch to a chaste matron." It's possible Mary translated more of Petrarch's *Trionfi* than the single *Triumph of Death*—after all, only three of her 150 Psalms were in Harington's manuscript—but no other poems from the series have been found.

Whatever Mary was working on at Spa, it's clear from the letters attributed to her in the Matthew collection that her writing went beyond a single translation. "And now I send you enclosed this Nothing," she wrote in a second letter, "which yet is all that I have been able to get." Apologizing for not having made more progress on whatever it was she was writing, she promised to send more very soon:

> Within a few days (and yet but a few days), which indeed had yet been fewer, but that I have been sick (as I am yet not well), I shall be there, where, I hope, I may prove much more able to say something of this new world to you.

She then acknowledged "those things which I received from you, which are all most excellent," and expressed her concern that her own output wasn't matching his: "And though my desires prove not yet so fruitful, as I would they did, yet let me still receive commands from you by your Letters, for they are all extremely welcome to me." This section of her letter ends with her asking Matthew to look kindly upon what she was sending him, "because they have parted from me to none but yourself." The use of the plural "they" to describe her work suggests she may have been writing poems. Whatever she was writing, she imagined Matthew as her only reader: "and as this copy is the first, so also is it to be the last."

The image of Mary that emerges from this correspondence—a

woman revitalized by her time at Spa, immersed in new work that she was striving to improve, and engaged in a literary exchange with a fellow writer—is otherwise entirely missing from her biography. But Mary had one further burst of creativity in her final years that has been recorded, which took an entirely new form. In the late summer of 1616 Mary intended to return from Spa to England, spurred by the upcoming birth of a grandchild (Philip Herbert's first son) for whom she was to serve as godmother. Her travels were delayed and she missed the christening, waiting several months in Calais before she could cross the Channel. Once back in London in December, she received an entirely unexpected gift from the king. James gave to Mary life interest in Houghton Park, a splendid property that belonged to the Crown in Bedfordshire, around fifty miles north of London.

For the first time in her life, Mary had the chance to live in a house that belonged to neither her father nor her husband: Houghton was entirely her own. Hiring the most talented architects from England and Italy—including the celebrated Inigo Jones, who several years later would redesign Whitehall's Banqueting House into one of the masterpieces of Palladian architecture—she built a beautiful three-story mansion that became famous throughout the region. Legend has it that the writer John Bunyan, who was a native of Bedfordshire, used it as the model for his "House Beautiful" in his 1678 allegorical novel, *The Pilgrim's Progress*.

Houghton House was both ambitious and quirky in its style, combining contemporary English architecture with distinctly classical features. There were two Italianate loggias, or covered exterior galleries, set amid English gables and turrets; according to the seventeenth-century biographer John Aubrey, the result was a "curious" if not aesthetically altogether coherent house. Aubrey also acknowledged it was "the most pleasantly situated" home in the area, "with four vistas, each prospect twenty-five or thirty miles." The sweeping views may have reminded Mary of her childhood home at Ludlow Castle, where she and her siblings had climbed the narrow stairway of the medieval tower to glimpse the Welsh countryside around them.

As her father had done at Ludlow, Mary carved the family's coat of arms into the medallion on her exterior wall, announcing to all who came there her proud identity as a Sidney. On the west loggia, she expanded this single identification with a frieze made up of three heraldic motifs: the Sidney porcupine, which had been adopted as a family crest by her grandfather, Sir William Sidney; the bear and ragged staff associated with her uncle Robert Dudley, Earl of Leicester; and her personal device of two interlocked pheons, or arrowheads, to make an *M* for Mary, which were crossed by an *H* for Herbert. The house is now in ruins, having been pulled down in 1794 by its owner, the Duke of Bedford, who wanted to lease the adjoining hunting park to a neighboring estate. But visitors to the park today can still take in the stunning landscape and imagine what it felt like for Mary to have made this her final home.

Around the same time Mary's architects were designing her house at Houghton, the Dutch artist Simon van de Passe made an engraving that became her most enduring portrait. As she indicated in one of her letters to Matthew, there were multiple pictures of her in circulation that to her mind showed her in a less improved state than she was at Spa ("for, believe me, I am not now as I was then"). The engraving, dated to around 1618, not only captured her rejuvenated self: it also recovered her status as a celebrated poet. In the only other portrait made during her lifetime that has survived—a 1590 miniature done by Nicholas Hilliard—Mary was shown as an aristocratic lady whose most conspicuous feature was her fashionable cartwheel ruff, an elaborate lace collar with a wire support that kept it elevated (and awkwardly stiff) around her head. The roses and honeysuckle decorating Mary's hair conveyed a carefree, youthful demeanor, and there was no hint of the serious literary work she had recently embarked upon.

The Van de Passe image made nearly thirty years later certainly affirms Mary's role as a noblewoman: her marriage to the Earl of Pembroke is mentioned in both the Latin and English inscriptions, and she's dressed in luxurious materials, with expensive lace around her wrists and collar, pearls hanging from her neck, and a dress of velvet and ermine. But departing from any ordinary iconographic conventions for female portraiture, above her head is a crown topped with the laurel wreath of poets, around the frame (officially known as a "cartouche") there seem to be quill pens resting in inkwells, and in her hand is an open book marked on the edges "David's

The last surviving image of Mary Sidney,
triumphantly shown as a poet

Psalms." It's not clear whether Mary commissioned the portrait and sat for it herself, or whether it was copied after another contemporary picture of her. However the engraving came to be made, there can be no doubt of its message: Mary's translation of the Psalms was her defining achievement. Many paintings of English aristocratic women showed them holding books of devotion; Mary would no doubt have known the portrait of her mother, Lady Sidney, with a small prayer book in her hand. But in the Van de Passe engraving, Mary isn't holding the book labeled "David's Psalms" to convey her piety. She's holding it to show her authorship.

In the late summer of 1621, Mary fell ill with smallpox. She died at her London house in Aldersgate Street on September 25, a month shy of her sixtieth birthday. As Chamberlain related it in his October 13 letter to Carleton, "The old countess of Pembroke died here some ten days since of the small pox, and on Wednesday night was carried with a great store of coaches and torch-light toward Wilton where she is to be buried." The ceremony was held at St. Paul's Cathedral in what Mary's brother Robert described as "a funeral made according to her quality"; the burial took place near Wilton at Salisbury Cathedral, where she lies at the east end of the choir in the Herbert vault next to her husband.

Among the many tributes paid to Mary, the most often repeated was an epitaph by William Browne, a minor poet seeking her son William's patronage. His description of Mary as "Sidney's sister, Pembroke's mother" was inscribed on a small diamond-shaped tablet of brass placed over her casket. To this crushingly male definition of her identity, Aemilia Lanyer might have countered with her lines from the dedicatory poem "The Author's Dream to the Lady Mary, the Countess Dowager of Pembroke" in *Salve Deus,* where she placed Mary above her famous brother Philip. After declaring that "Far before him is [she] to be esteemed / For virtue, wisdom, learning, dignity," she prophesied that it was Mary who would fill "the eyes, the hearts, the tongues, the ears / of after-coming ages."

It would take nearly four hundred years for Mary's reputation to arrive anywhere near Aemilia's estimation. But it's important not to imagine Browne's sexist epitaph as capturing either Mary's identity or her experience. She may not have published new work after becoming a widow, but judging from her letters to Matthew, she continued to write well into her fifties. She traveled abroad, where she moved from place to place as she chose, made new friends, and possibly had a love affair with a younger man. She built her own magnificent house where she enjoyed the tranquility of the countryside until illness brought her to London a month or so before she died. She was celebrated in her final portrait as the great translator of David's Psalms and a female poet laureate. She made her mark on the world.

CHAPTER TWELVE

November 11, 1620

Court of Chancery, Westminster Hall

Aemilia Lanyer

On November 11, 1620, the fifty-one-year-old Aemilia Lanyer filed a legal complaint at the Court of Chancery. Created in the fifteenth century to hear cases that fell outside the strict jurisdiction of common law, Chancery was an equity court that handled all sorts of business and property disputes, including issues of family inheritances and wills, marriage settlements, debts and bankruptcies, and fights over land. Located at the south end of Westminster Hall next to the Court of King's Bench, the Chancery Court was typically full of people ranging from ordinary laborers to the highest noblemen in the land. Petitioners submitted their claims to Chancery with the hope for quicker and more merciful rulings than they were likely to find in the Court of King's Bench, where the rigid application of common law limited the kinds of resolution available. Both courts were often in session at the same time, creating unpleasant crowds and poor acoustics: a rare surviving sketch from the early seventeenth century shows lawyers, judges, and spectators all packed together in the rear of the hall, with a few dogs wandering among them. Missing from the sketch are any women, although records show there were plenty of female petitioners like Aemilia.

Aemilia's petition from 1620 has survived thanks to the Chancery Court's extraordinary records, held today in Britain's National Archives. In the dusty map room on the Archives' second floor, oversize cardboard boxes stuffed with mostly illegible parchment and vellum—some narrow scraps, others enormous folios stretching several feet in width and length—contain the pleadings of plaintiffs and defendants, from 1558 until the dissolution of the court in 1875. In one such box, between Bridget Lewis's filing over a land dispute in Gloucestershire and Dorothy Lodge's request for a stay of legal proceedings, are two poster-size sheets of paper containing what remains of Aemilia's case.

Addressed to "The Right Honorable Francis Lord Verulam"— better known to modern readers as Sir Francis Bacon, who had become lord chancellor of England in 1618—the first document begins with Aemilia's account of her current circumstances. As the "late wife of captain Alfonso Lanier, his majesty's servant deceased [in 1613]," she had been left in "very poor estate, he having spent a great part of his estate in the serving of the late Queen in her wars of Ireland and other places." Given the minor role Alfonso played in Essex's expeditions, Aemilia wanted to make sure Bacon knew that he had nonetheless made sacrifices for the country, which in her estimation had been woefully undercompensated—with one notable exception.

In 1604, Robert Cecil, Earl of Salisbury and one of James's secretaries of state, had awarded Alfonso a lucrative patent for hay and grain, a form of monopoly over the weighing of these goods brought into London or its nearby suburbs. Alfonso seems to have gotten the patent thanks to the intervention of Richard Bancroft, bishop of London (and future archbishop of Canterbury), who in 1604 wrote a letter praising Alfonso's service in Ireland and calling him "mine old fellow and loving friend." The grant stipulated that Alfonso or his deputies be paid up to 6 pennies per load of hay and grain (there were 240 pennies in a pound) for a period of twenty-two years, bringing a much-needed stream of income into the Lanier household. When Alfonso died, the patent was Aemilia's only real inheritance, and she handed its management over to one of her brothers-in-law with the expectation that they would split the income.

There's no record of how much money the patent generated. But in her 1620 pleading before the Chancery Court, Aemilia represented herself as having been so impoverished that in 1617, for her own "maintenance and relief," she was "compelled to teach and educate the children of diverse persons of worth and understanding." Her son, Henry, who had followed in his father's and both grandfathers' path as a musician, received an official post at court only in 1629, so it's unlikely he was supporting his mother in 1617 (she may well have been supporting him); *Salve Deus* had produced neither income nor a position in a household of one of her many dedicatees, and she had no regular income outside of the patent.

It's also important to note that Aemilia was far from desperate. According to the 1601 Poor Law, anyone without adequate means was given either a "dole" from their local parish or, in more extreme cases of poverty, taken into the local almshouse to live (in the royal funerals for both Elizabeth and Anna, we might recall, poor women from almshouses led the procession). There's no indication Aemilia was in anywhere near so dire a state, and there's something jarring about her claim to need "maintenance and relief" and the risky decision she made to venture out on her own, as we'll see. Becoming a teacher in an already established school would have been a way of keeping her dignity while gaining stable employment—John Milton himself was a successful schoolmaster at the beginning of his career. But far from assuming a reliable job, Aemilia had rented a farmhouse in St. Giles in the Fields, a well-to-do suburb of London, to set up a school of her own.

The idea of a woman schoolmistress wasn't so uncommon as we may imagine it to have been. Starting in the late sixteenth century, a new crop of "domestic" schools began to surface, typically in rural areas—as St. Giles was—where there were often shortages of endowed grammar schools. These alternative schools were entrepreneurial ventures initiated by the schoolteachers who took on the financial risks in exchange for fees paid by the parents directly; the parents, in turn, paid significantly less than they would to send their children to established boarding schools or to hire private tutors. Unlike the endowed grammar schools, there were women as well as men running them. According to official records from the County of Essex, for example, between 1560 and 1603 there were forty-seven schoolmistresses teaching in twenty-eight different parishes in the diocese.

Aemilia's school at St. Giles was in operation for two years before things came to a halt due to a conflict with her landlord, Edward Smith. Smith, she declared in her 1620 petition, was "a counselor at law who [had] professed much friendship and kindness to her." In 1617, he'd leased her the farmhouse where she ran the school "with all the appurtenances whatsoever except one stable and hayloft" for £22 a year. This was not a trivial sum: Alfonso's annual salary as a court musician had been around £30. There's no record of how many students Aemilia had or what they were paying in fees; one of the few advertisements for a woman's school that has survived from the seventeenth century—from 1673, so more than fifty years after Aemilia's venture—lists annual fees of £20 a year. Whatever she may have been earning, she was chased off Smith's property in 1619 by a "better tenant who would give him more rent and take the stables and hayloft," the two outbuildings that had been exempted from her lease. Aemilia was suing Smith for "the sum of ten pounds and upwards for repairs"; she also requested that any countersuits of common law be stayed until she received a hearing in the Court of Chancery.

In addition to Aemilia's suit against Smith, a second document related to the case has survived. Entitled "The Joint and Several Answers of Edward Smith, Esquire . . . to the Bill of Complaint of Emilia Lanyer, widow complainant," it contains Smith's lengthy response. Scribbled on a sprawling sheet of paper nearly double the size of Aemilia's petition—my eyes strained to stay on the right line across the seemingly endless page—Smith admitted that he found a better tenant, Sir Edmund Morgan. Far from acknowledging any wrongdoing, however, he issued a counter-complaint. Aemilia, he claimed, owed him rent and money for repairs. There's no record of how the case was resolved; outside of Aemilia's and Smith's pleadings, no other materials have survived. As is so often the case, we're left with many more questions than answers. What was Aemilia teaching her students, and were there boys as well as girls? Did she hire other teachers, or run the school entirely herself? Who if anyone supported her, and how did she feel when things came to an abrupt end?

Once Aemilia's lease with Smith was terminated, there's no further mention of her working in the remaining twenty-five years of her life. It's hard not to feel sad about her life story: a woman who was once the mistress of the lord chamberlain and "maintained in great pomp," who had lived with the Countess of Cumberland and the future Countess of Dorset, and who went on to become the first woman in seventeenth-century England to publish her own book of poems, was reduced to fighting petty lawsuits and struggling to make ends meet. She could easily have ended up like Jane Shore, the famous mistress of Edward IV whom Thomas More wrote about in his *History of King Richard III.* Mistress Shore had been a beautiful woman—"nothing in her body that you would have changed," More noted, "say they who knew her in her youth"—whom the king favored above his other concubines, but as an old lady she was left "lean, withered, and dried up," without friends or acquaintance, begging for her living on the streets. But there's no evidence anything of this kind happened in Aemilia's case, and her final decades seem to have been stable, if not entirely conflict-free.

By 1630 Aemilia's son was married with two children and living in Clerkenwell, a relatively affluent London suburb with a good water supply (it was named for one of its many wells); at some point in the 1630s, she moved to Clerkenwell to live either with or near him. After Henry's death in 1633, at the age of forty, from unknown causes, she entered into new litigation with Alfonso's brothers, Innocent and Clement Lanyer, over the proceeds from the hay and grain patent. By this point she had clearly become adept in petitioning at the Court of Chancery, and multiple bulky and nearly indecipherable records from these lawsuits have also survived. Unlike her earlier lawsuit against her landlord, these petitions were made not only on her own behalf, but also on behalf of her two grandchildren. This time, she was successful: the ruling came down in her favor in 1637.

Aemilia died on April 3, 1645, at the age of seventy-six. In the parish records of St. James Clerkenwell, where she was buried on April 3, 1645, she was listed as a "pensioner" and not merely as a widow, which means she was still receiving a regular income of some kind at the time of her death (presumably from Alfonso's patent). In the late 1700s St. James Clerkenwell was destroyed and replaced with a new church, leaving very little of the dilapidated twelfth-century structure intact. A number of funerary monuments survived the rebuilding and were reinstalled in the body of the church or the crypt, including the mutilated effigy of Elizabeth Berkeley, one of the ladies of Queen Elizabeth's bedchamber, and the grand marble tablet to Elizabeth Drury, Countess Dowager of Exeter. Aemilia's tombstone wasn't among those preserved, and there's no way to know what may have been inscribed on it. But it's unlikely that it mentioned *Salve Deus,* which had already been out of print for over thirty years. Had this pioneering book never been redis-covered, nothing more of Aemilia would have remained outside of the heap of illegible legal petitions and the equally illegible and one-sided records kept by her astrologer, Simon Forman. She would have disappeared from history altogether.

And then, three centuries later, Aemilia made a surprising come-back—if for all the wrong reasons. A British literary historian who was studying Forman's casebooks read his notes on Aemilia's back-ground and came to the conclusion that she was the answer to one of English literature's greatest mysteries. Ever since Shakespeare's *Sonnets* were published in 1609, readers have tried to uncover the identity of the "Dark Lady"—the black-haired woman Shakespeare wrote about in his tortured, final poems. On January 29, 1973, in *The Times of London,* the scholar A. L. Rowse announced to the world that he had figured it out. Under the headline "Revealed at Last, Shakespeare's Dark Lady," Rowse explained what he regarded as his extraordinary discovery. "I myself," he wrote, "thought that she never would be discovered . . . but all the time the secret was waiting for me among the manuscripts in the Bodleian Library."

The combination of Aemilia's sexual promiscuity, her ties to the court and especially to Shakespeare's sometime patron Lord Huns-don, her Italian and possibly Jewish background (both unreliably suggesting dark coloring), and her musical family (one of Shake-speare's sonnets describes his mistress playing music for him) all seemed to Rowse to match up perfectly with Shakespeare's mysteri-ous lover. "We now have the answer," he triumphantly declared, "to the last and most inscrutable of the Sonnet's problems." For-man's account of his sexual relations with Aemilia alongside Shake-speare's depiction of a cruel and deceptive mistress led Rowse to brand Aemilia as "a bad lot" who "dragged [the poet] through hell." Shakespeare "was infatuated, under her spell, with his eyes open," he concluded, "and she led him a fearful dance." Just as Forman had done nearly four centuries earlier, Rowse projected all sorts of sexual fantasies upon Aemilia.

As it turned out, there was absolutely no basis for Rowse's identification of Aemilia as Shakespeare's mistress. The only solid piece of evidence linking the two of them was their common acquaintance with Lord Hunsdon. In 1594, Shakespeare joined Hunsdon's new theater company, the Lord Chamberlain's Men, and the company began staging some of his early plays. But whether Aemilia attended any of these performances or was ever introduced to the playwright remains unknown; even if Aemilia's affair with Hunsdon continued after her marriage to Alfonso, she presumably was no longer seen with him in public. The rest of Rowse's proofs were based on errors in his transcription of Forman's admittedly difficult scrawl: Rowse thought Forman wrote that Aemilia was very "brown," from which he concluded she fit the description of Shakespeare's mistress with her hair of "black wires" and her "raven black" eyes. But the word Forman used was not "brown" but "brave," meaning Aemilia was proud or showy. Rowse also mistakenly thought her husband's name was Will (and not Alfonso), allowing him to make all sorts of false connections to Shakespeare's punning on his name in the poems.

However misguided Rowse was in his research—and the bold surety with which he made his announcements is truly breathtaking—it's ironically to him that we owe *Salve Deus*'s reappearance in print. For after coming to his conclusions about Aemilia's role in Shakespeare's life, he learned that she was herself a poet. In 1978, under the sensational title *The Poems of Shakespeare's Dark Lady*, he published the first edition of *Salve Deus* to appear since 1611. By the 1990s, Rowse's theory about Aemilia had been largely debunked by scholars, and a serious edition of her poems was published by Oxford University Press, properly entitled *The Poems of Aemilia Lanyer*. But this didn't stop the public's fascination with the idea that Aemilia might be Shakespeare's missing lover. Somehow the allure of using her to fill the role of this fictional character in the sonnets—there's no proof that Shakespeare even had a "dark lady" in the first place—seems irresistible, especially to men.

In 2003, an article ran in the British newspaper *The Independent* with the title "Unmasked: The Identity of Shakespeare's Dark

Lady," after Aemilia was identified as the subject of a beautiful min-iature by Nicholas Hilliard in the Victoria and Albert Museum. This apparent discovery was made by the actor and playwright Tony Haygarth while working on a play, *Dark Meaning Mouse,* focused on Shakespeare's relationship with his supposed female lover. The portrait, dated 1593, shows a dark-haired, pale-skinned woman whose dress is decorated with tiny bees and stags; according to Hay-garth, these were, respectively, the silkworm moths of the Bassano coat of arms and the stags of the Earl of Essex's. There are multiple problems with this conclusion as well: the insects may or may not be moths, and Aemilia had no ties in 1593 to the Earl of Essex: Alfonso first served Essex on his expedition to the Azores four years later. The portrait also indicates that the sitter was twenty-six years old, whereas Aemilia would have turned twenty-four the year the portrait was made. A second Hilliard miniature, also in the Victoria and Albert Museum and dated 1590, was identified as Aemilia in 2014 by a theater director, John Hudson, who had even flimsier grounds than Haygarth—there are no silkworm moths or stags in this portrait, only a woman with dark hair. This was part of a much larger argument on Hudson's part: he claimed Aemilia wrote all of Shakespeare's plays.

Perhaps the reason Aemilia has been the subject of so much extravagant fantasizing is that, in the absence of sure knowledge, there's room for invention: none of these theories would have gone anywhere if she'd left behind a fuller record of her own. For aristo-cratic women with secretaries keeping track of their personal writ-ing, husbands in public office, and families immersed in life at court, the possibility of falling prey to wild biographical invention without competing pieces of evidence was unlikely. To tell Aemilia's history well with no letters or diaries in her own voice is a more complicated enterprise. But the more our focus falls on what we learn from her poems—about her experiences with Margaret and Anne Clifford, her hopes for a female readership and her belief in women's right to independence, her dream of women writers being recognized on their own terms—the more secure her legacy becomes.

CHAPTER THIRTEEN

February 20, 1627

Ten Miles from London

Elizabeth Cary

In "a little old house" outside of London—very far from the castle in Dublin where she'd recently lived in grand style—Elizabeth
Cary was busy at work. "About this time," her daughters related
in *The Lady Falkland,* "she wrote the lives of St. Mary Magdalene,
St. Agnes Martyr, and St. Elizabeth of Portugal in verse," as well
as "many verses of our Blessed Lady." Wrapped up in the lives of
Catholic saints, Elizabeth was exploring what it felt like to be a holy
woman in her new faith following her conversion in 1626. Unfortunately, none of these poems has survived. But on February 20, 1627,
she finished writing a book of a very different sort: a long history of
the profligate and irresponsible medieval king, Edward II.

Elizabeth's *History of the Life, Reign and Death of Edward II*
received no mention in her biography, nor did it appear in any contemporary references. When it was first printed in 1680—more than
forty years after Elizabeth's death—it was attributed to her husband,
Henry Cary, Lord Falkland, on the grounds that one of the two surviving manuscripts was found among his papers. The fact that Henry
had no record of being a writer didn't faze the late-seventeenth-
century publishers, Charles Harper, Samuel Crouch, and Thomas
Fox, who claimed the work belonged to a "gentleman . . . above
fifty years since" whose writing was unusually virile. "Those days,"
they observed, "produced very few who were able to express their

conceptions in so masculine a style." In their enthusiasm for the work's masculinity, they failed to read the "Author's Preface to the Reader" printed on the very next page, which describes the conditions in which the work was written:

> To out-run those weary hours of a deep and sad passion, my melancholy Pen fell accidentally on this Historical Relation . . . I have not herein followed the dull character of our historians, nor amplified more than they infer, by circumstance . . . If you so hap to view it, tax not my Errors; I myself confess them.

The preface was dated and signed: "20 Feb. 1627 Elizabeth Falkland."

In 1627, Elizabeth's life was in tatters. Denounced by her husband, rejected by her mother, and stripped of her children, she found herself alone in a way she hadn't experienced since she was locked up in a room by her mother-in-law more than twenty years earlier. Besides spending her "weary hours" crafting petitions to privy councilors with the hope of regaining some of the fortune Henry had squandered—her father, we will recall, disinherited her after Henry mortgaged most of her jointure properties—she decided to use her "melancholy pen" to write history.

According to her daughters, Elizabeth loved to read history "very universally, especially all ancient Greek and Roman historians; all Chronicles whatsoever of her own country; and the French histories very thoroughly." Beginning with the translation she did at age twelve of Ortelius's atlas, *Le Miroir du Monde,* she had shown a keen interest in the world around her; her plays set in ancient Judaea and Syracuse speak to her curiosity about cultures and eras far from her own. In her history of Edward II, Elizabeth drew on her reading of English Chronicles to explore a subject closer to home.

The story of this ill-fated king, whose twenty-year reign (1307–27) ended in the loss of his throne and his subsequent murder, was well known to Renaissance English audiences. In the early 1590s, Christopher Marlowe wrote a popular play on the subject that was performed on the London stage and subsequently printed in a cheap quarto edition in 1594 with the lengthy title *The Trouble-*

some Reign and Lamentable Death of Edward the Second, King of England, with the Tragical Fall of Proud Mortimer. Elizabeth seems to have been an admirer of Marlowe's works, or at least of the subjects he chose to write about: in the first few years of her marriage, her daughters claimed she wrote a "life of Tamburlaine in verse" that "was said to be the best" of her early writing. There's no way to evaluate this claim, as Elizabeth's history of the fourteenth-century Turko-Mongol conqueror Tamerlane or Tamburlaine, the violent hero of Marlowe's famous two-part play, has never been found. It's hard to imagine that any account of the brutal and savage ruler of the Persian empire would have appealed to Elizabeth's pious daughters in the Benedictine convent. But given Elizabeth's interest in Mariam and Salome, it's possible she found Zenocrate, the daughter of the Egyptian sultan whom Tamburlaine kidnaps and then successfully woos to become his wife, an intriguing heroine.

In writing about Edward II, Elizabeth wasn't following only in Marlowe's wake. She would also likely have read about Edward in a poem written by her tutor Michael Drayton, *The Legend of Piers Gaveston.* As the title makes clear, Drayton narrowed his focus to the king's young and seductive male favorite. According to contemporary chronicles, Edward's love for Gaveston was "immoderate" and "beyond measure." As Drayton's Gaveston describes it:

> *I lived, enjoying whatsoever was [the king's]*
> *who never my pleasure anything denied . . .*
> *For still I spurred up his untamed desire . . .*
> *till having lost the clue which led us in*
> *We wandered in the labyrinth of lust.*

Gaveston's intimacy with Edward, combined with his great arrogance and ambition, earned him the loathing of nearly everyone else in the kingdom. After violating multiple ordinances of the ruling lords, Gaveston was condemned to death and beheaded on the property of the Earl of Lancaster. When Edward found out what had happened, he was both utterly despondent and filled with the desire for revenge.

There's no way to know if Drayton shared his poem telling this grim tale with his pupil or whether Elizabeth read Marlowe's play in her youth. Thirty years would pass before she chose to tell Edward's story herself. It's notable that at this particular moment in her life—just after she'd announced her conversion and separated from her husband—she became interested in the tragically flawed medieval king; the subject fit more obviously with her secular plays from the early 1600s than with the religious questions that had come to preoccupy her twenty years later. But what's striking—and timely—about Elizabeth's *History of the Life, Reign and Death of Edward II* is its implicit critique of her king, Charles, as well as of his father. Edward's promotion of his male favorites clearly resonated with Charles's extreme dependence on George Villiers, Duke of Buckingham, as his most trusted adviser; the widespread belief that Buckingham had been King James's lover made the comparisons all the more powerful. When in a long aside in the *History* Elizabeth breaks out of her narrative to caution anyone who enjoys a "fair and large room in the royal affections" not to count blindly on the king's protection, her awareness of the parallels between the circumstances in the fourteenth and seventeenth centuries becomes indisputable. "Let him then that out of his master's love, more than his own desert, hath made himself a fortune be precisely careful," she warns, "that by his disorder he endanger not the stair and prop of his preferment."

It's possible Elizabeth never published her work because of its potential offense to both Charles and Buckingham, who was himself an important figure in her life. Not only was he her husband's chief patron in Ireland, but the women in his immediate family—his mother, wife, and sister—were also among Elizabeth's strongest allies when she announced her conversion (all three ultimately converted to Catholicism themselves). Nothing in Elizabeth's "Preface to the Reader," moreover, suggested she hoped the book would appear in print: she described it as a private exercise to occupy her mind at a difficult time. Just as Mariam might have helped Elizabeth think through the possible limits of wifely obedience early in her marriage, Edward's aggrieved wife, Isabella, may well have spoken to Elizabeth's experience in the aftermath of her separation from Henry. Given how prominent a role Isabella played in Edward's history, it's possible that Elizabeth's fascination with the story began not with the king, but with his queen.

As with Elizabeth's own marriage to Henry, the match between Edward and Isabella was made with complete indifference to the spouses' feelings. In this case, the twenty-three-year-old king was married off to the twelve-year-old French princess in a futile effort to wrest him from Gaveston. In the words of a contemporary chronicle, Edward "immediately felt such love for [Gaveston] that he entered into a covenant of constancy, and bound himself with him before all other mortals with a bond of indissoluble love, firmly drawn up and fastened with a knot." The use of sacramental language— "covenant of constancy," "bond of indissoluble love"—is certainly not accidental: Edward and Gaveston were effectively pledged in a marriage of their own. Edward even sent Isabella's father Philippe IV's wedding gifts to Gaveston before he and his bride returned to England from the wedding. Despite all of this, the union was functional enough to produce an heir: the future Edward III was born in November 1312, a few months after Gaveston's brutal murder. Over the course of the next decade, three more children—John in 1316, Eleanor in 1318, and Joan in 1321—would follow.

In Elizabeth's version of the story, Isabella hoped that Gaveston's death would bring Edward closer to her, and she took very hard his withdrawal into "his melancholy chamber" where he "ma[de] himself a recluse from the daylight." "The lovely queen," Elizabeth declares, "is truly pensive at [the king's] strange distraction, which seemed without the hope of reconcilement." When Edward's sorrow finally lifted, he turned not to Isabella, but instead to a new male favorite, Hugh Despenser the younger (whom Elizabeth, following Marlowe, called simply "Spencer"). At this point the queen, who "had no great cause to like those sirens that caused her grief, and did seduce her husband," seems to have given up hope: she recognized she was destined to be only "in name a wife, in truth a handmaid."

Isabella's behavior now strayed from the clearly virtuous path into muddier waters, although Elizabeth stressed that she was, as King Lear says of himself, "more sinned against than sinning." Fully ignored by her husband, who was not only "a stranger to her bed" but actively "revel[ed] in the wanton embraces of his stolen pleasures, without a glance on her deserving beauty," the queen began to look for love elsewhere:

[Edward's] contempt had begot a like change in her, though in a more modest nature, her youthful affections wanting a fit subject to work on, and being debarred of that warmth that should have still preserved their temper, she had cast her wandering eye upon the gallant Mortimer, a piece of masculine bravery without exception.

Isabella entered into a secret correspondence with her soon-to-be lover and agreed to flee with him and her eldest son, Edward, to France, where her brother had taken the throne as Charles IV. (Isabella's other children remained in England in the care of servants.) Upon reaching the royal palace in Paris—the "sanctuary of her hopes" and her "dearest refuge"—and receiving her brother's warm welcome, she delivers a rhetorically powerful speech that shows off Elizabeth's earlier gifts as a playwright. "Behold in me (dear Sir) your most unhappy sister," Isabella declares, "the true picture of a dejected greatness, that bears the grief of a despised wedlock, which makes me fly to you for help and succor." "I have," she exclaims, "with a sufferance beyond the belief of my sex, outrun a world of trials: time lessens not, but adds to my afflictions; my burden is grown greater than my patience." After describing the hardships she'd endured, she makes a final plea for Charles to intervene on her behalf, warning: "let not succeeding ages in your story read such a taint, that you forsook a sister, a sister justly grieved, that sought your succor." Behind the words of her heroine we might hear Elizabeth's own cry for help, although she had no one nearly so important as the king of France to listen.

In the final episodes of this history, Isabella and Mortimer—with a small army of around a thousand men—invaded England, where they were met with little resistance; Edward and Spencer fled to Wales, where they were soon taken into custody. Elizabeth dwelled at length on Isabella's cruelty toward Spencer, which she judged excessive. The queen treated him, she observes, with "a kind of insulting tyranny, far short of the belief of her former virtue and goodness." She went out of her way, however, to exculpate Isabella from any responsibility for Edward's subsequent murder, laying the blame squarely on Mortimer.

As recounted in the sixteenth-century historian Raphael Holinshed's *Chronicles of England, Scotland, and Ireland*—the primary source for Marlowe's play, and a work Elizabeth almost certainly relied on—the king was sleeping quietly in his bedchamber at Berkeley Castle when a group of assassins entered the room, pressed him down "with heavy featherbeds or a table," and then began their dirty work:

> [they] put into his fundament [i.e., his anus] a horn, and through the same they thrust up into his body a hot spit, or . . . through the pipe of a trumpet a plumber's instrument of iron made very hot, the which passing up into his entrails, and being rolled to and fro, burnt the same, but so as no appearance of any wound or hurt outwardly might once be perceived.

Elizabeth spared her readers all details of the violent act, instead simply stating that "the historians of these times differ both in the time, place, and manner of his death, yet all agree that he was foully and inhumanly murdered." Unlike Holinshed and Marlowe, however, who described Isabella as an accomplice to Mortimer, Elizabeth made a subtle legal distinction: she judged the queen "guilty but in circumstance, and but an accessory to the intention, not the fact." In her version, after Mortimer announces that "Edward must die," Isabella begs him to proceed no further with his treacherous plan: "Let us resolve (dear friend)," she pleads, "to run all hazards rather than this that is so foul and cruel; let us not stain our souls with royal blood and murder." After the deed was done, Elizabeth tried to conjure up how Isabella must have felt: the queen "tasted with a bitter time of repentance what it was but to be quoted in the margin of such a story."

"But to be quoted in the margin": what better description could there be of women's role in history? To move even a few of these figures from the periphery to the center—to focus on Mariam and Isabella, not Herod and Edward—is one way to understand the choices Elizabeth made over the course of her career. Something similar could be said of Aemilia Lanyer, who put Pontius Pilate's wife at the heart of her retelling of Christ's crucifixion, or Anne Clifford, who pulled from the archives female ancestors like Isabella de Veteripont, whose contributions to her family's wealth and power had been overlooked for centuries. Until history could be rewritten by women, these figures were relegated to the margins.

After finishing the *History of the Life, Reign and Death of Edward II,* Elizabeth was exhausted. "My weary pen," she proclaimed on the book's last page, "doth now desire a respite." If the date—February 20, 1627—scribbled next to her name at the bottom of the "Author's Preface" is correct, she had no rest in sight. By 1628, relations between Elizabeth and Henry had reached a new level of hostility, and as he had done before, Henry appealed to no lesser authority than the king. In a letter to Charles dated January 14, he laid out the risks Elizabeth posed in the broadest possible terms. "The universal toleration of religion in this kingdom," he began, "now and too long enjoys [free rein] without control or distinction; being become intolerably dangerous [it] ought for safety sake to be presently interrupted."

Five months later, Henry formally requested that Charles forbid Elizabeth to come within ten miles of London or the court before he would pay the requested allowance, describing the precaution as protecting both himself and Charles, whom he imagined as suffering "from the clamorous trouble of her importunities." Henry hadn't invented the idea of keeping Elizabeth, as a practicing Catholic, out of the city: in 1610, James had issued a proclamation banning Catholic recusants from London and the court unless they obtained a special license. Whatever the risk posed by Catholics at court might have been under James, it was greatly increased under Charles, whose wife, Henrietta Maria, did nothing to hide her faith. Elizabeth's decision to convert was part of an urgent national crisis: it was the religious equivalent of the plague.

At this point Elizabeth made another bold—and in many respects, imprudent—decision. Far from keeping a low profile, she decided to blazon her Catholicism to the world in the only way that she, as a woman and writer, could do. She took on the translation of a Catholic book written a decade earlier by a cardinal in France, whose central purpose was to refute religious claims made by King James. The 1618 treatise by Jacques du Perron bore the unpromising title *A Reply of the most illustrious Cardinal of Perron to the answer of the King of Great Britain,* and contained a long exposition of the differences between Protestants and Catholics. Elizabeth's translation, like her history of Edward II, was a direct provocation to Charles, whose realm had been beset from the start with tensions over his unapologetically Catholic queen, who had direct ties to Perron (he was the uncle of her personal almoner).

Elizabeth apparently completed her translation of the 464-page tome in a mere thirty days. "One woman, in one month, so large a book / In such a full emphatic style to turn," declares the anonymous author of a poem included in the book's prefatory pages. A second poem, addressed "To the most noble translator," describes the astonishing feat as a source for men's jealousy:

> But that a woman's hand alone should raise
> So vast a monument in thirty days
> Breeds envy and amazement in our sex.

Once the manuscript was done, it was sent off either by Elizabeth or by one of her Catholic friends to be printed in the northern city of Douai in France. Home to the English College for Catholic priests and a lively community of Catholic exiles from the British Isles, Douai was a publishing center for books that would never have made it past the English censors.

In London, all English books had to be approved by ecclesiastical or civil authorities and then licensed by the Stationers' Company before they could legally be printed. Works deemed seditious or in any way contrary to the king or church were produced only illegally; if discovered, they were confiscated (this was Queen Elizabeth's usual preference) or, more often under James and Charles, publicly burned. Among many other examples, in 1613 a treatise by the Jesuit theologian Francisco Suárez refuting James's right to demand obedience from his Catholic subjects was thrown on the pyre before a large audience at St. Paul's Cross. Only a "good number" of the books—and not all available copies—were destroyed, suggesting that James was more interested in sending a political message than he was in the risk of Suárez's book finding readers. That the treatise was written in Latin clearly minimized the risk, since only a very small percentage of the population would have been able to read the book, whereas everyone could understand from the fiery spectacle at St. Paul's that attacks on the monarchy were not to be tolerated.

Elizabeth's name didn't appear on the *Reply*'s title page—a small gesture of self-protection—but for those in her circle, her identity as the translator would have been reasonably easy to guess. In two separate letters included in the prefatory materials, she described her aims for the book in ways that revealed her gender, her faith, and her ambition. The first of the letters was addressed "To the Majesty of Henrietta Maria of Bourbon, Queen of Great Britain," whose title was printed in a conspicuously large font at the top of the page. (As her publisher in Douai no doubt understood, the best hope for the book's successful circulation in England would be the support of the kingdom's most prominent Catholic.) In the body of the letter, Elizabeth drew out the multiple reasons why Henrietta Maria should champion her work. As a "daughter of France," the queen deserved to possess the writing of so prominent a theologian, who had been "an ornament of your country." Next, as Charles's wife, the queen was "fittest to receive [the book] for him" who deserves "the inheritance of this work" written for his own father (no matter that James was Perron's target of attack).

Above all, it was Henrietta Maria's identity as a woman that made her the perfect dedicatee:

> And for the honor of my sex, let me say it, you are a woman, though far above other women, therefore fittest to protect a woman's work, if a plain translation wherein there is nothing aimed at but rightly to express the author's intention may be called a work.

In a spirit similar to Aemilia Lanyer's dedications in *Salve Deus,* Elizabeth fantasized about a world in which women would support one another in their intellectual endeavors. However elevated her status, the queen was "fittest to protect a woman's work" simply by virtue of her sex. This was more of a wish than a recognition of anything Henrietta Maria had done: she would become a great patron of music and art, but she wasn't particularly engaged in defenses of women.

Elizabeth's second prefatory letter was addressed "To the Reader," and its aim was to justify her purpose in doing the translation in the first place. "To look for glory from translation is beneath my intention," she professed, adding, "If I had aimed at that, I would not have chosen so late [i.e., recent] a writer." Translating Virgil or Livy would no doubt have brought her more recognition, but her purpose was otherwise: "I desire to have no more guessed at of me, but that I am a Catholic, and a Woman." This is how Elizabeth wanted to be known—not, for example, as a writer or scholar—and she explained the significance she attached to each of the two roles. "The first," she declared, "serves for mine honor, and the second, for my excuse, since if the work be but meanly done, it is no wonder, for my sex can raise no great expectations of anything that shall come from me."

The insult to her sex is hard to take too seriously: like so many women writers, Elizabeth tried to minimize her talent by asserting her natural inferiority. Once these disclaimers were out of the way, she contradicted herself by emphasizing the quality of her work: "Therefore will I confess, I think it well done," even if "it hath been four times as long in transcribing [i.e., preparing the manuscript for print] as it was in translating." The letter concluded with an unusually frank declaration—for a male or female writer—of her desire to see the book in print:

> I will not make use of that worn out form of saying I printed it against my will, moved by the importunity of friends: I was moved to it by my belief that it might make those English that understand not French, whereof there are many, even in our universities, read Perron.

Elizabeth was announcing herself to the world as a Catholic proselytizer.

No sooner did the heavy, folio-size tomes arrive on English shores than they were seized by the church authorities. George Abbot, the Calvinist archbishop of Canterbury, ordered all copies of the *Reply* to be burned. There's no record of a public burning or of any punishment doled out to Elizabeth—and her daughters, always interested in Elizabeth's saintly sacrifices, were unlikely to omit from their memoir any events of the kind. But wherever the books were destroyed (probably at a smaller venue than St. Paul's, like the Stationers' Hall or the archbishop's palace)—only a "few copies came to [Elizabeth's] hands."

Four years after her public conversion to a forbidden faith, Elizabeth had risked alienating the king and his councilors by publishing a work deemed too dangerous to circulate on English soil. It's hard to know whether she was simply indifferent to her reputation or so fired up with religious fervor that she threw all caution to the wind. The opening lines of *The Tragedy of Mariam,* in which Mariam berates herself for speaking too rashly with a "public voice," come to mind: like her heroine, Elizabeth had ventured very far from the prescribed silence that obedient wives were supposed to maintain. While concealed behind the words of a French cardinal, she had criticized the English Church and her former king.

Around thirty copies of Elizabeth's *Reply* have survived, including one donated to the Bodleian Library at Oxford by Elizabeth's friend James Clayton. A fellow Catholic, Clayton had lent Elizabeth money when she was first cut off from her husband's support following her conversion—in a record of her debts submitted to the Privy Council in 1627, he's listed as being owed £30. According to *The Lady Falkland,* he was also the author of at least one of the anonymous poems in the *Reply* that expressed amazement at Elizabeth's speed in doing the translation. Clayton's copy of the book was given to the Bodleian in 1635, and his name and details of the gift are neatly inscribed in Latin on the inside cover. Given that this was the only volume in his name bequeathed to the library—he wasn't, in other words, the donor of a large collection— it's tempting to think he was trying to preserve the banned book for posterity.

Of the other surviving books, six were so-called presentation copies prepared by Elizabeth or someone working alongside her as gifts for special recipients. All six have careful and nearly identical handwritten corrections scattered throughout the pages, and they all accordingly lack the "Admonition to the Reader" found in the other copies. There, the publisher apologized for the book's many typographical errors, blaming them on "the printers being Walloons [Belgians], and our English strange unto them it was incredible to see how many faults they committed in setting." In four of the presentation copies, there are several additional pages, containing an anonymous sonnet addressed "To the Queen's Most Excellent Majesty" written out in a beautiful hand and a copy of an engraved portrait of Perron with verses of praise below it. These pages are smaller than the ordinary folio pages used in the rest of the book, indicating they were "tipped in" between the title page and the printed dedication to Henrietta Maria.

Unlike Aemilia's presentation copies of *Salve Deus,* which were prepared in the printing shop—hence the adjustments in what was included were made before the books were bound—the changes to the *Reply* were done after the books had been printed, giving them the look of something handmade. Considering how small Elizabeth's household was at the time the book was printed (she had only her maid Besse with her), it's unlikely the carefully written corrections and pasting in of the pages were done in her new home. She must have found someone—the secretary of one of her Catholic friends, perhaps—to do this work for her.

In April 1630, with the *Reply* either fresh off the press or about to appear in print, Elizabeth might have chosen to keep a low profile. Instead, she continued to rail against her husband's treatment of her, submitting a second formal petition to the Privy Council to request that Henry pay "such debts as have grown due for necessaries since the taking of her children from her, and treating her as a loving husband ought to do and treat his wife." Henry, hardly interested in behaving as a "loving husband" to his disobedient wife, remained unwilling to budge, forcing King Charles—who continued to show kindness to Elizabeth despite her polemical activities—to instruct his councilors that some of the money budgeted for Henry in Ireland be used to cover Elizabeth's allowance (the Renaissance equivalent of alimony).

By this time Henry was in fact back in London, having been recalled from Dublin after being accused of helping to falsify testimony against a powerful Irish clan, the O'Byrnes of Wicklow. This turned out to be just the tip of the iceberg: Henry had been implicated in one despicable scheme after another to appropriate Irish lands from their owners in order to create profitable estates for English lords. Among the most egregious examples, he had helped to seize 11,000 acres of fertile land for Buckingham, who regarded Ireland as his own private territory to be exploited as much as possible. To cover his enormous debts and keep up his extravagant lifestyle, Buckingham had taken to all sorts of illegal activity, including the creation (and sale) of Irish titles. After Buckingham was brought up on impeachment charges in 1626—he was accused, among other things, of selling offices and honors, delivering English ships into French hands, handing over positions and titles to family members, and even poisoning his beloved King James—Charles chose to dissolve Parliament rather than see his most trusted adviser publicly punished. But in the summer of 1628 Buckingham was murdered by a disgruntled soldier, who took it upon himself to act for the good of the nation after "reading the remonstrance of the house of Parliament."

With the assassination of Buckingham, Henry lost his greatest advocate at court. When he returned from Ireland, he was left on his own to fight two different legal battles. First, he launched a counterattack in the Star Chamber—the court made up of privy councilors and judges free from all restrictions of common law—to keep his job as lord deputy in Ireland. Second, he sought to defend himself against the Privy Council's demands that he pay Elizabeth her allowance. The Star Chamber case took a year or so to resolve, and it ended with his losing his job. In his marital dispute, Henry had more success, or at least he managed to continue his pattern of evasion: evidence shows Elizabeth never received any payments from him.

In addition to his charges of Elizabeth's disobedience by virtue of her religious conversion, Henry also made the more practical claim that she grossly exaggerated her needs. All the wealth of "an Indies," he quipped, "will no more suffice her vanity than the meanest limited portion." Whether there was any truth to this is hard to judge, but in 1631 a woman named Margaret Williams who was boarding Elizabeth's horses in London filed her own petition to the Privy Council, testifying that "the charges of all her horses amounted to thirteen pounds, whereof [Lady Falkland] paid your petitioner five pounds promising from time to time to pay the rest, which she the said Lady hath not done, to the utter undoing of your poor petitioner." If Elizabeth wasn't able to muster the £8 she owed for her horses, it seems unlikely she was faking her poverty.

On September 20, 1633, Henry was hunting with the king at

Theobalds Park in Hertfordshire when he fell off a tree stand and broke his leg. A botched procedure to reset the bone led to gangrene, which began to spread so quickly that the surgeons decided his leg needed to be amputated. Elizabeth was called to his side immediately after the accident, and she "stayed with him night and day, watching with him and never putting off her clothes in all the time." According to *The Lady Falkland,* Henry asked her to call a Catholic priest to administer last rites, speaking to her in French so that the Protestant servants wouldn't understand. He bled to death the next day.

There's nothing in Henry's letters or papers to suggest he had any interest in converting: on the contrary, he'd spent much of his career fighting against Catholic worship in Ireland, not to mention in his own household. The only evidence of Henry's Catholic sympathies mentioned in Elizabeth's biography was the sheer fact that a copy of her Perron translation was found in his closet. Based on this, their daughters came up with the idea that the book "might have chiefly inclined him to have a desire of being a Catholic." Henry's copy of the *Reply* has probably survived—the copy that is now at Queen's College, Oxford, has extensive marginal symbols and notes that seem to be in his hand. But anyone looking to find proof of his Catholic fervor from this scribbling will be sorely disappointed: the vast majority of the comments have to do with typographical errors, pointing out sentences that should or shouldn't have been in italics.

There's no record in *The Lady Falkland* of how Elizabeth responded to Henry's death. After nearly thirty years of marriage in which she bore him eleven children, tried her best to accommodate his habits and tastes (if not his religion), lost her inheritance paying for his debts, and was ultimately dragged into a bitter financial struggle to receive even the minimum level of support, it's possible she felt relief as much as sorrow. Her daughters noted only that following his death, Elizabeth became more reclusive than ever before. "She never went to masques nor plays," her daughters related, "not so much as at the court, though she loved them very much especially the last [plays] extremely." She also gave up entirely on making herself presentable: she wore "anything that was cheapest and would last longest" and put away her chopines—a high platform

shoe that came into fashion in Venice in the sixteenth century—
"which she had ever worn, being very low [i.e., short]."

Having now regained the custody of her younger children—she
had four daughters and two young sons at home—Elizabeth's aim
was to bring as many of them as possible into the Catholic fold.
Over her two adult sons, Lucius and Lorenzo, and her fourteen-
year-old daughter, Victoria, who lived at court, she had little sway.
But the rest of the brood remained for the time under her roof, and
she took full advantage. Refusing all invitations to "dine and sup
abroad," she chose instead to "have her children at home at those
times, chiefly because at her table she only hoped to have them hear
of religion." By 1634, she'd succeeded in converting her daughters
Anne, Elizabeth, Lucy, and Mary, and paved the way for the two
little boys, Henry and Patrick.

The conversion of Elizabeth's daughters was enough to raise
alarms once again at the highest level of state. Charles was frequently accused of being too lenient on English Catholics, but he
was only lenient on those who kept their faith to themselves; fines
on practicing Catholics continued to rise throughout the 1630s. The
fact that Henrietta Maria was attracting more and more aristocratic
women to convert to her faith and join her for Mass in her private
chapel at Somerset House no doubt made the conversion of Elizabeth's four daughters more threatening. On July 20, 1634, the new
archbishop of Canterbury, William Laud—who would himself be
accused a few years later of introducing Catholic ceremonies back
into the English Church—sent a letter to the king urging him to
order that the girls be removed from Elizabeth's home. "The greatest thing I fear is that the mother will still be practicing, and do all
she can to hinder [their departure]." Laud therefore also requested
permission to "call the old Lady," whom he described as having a
"dangerous disposition," before the High Commission, the highest
ecclesiastical court in the land.

What Laud didn't know was how much difficulty Elizabeth was
having just keeping her family afloat. Whatever success she had
with religious persuasion didn't extend to her finances: despite using
all possible means to gather more income, even "disfurnish[ing] her
own chamber wholly, even of her very bed, being fain to sleep in a
chair," she found herself at "the last extremity, not being able to find

any way to hold out longer." Not only had she been disinherited by her father, but Henry had also failed to leave her a dowager portion and had taken away her access to her jointure properties. After becoming physically ill with what *The Lady Falkland* described as "grief and apprehension," she ultimately sent her six younger children to live with their older brother Lucius toward the end of 1634. Heir to both his father and grandfather, Sir Lawrence Tanfield, the twenty-five-year-old Lord Falkland was a wealthy young man: his inheritance from Henry's estates alone was valued at £57,000. Following his marriage in 1630 to the penniless Lettice Morrison, Lucius established his household at his grandmother's former home in Great Tew, Oxfordshire (Lady Tanfield had died two years before).

In a life filled with drama, Elizabeth's biography now came to possibly its most unusual episode. During the spring of 1636, in coordination with her already converted daughters, Elizabeth arranged for her sons Patrick and Henry (aged twelve and thirteen, respectively) to sneak away from Lucius's house where they'd been living for the past two years. A crisis had arisen over the boys' education: in an effort to keep them from becoming Catholics, Lucius was "resolved to send them further off, amongst Puritans." To counter this plan, and any other attempts on Lucius's part to keep his brothers within the Protestant faith, Elizabeth was plotting to send them across the Channel to a Catholic seminary. In a striking display of the cunning Henry had accused her of possessing, she commissioned two lowly servants—total strangers to the boys—to take them from Lucius's home in Great Tew to Abingdon, fifteen miles away, where they were to be met by a "gentleman that had served her (who was very young) with a pair of rowers to be brought from thence to London by water, a thing unusual enough." To avoid raising suspicion, the group traveled "at dark night, with watermen not only not able to row, but ready every minute to overturn the boat with reeling and nodding."

Patrick and Henry were fully complicit in the plot: together with their sisters they "kept all very secret" as they packed their things and made up a plan to leave very early in the morning. As related in *The Lady Falkland*, "the children's desire to go was so great that it gave them not leave to oversleep, but rising at three . . . went to call their sisters." Once the boys reached London, Elizabeth moved them from place to place in a game of cat and mouse while the authorities, informed of the kidnapping by Lucius's wife, Lettice, desperately tried to find them. Lucius didn't have legal custody of his brothers—they were living with him by Elizabeth's consent. In this respect, the law was on her side. But the threat of her sending the boys to a seminary in France was enough to get the attention of the Privy Council.

On May 16, 1636, Elizabeth was brought before the King's Bench, the highest common law court in the kingdom. Despite being subjected to a harsh interrogation by the chief justice, Sir John Bramston, she remained unshakable. She even perjured herself by claiming she didn't know "what [had] become of her two sons" and had no idea "whether they be in England or out of England beyond the sea." Nine days later, she was summoned to the Star Chamber—the same court that had heard Henry's case regarding his removal from Ireland five years earlier. There, under examination by a panel of fourteen men including Archbishop Laud, she was accused of "sending over into foreign parts two of her sons, without license to be educated there (as is conceived) in the Romish religion."

Not only did Elizabeth refuse to cooperate with the court, but according to her daughters' detailed account, she brazenly challenged the legal basis of the judges' charge against her. Even if she had sent the boys to France, which in fact she hadn't yet done, she argued it would have been up to the officers at the port to check for their licenses to travel, but not up to her to obtain them. Irate, one of the lawyers asked whether "she meant to teach them law." She responded that they shouldn't fail to "remember what she made no question they knew before, and that she being a lawyer's daughter was not wholly ignorant of." Her hours spent as a child in Lawrence's courtroom—the closest thing to a legal education a woman could have—had paid off.

It's hard to know how Elizabeth found the courage to defy the leading jurists and bishops of the era. Like Anne Clifford, who had stood up to James and his courtiers twenty years earlier when they pressured her to sign the King's Award, Elizabeth was one of those rare women who refused to bow to male authority when it came to defending what mattered to her most. It's probably not a coincidence that both women took solace, and found strength, in their writing: whether in diaries, religious treatises, or political histories, Anne and Elizabeth had found a means to protest the world around them and had meaningfully honed their gifts of self-expression. The act of writing itself had in turn empowered them to speak, however dangerously.

When Elizabeth's protesting left the page and entered the courtroom, however, she found herself in real trouble. Accused of withholding information, she was sent back to the King's Bench for re-examination by the chief justice three days later and warned that any further "subterfuge or evasion" would lead her to be "committed prisoner to the Tower." At this point she conceded a bit, providing the names of the two servants who had taken the boys from Lucius—Henry Axley and George Spurrier—and declaring that her sons were now in France, "but in what part of France she knoweth not." (In fact, they were still in London.) When pressed to reveal "by whom her said sons were conveyed thither," she didn't respond.

Elizabeth's answers this time were sufficient to keep her out of prison, while Axley and Spurrier were taken to the Tower for two days. Meanwhile, after three weeks of hiding the boys in London, Elizabeth received welcome news: Francis Tresham, an English Benedictine monk in Douai, had raised the money for Patrick and Henry to travel first to Rouen and then on to Paris, where they would be placed at the Benedictine priory in that city. All of these moves were made possible by the network of English Benedictine monasteries cropping up on the Continent, justifiably raising fears in England of secret alliances between Catholics at home and abroad. For the boys' maintenance at the monastery, Elizabeth received a gift from none other than the queen.

Elizabeth's four converted daughters made their way to France a few years after their brothers. There are surprisingly no details in *The Lady Falkland* as to how they got there or who paid their way. But in August 1638 Mary and Lucy were "professed" at Our Lady of Consolation, Cambrai, as Dame Maria and Dame Magdalena, respectively; their sister Elizabeth joined them, as Dame Elizabetha, two months later, and Anne came the following March, becoming Dame Clementia. In a 1637 exchange of letters written in Italian between the pope's secretary, Antonio Ferragalli, and the

English papal emissary, George Con, the two men nervously discussed Elizabeth's own plan to travel to the Continent: she wanted to make a pilgrimage to Rome. Ferragalli described Elizabeth as *"lunatica"* (crazy or unstable), and as having *"poco cervello"* (little brain, i.e., lacking in her head). Con promised to do his best to "oppose her plan" and protect Ferragalli and his colleagues from *"ogni molestia"* (any harm).

It's hard to understand Con's reaction to Elizabeth's desire to come to Rome, especially since she had earned a strong reputation as a learned and committed Catholic. Indeed, in a 1636 report to the Vatican, Con had referred to her as "she who has translated into English the works of Cardinal Perron"; five years later, the English Benedictine monk David Codner would send a letter to Cardinal Barberini (the grand inquisitor of the Roman Inquisition) in which he acknowledged that in addition to the enormous sacrifices Elizabeth had made to bring her children into the Catholic fold, she had an "intellect far above other women" as shown in her "most erudite" translation of Perron's *Reply*. It's not clear, therefore, what harm Ferragalli and Con feared that Elizabeth might cause, although Con suggested that her desire to travel to Rome "was born out of her poverty." There's no further mention of the trip in any of the surviving documents, so he must have been successful in calling it off. Elizabeth's only recorded pilgrimages were to local English shrines.

The last few years of Elizabeth's life were her quietest. After a period of conflict over her younger children, her conversion, and her constant need for money, she and her eldest son finally made peace. Lucius had in fact been supporting Elizabeth since his father's death: as he detailed in a December 1636 letter to the Privy Council, he had been giving her an annual allowance of £150, "not to speak of accidental additions, which have not been so small." He was also finalizing arrangements for her to receive "the better part of fifteen hundred pounds" from Aldenham, one of her jointure properties, but he explained he thought it best not to share this news with her: "my mother having no over-frugal disposition (which is the most that it will be fit for me to say of any expense of hers) a little which she expects now will more help her, than much more which, she knowing, would intend to spend." His account of Elizabeth's prodigality wasn't far from her husband's.

Elizabeth's daughters saw it otherwise. From their perspective, the only luxury that interested their mother was the freedom to spend her time "writing and reading." This, they claimed, was "her whole employment." The intellectual project she immersed herself in was likewise tied to her withdrawal from worldly concerns: she was translating some of the Latin writings of Ludovicus Blosius, a sixteenth-century Flemish monk and mystic. It's not clear how strong her Latin was at this point—as a girl, we might recall, she had translated Seneca's *Epistles*—but her daughters reported that she had a Spanish translation of Blosius's text at her side for occasional consultation. Ever a lover of foreign tongues, she also apparently began to study Hebrew. Our final image of Elizabeth is of a stout if not obese woman in her mid-fifties living alone, wearing comfortable shoes, and fully immersed in her books. Despite her having been the mother of eleven children and the wife of an ambitious courtier, it's hard not to think she would have been happier as a cloistered nun.

Elizabeth died on October 19, 1639, from "consumption," a catchall term for any number of diseases that wasted away the body but most often meant tuberculosis. She was fifty-four or fifty-five years old. In death, she received her last favor from the queen, who seems to have arranged both for Elizabeth's funeral at Somerset House in her private chapel, and for her burial most likely in the cemetery adjacent to the chapel (both the chapel and the cemetery were destroyed during the Civil War, so there's no way to know for sure). According to *The Lady Falkland*, Elizabeth's last rites were administered by a Benedictine monk, and the funeral was performed by the Capuchin friars who maintained the queen's chapel. Everything was as Catholic as it could possibly be.

As her daughters saw it, Elizabeth died just in time. In December 1640, Archbishop Laud was impeached by Parliament for high treason. Among the many charges against him, the most damning was that he sought to introduce papist ceremonies into England with the aim of reconciling the English Church to Rome. A full-scale rebellion, meanwhile, had been raging for several years in Scotland over the king's decision to impose what he regarded as religious reforms on the Scottish "kirk." Unlike Ireland, where Elizabeth had found a very active if illegal world of Catholic worship, Scotland had taken a hard Calvinist path since the early days of the Reformation; by the 1630s the Presbyterian Scots were refusing to recognize the episcopal hierarchy, the Book of Common Prayer, and the religious "articles" of the English Church, let alone tolerate Roman Catholics. The Scottish "Covenanters" (joined in a covenant against the king) raised a significant army that included foreign mercenaries as well as local troops.

In July 1640, Charles made what turned out to be a catastrophic decision to invade his northern kingdom. The insufficiency of his troops became quickly apparent, and he was forced to call Parliament to raise money. This was the second time he'd called Parliament in less than a year, after a period of eleven years, from 1629 to 1640, known as the Personal Rule (or the "Eleven-Year Tyranny," depending on whose side you were on), in which Parliament never met at all. During that time, resentment over Charles's seemingly tyrannical rule rose exponentially, with particular outrage over his use of antiquated laws to raise ship money: invoking a medieval statute requiring coastal counties to provide ships to the Crown, he had created a new tax to be paid by all counties, coastal and inland. Once the so-called Long Parliament was convened, his position became immensely fragile.

By the spring of 1641, a powerful new leader pushing for religious liberty had arisen among the parliamentarians. A man from a modest background with an enormous talent for shaping both politics and war, Oliver Cromwell began attacking the king on every imaginable front. Charles tried to fight back: he charged six different members of Parliament (but not Cromwell) with treason, he authorized more than 450 pamphlets and broadsheets in defense of his reign, and he traveled around the north and the west midlands—the regions of the country most loyal to him—delivering speeches against Parliament. But he soon recognized there was no hope of a peaceful resolution in his favor. On August 22, 1642, the king raised his standard at Nottingham, and the country plunged into civil war.

In this political and religious chaos, the private civil war Elizabeth had experienced in her own household was now being played out on a national scale, with tragic consequences. As her daughters imagined it, had she still been alive she would have suffered "the most insupportable affliction she ever had, in the death of her two sons (killed in the wars) without any sign of hope." Lorenzo Cary was killed early in 1642 at the Battle of Swords outside of Dublin following a full-scale revolt in Ireland known as the Great Rebellion. The following year Lucius met his death at the Battle of Newbury in Berkshire, England. Both men were fighting for the king, although at least in Lucius's case without real conviction. Telling his friends before the battle he was "weary of the times, and foresaw much misery to his own country," he volunteered to serve in the front line of combat and rode his horse directly into enemy fire, effectively committing suicide. In the margins of *The Lady Falkland,* Elizabeth's daughter Mary noted, "God be thanked there is great hopes they both died Catholics," but there's no evidence to support this in either case.

Far from the battles being fought across the Channel, Mary and her sisters took up their pens at their convent in Cambrai to write their mother's life. In the monastic library, they would have found volumes on the lives of female saints as well as the books written by their own spiritual director, Father Augustine Baker, about two contemporary Englishwomen, Dame Gertrude More and Dame Margaret Gascoigne. During meals they would have listened to the Catholic martyrology—the official record of martyrs and saints arranged according to the calendar—read aloud on a daily basis. Surrounded as they were by the celebration of holy women, they must have been inspired to tell their own mother's story.

For around two hundred years, the manuscript of *The Lady Falkland* sat untouched in an archive in Lille, France. It was discovered in the 1850s when a writer for *The Rambler,* a Catholic monthly founded by liberal converts, was searching for documents related to English Catholicism in the sixteenth and seventeenth centuries. The London publisher that brought out the first edition of *The Lady Falkland* in 1861 combined it with a short biography of Francis Slingsby, an Englishman who became a Jesuit priest in the 1630s. For Catholic Publishing & Bookselling, Elizabeth was worthy of interest as a heroic religious figure, not as a pioneer in women's writing. Modern readers of *The Lady Falkland,* however, could hardly overlook her accomplishments as a playwright, historian, and translator, who left behind both her husband and her place in society to pursue the life she most desired. In *The Tragedy of Mariam,* Elizabeth put these words in the mouth of the daring Salome:

> *Why should such privilege to man be given?*
> *Or given to them, why barred from women then?*
> *Are men than we in greater grace with Heaven?*

Elizabeth's tombstone hasn't survived, but it's hard to imagine a better epitaph.

CHAPTER FOURTEEN

December 11, 1643

Baynard's Castle, London

Anne Clifford

After waiting thirty-eight years, two months, and thirteen days, Anne Clifford finally inherited her father's estates in the north of England. The long-anticipated day came with less of a bang than a whimper. According to the King's Award negotiated between her first husband, Richard Sackville, and James I in 1617, Anne's uncle Francis Clifford was to keep the Westmorland and Craven lands in his family line provided there were direct male heirs. Should no male heirs materialize, the lands would revert to Anne. When Francis died in 1641 at the age of eighty-one, he left behind his only son, Henry, who had only daughters (two sons had died in infancy). Henry's wife, Lady Frances Cecil, was by this time in her late forties, so the chances of her bearing another child were extremely slim. The fifty-three-year-old Anne knew her triumph was imminent: she was about to become one of the greatest landowners in the kingdom.

In December 1643, Henry died unexpectedly of a high fever. Although his death wasn't caused directly by the Civil War, the conflict had taken an enormous toll on his well-being. A staunch royalist, Henry was given command in 1639 of the king's troops in Cumberland and Westmorland; he was also appointed governor of Newcastle and tasked with raising cavalry troops and preparing the king's defenses there. It turned out he was neither a talented soldier nor a gifted military strategist, and after relying too heavily on his officers he ended up putting the whole area at risk. Henry retired to Skipton Castle at the end of 1642 in a state of frustration if not shame for his poor performance; he was forced to leave his home the following spring when the royalist army was defeated in nearby Lancashire. His last days were spent around forty miles from Skipton at his friend Sir William Robinson's house in York, where he died at the age of fifty-one.

News of Henry's death took a few days to reach Anne, who was living alone with her younger daughter, Isabella Sackville, at Baynard's Castle in London. A large fifteenth-century palace on the Thames that had been the official London residence of four of Henry VIII's wives, it was given in 1551 to William Herbert, first Earl of Pembroke, and it remained in the Herbert family until its destruction in 1666 from the Great Fire of London. Anne's diary from 1643 hasn't survived—all of her diaries from 1620 to 1675 are missing—so we can only imagine the celebrations that must have reverberated through the palace's vast corridors and chambers. When relating the event in her memoir, *The Life of Me,* which covered the years 1590–1649, she kept to the bare facts: "So by the death of this cousin-german [first cousin] of mine, Henry Clifford, Earl of Cumberland, without heirs male, the lands of mine inheritance in Craven and Westmorland reverted unto me without question or controversy."

Left to her own devices, Anne would no doubt have packed up her things immediately and set out for the north. Unfortunately, her hard-earned victory came right in the middle of the first phase of the Civil War, when, as she put it, the fighting was "very hot." The area around Westmorland was in a state of nearly constant warfare, and there was neither a protected route for Anne to travel nor any guarantee of safety once she arrived. Thus, she was stuck for the time being at Baynard's Castle, where her husband, Philip Herbert, Earl of Montgomery and Pembroke, had sent her as a safe haven. For passersby on the street, the castle was entirely hidden by a massive stone wall, with a gatehouse at one end. From Anne's perspective, Philip cared less about her well-being than about the property within the castle walls: "A house full of riches," she commented, it was "the more secured by my lying there."

In addition to Anne's keeping Baynard's Castle under watch, Philip also presumably wanted to keep her away from the north, which was largely a royalist stronghold. Having served Charles as lord chamberlain for many years, Philip had taken the parliamentarians' side after a series of disagreements with the king over religion had led to his losing his post in 1641. A fervent Protestant, he had no patience for Charles's indulgence of the queen's Catholicism, and it was ultimately Henrietta Maria who convinced Charles to push Philip out of his office. Given that Anne's own sympathies were almost certainly with the king—she defended the Church of England to a group of Cromwell's men in the 1650s and spoke admiringly of Charles in her annual chronicles for those years—Philip wouldn't have wanted his wife to form any alliances that could compromise his own position. The result for Anne was a very long stay in London that felt like a house arrest. As she complained in *The Life of Me,* "I continued to lie in my own chamber without removing for another six years and nine months." This, she noted bitterly, "was the longest time that ever I continued to lie in one house in all my life."

Frustrated by her immobility and desperate to mark her new status as the Clifford heiress even at a distance from her lands, Anne made an unusual decision: she commissioned a major work of art. The "Great Picture," as it came to be known, is attributed to the Dutch artist Jan van Belcamp and measures nine feet high and eighteen feet wide. Using a form generally reserved for religious art, the triptych is an unabashed celebration of Anne's personal biography. There is nothing quite like this in all of the painting of the period: aristocrats routinely had group portraits made with living members of their family, as Philip himself did in 1635 (more on this to come). But Anne's idea of creating a set of historical portraits marking crucial moments in her life was completely out of the ordinary. It speaks to her overarching project to ensure that she would be remembered—a project that took on an impressive variety of genres, mediums, and forms in the last decades of her life.

The central panel of the painting shows Anne's parents and her two brothers, both of whom died in early childhood. In her mother's right hand is a book of prayers; with her left hand she gestures at her stomach in a secular version of Piero della Francesca's *Madonna del Parto,* suggesting her pregnancy with Anne. In the long inscription in the upper right corner, Anne explained that the portraits of her four family members were copied from originals done in June 1589, when they were living in Westminster. It was there, she added, that "the said worthy countess conceived with child, the first of May, Ano. Dom. 1589, with her only daughter" (namely, Anne). On the wall behind her mother and brothers are four small, framed portraits of Anne's aunts: Margaret's two sisters, Anne, Countess of Warwick, and Elizabeth, Countess of Bath; and George's sister, Frances, Lady Wharton, and his half sister, Margaret, Countess of Derby. All of her uncles are conspicuously missing, as if the family were exclusively matriarchal. Lining the left and right borders of the panel is an impressive series of thirty-four coats of arms, each with its own inscription; together they supply a long view of the Clifford's dynastic history from the family's mid-twelfth-century ancestors through Anne's two sons-in-law.

Framing the central panel with its display of family history are two portraits of Anne. On the left, she's shown as a sumptuously dressed girl of fifteen, the age she was when her father died and she was officially disinherited. This is the painting that includes her many books with their titles proudly displayed—all presented in English or English translations—as well as other accouterments of an aristocratic childhood. Behind her on the wall are portraits of her childhood tutor Samuel Daniel and her beloved governess, Mrs. Taylor. The inscription on this panel whitewashes the forty years of litigation as if she'd come into inheritance at the time captured in the painting: "This is the picture of the Lady Anne Clifford at fifteen years of age, daughter and sole heir of George Clifford, earl of Cumberland."

The portrait of Anne on the right panel of the triptych depicts her on the other side of her inheritance battle. Almost certainly painted from life, she's seen here as a mature woman wearing a somber black satin dress with a prominent white collar and cuffs; two strands of pearls hang from her neck and another around her waist. Unlike Queen Elizabeth, who chose to depict herself as a young maiden until her dying days, the fifty-six-year-old Anne made no effort to disguise her age. In *The Life of Me,* she recounted the loss of her youthful looks. After a long exposition of her formerly lustrous "brown and very thick" hair, "full cheeks and round face," and "exquisite shape of body," she acknowledged that "time and age hath long since ended those beauties, which are to be compared to the death of the field."

Compounding the severity of the middle-aged portrait is the contrast not only with her own youthful image, where she wears a tightly fitted white dress elaborately embroidered, but also with her mother's rich gown of gold and brown. In her puritanical black, Anne seems at once stern and proud: she stands erect before us, her gaze serene and self-assured as she rests her long, elegant fingers on top of two books placed on the table beside her. The books confirm the seriousness of her occupation: stacked one on top of another are the Holy Bible and Pierre Charron's *Book of Wisdom,* a contemporary work of neo-Stoical philosophy. Behind her are two shelves packed with more books in a state of disarray, as if she'd recently been looking through them and hadn't yet bothered to put them back in place. Under the shelves in the far left side of the painting are framed portraits of her two husbands, treated in effect as if they were both dead (Philip was still living). A white dog nipping at her leg and a black cat sitting at her foot are more prominently shown than either of the two men. The overall impression the portrait gives is of an independent woman content with her place in the world.

Anne commissioned not one, but two copies of her monumental triptych—a fact that confirms her interest in the painting not as a work of art per se, but as a testament to her dynastic victory. She imagined each of her daughters would have her own copy, and that they would display them in the great halls at Appleby and Skipton, respectively. As it happened, she was smart to have two paintings made. What remained intact of the Skipton triptych was destroyed by fire in the nineteenth century, while the Appleby painting hung for centuries in the castle and can be seen today at Abbot Hall in nearby Kendal.

In 1649, Anne's moment to take possession of her father's lands finally came—at the expense, as it were, of the king's head. In her last few years in London, she would have followed the dramatic course of Charles's downfall. After Parliament created a centralized professional army of 22,000 trained soldiers known as the New Model Army, Charles's troops were definitively routed at the Battle of Naseby in June 1645; a series of further defeats in the following months brought the First Civil War to an end. Fearing capture by Cromwell's forces, in early 1646 Charles surrendered to the Scots at Newark. After refusing to agree to the terms of their National Covenant (drawn up in 1638 in opposition to the reforms proposed by the English Church), he was passed from Scottish to English hands. For the better part of two years Charles was held as a prisoner, although his circumstances were far from what we might imagine: he was kept for more than a year at Carisbrooke Castle on the Isle of Wight, where he had his library shipped and spent most of his days absorbed in reading (his heavily annotated copy of Shakespeare from this period has survived).

Giving up all other hope of regaining the throne, Charles ultimately agreed in 1648 to a secret deal with the Scots against the English parliamentarians. Thus began what came to be known as the Second Civil War, but it was short-lived: the Scots proved no match for the New Model Army, which crushed the invading royalist troops in August 1648 at the Battle of Preston. Charles was now given the choice of abdicating the throne in favor of his son or facing trial on charges of tyranny and treason. Imagining there was no way the army would actually go through with its plan to execute him—there was enormous opposition to regicide within Parliament as well as on the Continent—Charles chose to take his chances at trial. What he didn't anticipate was how far his enemies would go to ensure their victory: in December 1648 over half of the members of the House of Commons were purged by Cromwell's ally, Colonel Thomas Pride, for their opposition to the treason charges, leaving in place what came to be known as the Rump Parliament, which was eager to end the British monarchy altogether.

On January 20, 1649, Charles was tried before a specially constituted court at Westminster Hall. On January 27, after refusing to enter a plea, he was convicted. Three days later, on a bitter cold morning, a scaffold was set in front of Inigo Jones's magnificent Banqueting House at Whitehall, where Charles could glimpse on his way to his death the set of paintings on the ceiling that he had himself commissioned from Peter Paul Rubens twenty years earlier. In the central panels he would have seen the triumphant images celebrating his father's peaceful reign.

Before a large crowd divided between supporters and enemies—although those sympathetic to the king seem to have been in the majority—Charles rose to the occasion of his final performance. Wearing two shirts to keep from looking afraid by shivering, he made a short speech declaring his innocence and called himself a "martyr of the people." After forgiving his executioners and saying his final prayers, he gave the signal for the ax to come down. One eyewitness famously remarked that the execution was met with "such a groan as I have never heard before, and desire I may never hear again." Out of fear that his tomb would become a cult site for his loyal followers, the parliamentarians forbade his burial in Westminster Abbey. After his head was sewn back onto his body, Charles's remains were buried inside the castle walls of St. George's Chapel at Windsor.

In Anne's diary entry for January 30, 1676, she recalled the king's execution several decades past: "And this day was twenty-seven years our then King Charles (who was born in Scotland) was beheaded on a scaffold in the open air near the Banqueting House at White-hall and his dead body afterwards buried in the chapel at Windsor in Berkshire." By that time, the English monarchy had long been restored: Charles's son, Charles II, returned to the throne in 1660 after Cromwell's rule as Lord Protector came to an end with his death in 1658, which had been followed by a brief and unsuccessful attempt by his son, Richard, to keep the Protectorate going. Those in Parliament who had signed Charles's death warrant were hanged for treason, as was Cromwell's corpse, which was dug up in 1661 from its grave so that it could be publicly humiliated. The decapitated corpse was then cast in a lime-pit beneath the gallows while Cromwell's embalmed head was impaled on a spike placed outside Westminster Hall. There it remained for several decades until a strong gust of wind supposedly sent the head to the ground, where it was picked up by a guard. (Different versions of this story and the subsequent fate of the head have circulated for centuries.) The new Parliament, meanwhile, confirmed Charles I's self-description as a martyr, and he was subsequently added to the calendar of Anglican saints. By remembering Charles on the anniversary of his violent death, Anne was both displaying her loyalty to her former king and doing her duty as an obedient subject of his son.

When Anne arrived at Skipton Castle in July 1649, however, the king's execution six months earlier was far from her mind. This was the first time she'd been inside the gates of her birthplace "since she was nine or ten weeks old," and she found the castle in terrible shape, having been the site of multiple sieges in recent years. Skipton began the Civil War as a royalist garrison and had then fallen into the hands of the parliamentary army. A royalist uprising—and subsequent defeat—in 1648 had brought on more destruction. Anne claimed that "most of the old castle" had been pulled down; records show its defensive walls were dismantled, its roof stripped of lead, and a good deal of its timber and stone sold to local men for profit. After a stay of three weeks, she moved north to Appleby, which she had always regarded as the jewel in the Clifford crown. That castle, too, had been an active battleground—it had flipped from parliamentarian to royalist and then back to parliamentarian control—and it was in desperate need of repairs. For a period of time, it was even missing its roof. But in recording these first visits, Anne said nothing about her living conditions: what mattered was simply marking her territory. "So the eight[h] day of that August in 1649," she declared, "I came into Appleby Castle the most ancient seat of my inheritance and lay in my own chamber there where I used to lie with my dear mother."

Anne's move to the north coincided with another major change in her circumstances. After falling ill in the spring of 1649, Philip died in London on January 23, 1650 at the age of sixty-five, making Anne a widow for the second time. She was at Appleby when the news reached her, and she chose not to travel to Philip's funeral on February 9 in Salisbury Cathedral, where he was buried in grand style near his brother, William, and his parents, Mary Sidney and Pembroke. In the remaining twenty-six years of Anne's life, she never left the north again.

Looking back at her nearly two decades as Philip's wife, Anne expressed very little tenderness toward her husband, whom she described as "extremely choleric by nature." By all accounts, they had very little in common. According to the seventeenth-century historian John Aubrey, Philip "did not delight in books, or poetry" and spent most of his free time hunting. Anne's secretary George Sedgewick (who earlier worked for Philip) took this one step further, claiming Philip "could scarce either write or read; not that he wanted good breeding and education, but he would never be brought to mind his book, being addicted to all manner of sports and recreations." Sedgewick also noted that Philip was "much given to women."

Despite their obvious differences, the couple seems to have lived harmoniously for the first few years; Anne even bore Philip two sons, though they both died in infancy. By 1634, after four years of marriage, they had effectively separated. Philip lived in grand style at Whitehall Palace, where, as lord chamberlain, he was surrounded by a personal staff of eighty attendants. Anne stayed mostly at the Herberts' palatial home at Wilton, where she could enjoy her deceased mother-in-law Mary Sidney's library and the beautiful landscape conjured up in Mary's brother Philip's romance, *The Countess of Pembroke's Arcadia*. Whatever pleasure she took living in the countryside, however, didn't erase her bitterness about being excluded from Philip's world at court. To come to London, she explained in a letter to her cousin Francis Russell, she needed her husband's permission, "lest he take that occasion to turn me out of his house, as he did out of Whitehall."

Anne's account of the relationship's collapse turned on a fight over her daughter Isabella's marriage. Anne's older daughter, Margaret, had married John Tufton, Earl of Thanet, a year before Anne's marriage to Philip, making the arrangements much easier, as Anne was Margaret's sole guardian at the time. But the question of Isabella's future spouse was one that Philip wanted to negotiate—and benefit from—himself. As part of their own marital agreement, Philip promised Anne that he would raise the substantial sum of £5,000 for Isabella's marriage portion, but his offer came with a catch: he wanted Isabella to marry one of his younger sons. As Anne wrote in *The Life of Me,* she refused to comply, "my daughter being herself extremely averse from that match, though he believed it was in my power to have brought it to pass." Following in her own mother's path, Anne wasn't going to let the men decide whom her daughter should marry. She insisted on Isabella's consent.

Anne won the argument with Philip, and she ultimately arranged for Isabella to marry James Compton, Earl of Northampton. Both of her daughters were thus placed at the highest echelons of the aristocracy—they were both countesses, like their mother and grandmother—and the marriages created useful new ties for Anne. The quarrel with Philip, however, seems to have precipitated if not caused the end of their marriage, even if they remained a united front on paper. Philip continued to support Anne in her ongoing legal disputes, and in 1635 he agreed to make over to her the jointure properties in Kent that he'd given to his first wife, properties that would generate an income of roughly £2,000 a year during Anne's widowhood.

Keeping up appearances for posterity, Philip also included Anne in the magnificent family portrait he commissioned from the great Flemish artist Anthony van Dyck, who painted Philip on multiple occasions and enjoyed his patronage for years. However uninterested Philip may have been in literature, he was known to be a generous patron both to writers and artists. (Shakespeare's First Folio, we might recall, was dedicated to Philip and his brother, William.) At ten feet high and sixteen and a half feet wide, the Herbert family portrait was the largest and most ambitious painting Van Dyck would ever make.

Philip commissioned the portrait in 1634 to celebrate the upcoming marriage of his oldest son, Charles, to Lady Mary Villiers, the immensely wealthy daughter of the Duke of Buckingham, who was murdered in 1628, leaving Mary a stunning dowry of £25,000—the equivalent of around £3.5 million today. (The marriage, which had been arranged in 1626 when Charles was seven and Mary four, lasted less than a year before the fifteen-year-old groom died of smallpox in Florence.) Van Dyck painted Anne seated next to Philip, but her posture and demeanor are jarringly different from the rest of the group: she's wearing the least festive of garments (a plain black dress), her arms are folded in her lap in a gesture of resignation, and her gaze is blank and distracted. It looks as if her portrait may have been inserted after the painting was completed at a different sitting altogether. She was by this time a placeholder for Philip's wife, but nothing more.

With Philip's death in 1650, Anne was for the first time in her life truly free. An immensely wealthy widow with vast estates to manage, she embarked on a new career. To announce her status throughout the lands she now controlled, she began "riding the boundaries," a ritual of visiting each of her inherited estates and meeting with local tenants. She also began a long and costly process of repairs to her castles. When she was warned that if she restored their defenses Cromwell would have them destroyed, she supposedly quipped: "Let him destroy them if he will; as often as he levels them I will rebuild them, so long as he leaves me a shilling in my pocket." As early as 1651, she reported progress on three separate fronts: she was arranging for Brougham Castle to be made "as habitable as I could though it was very ruinous"; she helped "to lay the foundation stone of the middle wall in the great tower of Appleby Castle, called Caesar's Tower"; and she oversaw the "laying of the first foundation stone of my almshouse."

This last project, known as St. Anne's Hospital and located just beyond the outer gates of Appleby Castle, would become Anne's most enduring charitable work. Aimed at providing a home and sustenance for local widows and elderly women, the almshouse was built to accommodate twelve "sisters" and a supervising "mother." The first group Anne installed at St. Anne's between 1652 and 1654 included twelve widows and one maimed woman. On the surviving document only three of the thirteen women were able to sign their names to accept the Orders; the others made an "X" or mark.

According to Edward Rainbow, bishop of Carlisle, Anne immensely enjoyed the women's company, visiting them frequently at the almshouse and also inviting them to dine with her at the castle. "After meat," Rainbow wrote, the grand Dowager Countess of Dorset, Montgomery, and Pembroke could be seen "as freely and familiarly conversing with [the almswomen] in her chamber as if they had been her greatest guests." St. Anne's remains an almshouse today, with Anne and her mother Margaret's coats of arms proudly displayed at the gates. When I visited recently, one of the almswomen kindly brought me to the chapel, where the local vicar comes weekly to conduct services for the all-female residents. Hanging on the walls were framed copies of Anne's Orders, which (with small modifications) are still observed.

The easy relations Anne had with her almswomen were in stark contrast to her dealings with many of her male tenants, who refused to pay her back rents and entry fines—the charges made with a new lord to reaffirm the ties between tenant and lord—when she took control of her lands. "Suits and differences in law," Anne noted in her 1650 memoir, "began to grow hot betwixt my tenants in Westmorland and some of my tenants in Craven and me." These men had no idea whom they were dealing with: hardly a stranger to the English courts, Anne brought the same determination to her local disputes that she had used in her inheritance battle against the highest powers in the realm. To her mind, the stakes were roughly the same. As she explained in a letter to her steward, Christopher Marsh, "if I should be foiled in this suit-in-law between me and my attendants here in Westmorland, I and my posterity should have our fortunes in this country in a manner quite overthrown."

Several long years of litigation followed, with Anne's attempts to eject her tenants repeatedly dismissed in the Chancery courts. (Records of many of these cases, as with Aemilia Lanyer's lawsuits, are kept in the National Archives in London; in Anne's case, the documents are mostly small scraps of paper loosely tied together with string.) However strong a front Anne put up, the lawsuits took a toll on her peace of mind. In a January 1650 letter to her friend Elizabeth Grey, Countess of Kent, she wrote, "If I had not excellent Chaucer's book here to comfort me, I were a pitiful case, having so many troubles as I have here." Throughout every stage of her life— two marriages, seemingly endless litigation, and countless social and political upheavals—literature had remained one of Anne's greatest companions.

In 1656, the tide finally turned in Anne's favor when her case was brought before the Court of Common Pleas. In fact, the panel of judges seems to have been stacked: Anne's cousin Oliver St. John, who was the lord chief justice, and her personal adviser (and sometime lawyer) Matthew Hale were two of the four men hearing the case. In her 1657 memoir, she reported with great satisfaction that several more trials had followed in quick succession "where the verdict passed for me, and was so recorded in court, this being the fourth trial I have had and the fourth verdict I have had against my said tenants at the said common pleas bar in Westminster." Anne ended this entry with a citation of two verses aptly chosen from Psalm 116: "What shall I render unto the Lord for all benefits towards me? / I will take the cup of salvation, and call upon the name of the Lord."

Putting aside the trouble Anne had with her tenants, the experience of being—as she proudly called herself—the High Sheriffess of Westmorland seems to have given her deep satisfaction. "I do more and more fall in love with the contentments and innocent pleasures of a Country Life," she wrote in 1651, expressing her hope that "my posterity that are to succeed me in these places . . . [might] make their own houses the place of self-fruition." That her houses might be "the place of self-fruition" wonderfully captures Anne's aim for her life post-inheritance: her father's lands had been at the core of her identity since his death in 1605, but until she actually possessed the estates, this side of her hadn't had any opportunity to flourish. As she wistfully reflected in *The Life of Me,*

> The marble pillars of Knole in Kent and Wilton in Wiltshire were to me oftentimes but the gay harbors of anguish, insomuch as a wise man that knew the inside of my fortunes would often say that I lived in both these, my Lords' great families, as the river of Rhône or Rhodanus runs through the lake of Geneva, without mingling any part of its streams with that lake.

Knole and Wilton were counted among the greatest houses in the kingdom, but they never touched Anne's soul.

In her annual chronicles for the years 1650–75, Anne recorded her stays at each of her castles in minute detail: the number of days she spent, the room she slept in, the family members and guests she entertained, the amount of time that had passed since her last visit. She also carefully noted her leave-takings when she traveled from one castle to the next, treating these "removals" as formal ceremonies. Local gentry and tenants would assemble to send her off as she and her entourage—her lady's maids sitting with her in her coach, her male servants behind on horseback—rode away from the castle to the accompaniment of musicians and the ringing of bells. A typical journey from Appleby to nearby Brough, for instance, involved a train of forty-eight double carts filled with household goods. In addition to her clothing and jewels, she brought with her wall hangings, linens, kitchen tools, and bulky furniture. The trips were the equivalent of royal progresses, with Anne as the de facto queen.

Anne's relationship to her castles permeated her being so deeply that nearly all of her experiences were refracted through her physical location. When she read a book—and she continued to acquire new books through the final years of her life—she recorded inside its covers exactly where she was when she read it. On the back of the title page in her copy of *The Countess of Pembroke's Arcadia,* for example, Anne scribbled: "This book did I begin to read over at Skipton at Craven about the latter end of January and I made an end of reading it all over in Appleby Castle in Westmorland the 19 day of March following; in 1651." (In several books of hers from before 1650 she inscribed the date of her reading, but interestingly not the location—the latter took on meaning only when it was her own home.)

When Anne learned of major events in the world, she noted where she was when the news reached her: King James's daughter Elizabeth, Queen of Bohemia, died while "I now lying in Brougham Castle in Westmorland"; the fire of London, which raged through the city in the summer of 1666 and left most of it in ruins, took place while "my daughter of Thanet and her three youngest daughters lay here in Skipton Castle with me." The same was true for family news: a great-granddaughter was born while "I [was] lying now in my house or castle of Skipton in Craven"; her daughter Isabella died in 1661 while "I [did] lie in my own chamber in Appleby Castle," although, she added, she did not hear of the death until she moved to Pendragon Castle, "where I lay in the second story that looks east and south." What becomes clear, and oddly compelling, is the absolute lack of separation between her psyche and her estates.

On the one hand, Anne was deeply immersed in her daily life and focused on the present moment. She not only kept track of her reading, her travel, and her activities, but she also carefully oversaw her financial accounts, reviewing all income and expenses in elaborately maintained "books of receipts." On the other hand, Anne's gaze was toward the future as she embarked on the enormous task of securing her legacy. The first order of business was to commemorate her parents. Already in 1617, a year after her mother's death, Anne had erected a beautiful alabaster tomb at Margaret's burial place of St. Lawrence's in Appleby. On top of the tomb is a life-size effigy of Margaret lying supine with her elegant hands clasped together in a posture of prayer; on either side below are inscriptions carved into black marble with details of Margaret's life and piety. In 1654, Anne made a comparably impressive, if very different, monument for her father at his burial place at Holy Trinity Church in Skipton. George's grand tomb, erected in the church sanctuary near the tombs of his grandfather, Henry Clifford, and Anne's brother Francis, is covered on all sides with brightly decorated coats of arms laying out the Cliffords' heraldic history from the twelfth century on. Unlike Margaret's tomb, George's has no effigy gracing its black marble top. Maybe not surprisingly, Anne's emphasis here was on the family lineage, not the man himself.

Around the same time that she commissioned George's tomb, Anne made a second monument to her mother of an entirely unusual kind. Roughly a mile from Brougham Castle on the edge of the road that leads from Appleby to Penrith stands what came to be known as the Countess's Pillar, an octagonal stone shaft topped with a square block and a small pyramid, which measures fourteen feet high. (To get there today, you need to park off the highway on a dead end and walk up an unmarked path; if you didn't know where to look, there would be no chance of stumbling upon it.) On three sides of the block are carved sundials; on the fourth, which can be glimpsed from the road, are the shields of the Clifford and Russell families.

The monument would be completely mysterious were it not for the inscription on the base, which explains that the pillar

> was erected anno 1656 by the R. Honorable Anne Countess Dowager of Pembroke etc. and Daughter & Sole Heir of Right Honorable George Earl of Cumberland etc. for a memorial of her last parting in this place with her good and pious mother, the Right Honorable Margaret Countess Dowager of Cumberland the second day of April 1616.

It also records Anne's gift to the poor of Brougham parish, who received £4 a year (to be divided among them) on the anniversary of the final parting. Of all her relationships, Anne's bond with her mother seems to have been her strongest, and the poignancy of marking the spot where they said their final goodbyes was the most sentimental gesture the tough-minded Anne ever made.

Anne didn't stop with memorials for her parents: she also prepared her own burial site and tomb. While doing repairs to St. Lawrence's Church in 1655, she made "a bank in the northeast corner of the church for myself to be buried in"; two years later, she reported that the work was completed. Visitors today will still find in the church's north chapel Anne's imposing black marble tomb. Outdoing even the dynastic display on her father's monument in Skipton, the marble slab attached to the wall has twenty-four heraldic shields related to the Clifford family's history. At the top are Anne's oldest known ancestors; at the bottom, her own coat of arms flanked by those of her two husbands. On the base of the tomb she prepared as best she could her own funerary inscription (even she couldn't supply all the details of her own death), describing herself as being "by a long continued descent from her father and her noble ancestors . . . Baroness Clifford, Westmorland & Vescy, High Sheriffess of the County of Westmorland and Lady of the Honor of Skipton in Craven." As with George's memorial, there's no effigy or image incised in brass: Anne chose to be remembered through her lineage alone.

The only hint of Anne's actual person lay in St. Lawrence's vault, where she was buried in a simple leaden shroud sized to fit her body. At four feet and ten inches long, it confirms her diminutive figure: having been excluded at age thirteen from Queen Elizabeth's funeral because she "was not high enough," it seems she never reached five feet. A crude image carved on top of the shroud shows a woman with her eyes closed; affixed to her torso is a tablet identifying the corpse within as "the body of the most noble, virtuous & religious Lady Anne Countess Dowager of Pembroke, Dorset and Montgomery." Everything about this burial feels shockingly modest, but it corresponded to Anne's desire to "be buried decently, and with as little charge as may be, being sensible of the folly and vanity of superfluous pomp and solemnities." Her will left instructions for her corpse not to be disemboweled—like Queen Elizabeth, she didn't want to be opened up—but "wrapped only in cerecloth and lead, with an inscription on the breast whose body it is, and so to be interred in the vault in Appleby Church, in Westmorland, which I caused to be made there, with a tomb over it, for myself." The "pomp" of the marble monument in the chapel above, with its ostentatious display of heraldry, didn't count as part of her Christian burial. It was a piece of her secular history.

Anne's most ambitious project of self-commemoration wasn't done in marble or stone. It came in the form of books. By vocation, Anne was neither a builder nor an architect: she was a writer who processed everything that happened by putting it down on the page. As she grew older, she evolved from being only a diarist to becoming also a family historian. Her mother's search for documents to support Anne's legal claims gave her, already as a young girl, a taste of the treasures in the archives; when she set out for the north in 1649, she began to assemble all of the Clifford records dating back to the eleventh century. Anne's purpose was not to file the documents away in storage, but to incorporate them into a single written history. Over the course of the next few years, Anne oversaw the production of three massive volumes, which she aptly called the *Great Books of Record*. Written out by hand in "elephant" folios roughly the size of large modern atlases, the *Great Books* together run just over a thousand pages long. Never one for a single copy of anything, Anne had four sets of the manuscripts made, three of which have survived.

The *Great Books* consist mostly of transcriptions of original documents dating back to the late twelfth century when Robert de Veteripont was created Lord and Baron of Westmorland. (It was Robert's granddaughter, Isabella de Veteripont, who married Robert de Clifford, thereby merging the two families' estates to create the powerful Clifford dynasty.) The books proceed genealogically through the biographies of each of the subsequent Clifford lords, with special attention to wives and daughters. Charters, royal grants, petitions, inquisitions after deaths, deeds of land, reversions of property, wills, and any other relevant documents Anne could find are included both in their original languages (often Latin or Anglo-French) and in English translations. There are beautifully illuminated genealogical "descents" (a version of family trees), sometimes accompanied by drawings of the primogenitors at the bottom of the page. Personal and royal seals are meticulously reproduced in an effort to re-create as fully as possible the appearance of the original materials.

To amass the thousands of documents included in the *Great Books* was an enormous enterprise, and Anne drew upon a wide range of sources. On the title page of all three copies of the *Great Books* she credited her mother's "care and painful industry" in gathering the "chief" of the "records." It's certainly the case that Margaret's team of lawyers and antiquarians found many of the documents Anne used in her lawsuit, but there were many other contributors to the final project. Once Anne came into her inheritance, she had full access to the Muniment Room at Skipton—the very resource her uncle Francis had tried to keep from her and Margaret in 1607, when he denied them access to the castle—and she employed her own antiquarians to comb through the family's records. Anne's husband Philip, in his capacity as lord chamberlain, had also helped her obtain documents related to the Cliffords' centuries of interactions with the Crown. In assembling the books, Anne chose what to include and personally inspected all the records, including those written in Latin (a language, we will recall, which she'd never studied). She also reviewed the manuscripts once they were made, inserting comments in her own hand in the margins. In these respects, she was effectively the editor-in-chief of an elaborate family encyclopedia.

Anne's contribution to the *Great Books* wasn't limited, however, to her demanding editorial supervision. To bring the volumes to life as narrative history and not merely as a collection of documents, she decided to write biographical sketches of each of her ancestors. There was no precedent for doing this in the Clifford records themselves: this was a creative addition of her own. For the spouses and children of the Clifford lords, Anne wrote brief entries that were included in a "Summary" at the end of each section. For the primary lord himself, she wrote longer pieces. There were some notable exceptions to this division of things, reflecting her personal biases. The longest entry of all (nearly five thousand words) was reserved for her mother, a Clifford only by marriage, whereas those for her uncle Francis and her cousin Henry—both recognized as legitimate Clifford heirs by nearly everyone but Anne—were put under the compromised heading: "A summary (by way of digression) concerning Francis [or Henry] Clifford." What becomes clear from all of these entries, whatever their length or detail, is Anne's fascination with the art of biography. Reading through the dry archival records, she was drawn to conjure up the actual lives.

Remembering the lives of her ancestors was part of remembering herself: to preserve the full record of her own experience, Anne built on the entire apparatus of the past. When the *Great Books of Record* arrives at her own chapter as the Clifford heir, it's not surprising that she expanded her previous scope. This section, entitled "Baroness Clifford," takes up nearly half of the pages in the third volume, which covers the period from 1528 to the late seventeenth century. In the first part, she followed the ordinary pattern in the *Great Books* by providing the transcriptions of important documents: Anne's baptism record; the "letters patent" of the king granting Francis "all the lands that were the Cliffords"; court orders between Anne and Francis; trial records from the Court of Common Pleas in Westminster in 1615; a patent from Anne and Richard issued in 1616 requesting the "bayliffwick, or sheriffwick, of the county of Westmorland"; the "substance of King James his award" in 1617; Anne's petition in 1628 to King Charles "touching her right to the baronies"; and a series of "claims and entries" made in 1628, 1632, and 1637 by Anne's steward, Marsh, regarding Westmorland and Craven. After all of the records—again, following the standard form of the earlier chapters—she provided her own genealogical "descent" or family tree, which was updated for around fifty years after Anne's death to include the lives of several of her grandchildren.

At this point, Anne deviated from the format established in the chapters for all of the previous Clifford lords. Asserting her own role as both historical subject and author, she devoted a long second section (and not merely a page or two) to her autobiography. She began with the full text of *The Life of Me,* which ended with her arrival at the "decayed castles of Brough and Pendragon" in August 1649. Following this sweeping memoir, she included her annual summaries, which were copied at the end of each year directly into all four sets of the *Great Books* from 1650 through 1675, the last full year she lived. The books thus remained a work in progress, with materials added also here after Anne's death: below the 1675 summary is a paragraph written most likely by her grandson and eventual heir, Thomas Tufton, offering a brief eulogy of his "noble and pious" grandmother and providing details of her death.

The only part of Anne's life not covered in the *Great Books* is its very end. For her final months in 1676, her ordinary diary has survived, although it was written entirely by her secretary George Hasell, to whom she must have dictated the entries; the only thing in Anne's hand are the monthly headings for January through March. As with the 1616–19 diaries, the pages of the 1676 diary were laid out with two columns: the main entries were written horizontally in the middle with extra material put in the left margin, either horizontally or vertically. Anne recorded her final days in granular detail. She had a quarrel with "the deaf woman of my almshouse at Appleby" from whom she regularly bought lace ("I was very angry with her for bringing so much," Anne noted, "and told her I would have no more of her"); she watched her black-spotted dog, Quinny, "puppy in my bed and chamber four little puppies, but they were all dead"; she dined with Richard Jackson, the local schoolmaster of Appleby, and after dinner "had him in my chamber and took him by the hand and talked with him a good while." She also kept track of her own physical decline, paying special attention to her "fits of the wind" and swooning.

On March 21, Anne dictated to Hasell what turned out to be her final entry: "I went not out of the house nor out of my chamber all this day." This was followed by a citation of Psalm 121, which ends with the verse: "The Lord shall preserve thy going out and thy coming in from this time forth, and even for evermore." According to Hasell, who kept the original 1676 diary among his own papers (it's for this reason the diary survived, escaping the fate of the others), the very last words Anne spoke were "I thank God I am very well." She died the next day, at eighty-six years of age.

At St. Lawrence's Church in Appleby on April 14, Bishop Rainbow preached Anne's funeral sermon on Proverbs 14:1, "Every wise woman buildeth her house." This biblical verse had certainly met its match. Not only had Anne restored all of her father's castles, repaired local churches and bridges, created a new almshouse, and made significant improvements to the landscapes of Westmorland and Craven. She had also built a powerful legacy in words. Never before had a woman decided that her family's past was worthy of a narrative history comparable to Holinshed's *Chronicles;* never before had a woman carved from centuries of family records a starring role for herself and her female ancestors.

Had Anne's writing been published in the century or two after her death, it might have paved the way for other women to find similar inspiration in their own life experiences. As we've seen, it would be centuries before Vita Sackville-West decided to bring Anne's earliest diaries into print. But even if generations of writers had no access to her story, it was never really lost. Like the works of Mary Sidney, Aemilia Lanyer, and Elizabeth Cary, it was waiting to be pulled from the archives and given the attention it deserves.

May 29, 1989

Linsly-Chittenden Hall
New Haven, Connecticut

I was a student at Yale in the late 1980s when I fell in love with Renaissance literature. In a yearlong course entitled "Major English Poets," the prerequisite for the English major, I was introduced to Spenser, Donne, and Milton; I studied Shakespeare in large lecture halls and in small seminars; I read lots of sonnets. But when I graduated with a BA in English in May 1989, I had never read a word written by a woman before the nineteenth century. Nor did I imagine there were things to be read. To the extent that the question ever crossed my mind, I took Virginia Woolf at her word when she told me in *A Room of One's Own* that no woman could ever have made it as a writer in Shakespeare's England.

Six years as a graduate student in English at the University of California, Berkeley, only confirmed this impression. There, I plunged into classes on Renaissance theater, expanding my horizons from Shakespeare to Marlowe, Jonson, Dekker, and Webster. I studied the "invention of privacy" and the deepening of poetic inwardness. I learned about the Reformation and the Counter-Reformation and the witchcraft craze that swept over Europe. I read sermons, political treatises, prayer books, and travel narratives. But when I received my PhD in 1996, I still hadn't encountered a single woman writer from the Renaissance.

Part of this was my own fault. I never asked any of my professors whether it was really the case that there were no women who might be included in their exclusively male syllabi. But had I been more curious, I would largely have been thwarted. Until the 1990s, most Renaissance women writers were unpublished, out of print, or appeared in books that obscured their authorship. Elizabeth Cary's 1613 *Tragedy of Mariam* hadn't been reissued outside of a scholarly facsimile in 1913; Aemilia Lanyer's *Salve Deus* first surfaced after more than three hundred years, as we've seen, under the misleading title *The Poems of Shakespeare's Dark Lady;* Mary Sidney's Psalms were published in the nineteenth and early twentieth centuries under her brother's name or with her name subordinated to his; Anne Clifford's early diaries came out in Sackville-West's 1923 edition, but her other autobiographical writings—the diaries for 1650–1676 and her memoir, *The Life of Me*—were completely unavailable.

And then everything changed. Thanks to the amazing work of feminist scholars and editors in the last few decades—among many others, Margaret W. Ferguson, Margaret P. Hannay, Jessica L. Malay, Leah S. Marcus, Janel Mueller, Heather Wolfe, and Susanne Woods come first to mind—Renaissance women writers have been resurrected from the dead. A full edition of *The Diaries of Lady Anne Clifford* was first printed in 1990 and a monumental transcription of the *Great Books of Record* in 2015; a critical edition of Aemilia's *Salve Deus* in 1993; Elizabeth's *Tragedy of Mariam* and her daughters' memoir of her life, *The Lady Falkland,* in 1994; and *The Collected Works of Mary Sidney Herbert, Countess of Pembroke*—in two significant volumes—in 1998. Scholarly essays and books on these women and a group of their contemporaries began to appear. A new field was born. But unless you found yourself at a university where someone was doing this work, it was entirely possible to hear nothing about it.

Today, the situation has in many ways changed again. In addition to the critical editions of individual authors, there are anthologies of women's writing that include materials far beyond poems and plays, giving readers access to letters, prayers, pamphlets, diaries, domestic treatises, and all sorts of occasional writing by women whose names we'd never heard before. Dissertations, essays, and scholarly monographs have been published on the women now considered, to return to the language of Yale's curriculum, "Major

Authors"; in the classroom, these women now frequently show up in syllabi otherwise dedicated to works by men. A course on Renaissance devotional literature may include Aemilia's *Salve Deus* and a selection of Mary Sidney's Psalms; a course on Renaissance lyric might pair Aemilia's "Ode to Cooke-ham" with Jonson's "To Penshurst." There are thriving professional organizations dedicated to the study of Renaissance women's writing, and regular panels at major conferences. In all of these ways, the situation has certainly improved from my time at Yale thirty-five years ago.

And yet. When a young friend of mine taking a class on tragedy at Cambridge University in the fall of 2021 asked her professor if she could write about Elizabeth Cary's play, he told her he'd never heard of it. To his credit, he gave her permission—and maybe next time he'll even include *The Tragedy of Mariam* in his course—but the anecdote is by no means unusual. Many scholars working in the field still never teach anything written by Renaissance women, and this means students taking literature classes can still graduate with a degree in English without knowing anything about them. In the larger public, it's rare for anyone without a specialized degree to have heard of any of the women in this book, and therefore—and possibly more importantly—it's also rare for them to know anything about what it was like to be a woman in Shakespeare's England.

I put the issue this way because I think the rewards of reading literature aren't solely literary. In particular, there's so much more to learn through reading women's writing than we can measure on strictly aesthetic or formal grounds. At the same time, it's important to affirm that the women in this book absolutely stand up to their male counterparts. One of the questions I'm frequently asked when I talk about these writers is, are they any good? Is there a reason, people want to know, why we should bother to read them? Putting aside the offensiveness of the question, with its underlying assumption that the canon has done its work and kept out the lesser talents, it's important to affirm that they are indeed "good" by literary standards: Aemilia Lanyer and Mary Sidney are brilliant poets, Elizabeth Cary is a first-rate playwright, and Anne Clifford is one of the great diarists of the era.

And the list by no means stops here. I've chosen these four women to anchor this book, but there are many more who deserve our attention and who could fairly have claimed a place. During Mary Sidney's childhood, Isabella Whitney, a woman who worked for a while as a servant and who described herself as "whole in body and in mind, but very weak in purse," published a small book of love poems entitled *The Copy of a Letter* in 1566 or 1567, and a second collection of verse and prose entitled *A Sweet Nosegay* in 1573. Whitney professed to write poetry because, as an unmarried woman, she had no other work to do. In a verse letter to her sister in *A Sweet Nosegay*, she declared:

> *Had I a husband or a house*
> *and all that longs thereto*
> *My self could frame about to rouse*
> *as other women do:*
> *But till some household cares me tie*
> *My books and pen I will apply.*

Whitney's contemporary Anne Vaughan Lock was a religious writer in the mid-sixteenth century: a passionate supporter of Protestantism who fled to Geneva to escape from the Catholic Mary I, Lock translated several of Calvin's sermons into English and wrote a paraphrase of Psalm 51—a plaintive confession of David's after his adultery with Bathsheba—in the form of twenty-one sonnets. Lock's sermons and poems, which were dedicated to Katherine Willoughby, Countess of Suffolk, were published anonymously in 1560. Four hundred years later, she was identified as the author.

In the generation of Elizabeth Cary and Anne Clifford came Mary Sidney's niece Lady Mary Wroth, who followed in her aunt's path to write several major works of her own. Wroth's *Countess of Montgomery's Urania,* named for her cousin Philip Herbert's first wife, Susan de Vere, and published in 1621, was the first prose romance ever published by an Englishwoman. This dense and complex tale involving hundreds of characters, some of whom were only loosely disguised from Wroth's contemporaries, created a scandal at court, leading Wroth to claim she never intended for the book to be published and to recall as many copies as she could. Appended to the *Urania* was Wroth's collection of poems, *Pamphilia to Amphilanthus,* which consisted of 103 sonnets and songs. For the first time in

English literary history a woman took on the most celebrated tradition in love poetry—the sonnet series made famous by Francesco
Petrarch—but reversed the gender roles so that now a female poet
was describing her unrequited love for her male beloved, not vice
versa.

If we cast our gaze just a bit later, two significant women writers stand out. Margaret Lucas Cavendish, a passionate intellectual
who published no fewer than fourteen books between 1653 and
1668, ranging in genres from natural philosophy and satire to poetry,
plays, and romance, became famous for her work of science fiction,
The Blazing World. Set in a utopian land reached by crossing over
the North Pole, the story focuses on the intergalactic adventures
of a shipwrecked woman who becomes empress of her new land.
A decade or so after Cavendish's works appeared in print, the first
truly professional woman writer came on to the scene. Born around
1640 to a mother who worked as a wet nurse and a father who
was a barber, Aphra Behn lived for a while in the Dutch colony of
Surinam before becoming a spy for Charles II in Antwerp. Due to
her inadequate pay—she may even have served time in a debtor's
prison—Behn took up her pen to earn her living through writing. Starting in 1670 she wrote no fewer than nineteen plays—first
mostly tragicomedies, and later more straightforward comedies and
farces—which were performed on the London stage. Behn's best-
known work was her novel, *Oroonoko,* which she published in 1688,
a year before her death. *Oroonoko* tells the story of an African prince
who was abducted and sold into slavery in Surinam. Drawing upon
Behn's own experiences in the colony, the novel took what was considered a radical abolitionist stance.

It's tempting to imagine what it would have been like if Behn
or any of the other extraordinary women who followed in her wake
in the eighteenth century—Fanny Burney, Mary Wortley Montagu,
Mary Wollstonecraft, to name a few—had had easy access to the
works of their Renaissance sisters. What would they have made of
Pontius Pilate's wife demanding on behalf of her sex in *Salve Deus,*
"Then let us have our Liberty again," or of Elizabeth Cary's heroine, Mariam, brazenly announcing that she would no longer obey
her husband's will? How might they have responded to Mary Sidney's working through her grief over her brother Philip's death by

becoming a poet, or to Anne Clifford's forging her legacy through a lifetime of autobiographical writing as she battled against patriarchy? Generations of women writers who came after them couldn't access their work; they were forced instead to turn inward for inspiration without models to emulate and surpass. But we can access them. We can hear their words and learn their lessons, and the more of these voices we can uncover, the richer our own history becomes.

The future of the past is full of women.

Acknowledgments

In a book about women writers who so rarely had support from the world around them, I want to begin by acknowledging the extraordinary women who helped me to bring this project to fruition. First, my most profound gratitude is to my beloved agent and friend, Jill Kneerim, who passed away just as I was finishing the manuscript. I could never have written this book without Jill's extraordinary dedication and passion, which kept her closely involved from the earliest draft of the book proposal through her very last days. I am grateful to my new agent, Lucy Cleland, who graciously took up the helm and has shepherded the book through with great attention. LuAnn Walther was my first editor at Knopf, who believed in the book from the start and gave me the encouragement to write it. Deborah Garrison, who became my editor upon LuAnn's retirement, has embraced the project with amazing generosity and enthusiasm, and I am deeply indebted to her careful, intelligent readings and her engagement with every aspect of the book's production. Many thanks to Zuleima Ugalde for making the editorial process run so smoothly, and to Susanna Sturgis for her excellent copyediting. I am also very grateful to Katie Adams for her brilliant early reading of the full manuscript.

This book builds upon several decades of research by pioneering feminist scholars who have brought Renaissance women writers into print after centuries of neglect. Without the editorial and critical work by Margaret W. Ferguson, Margaret P. Hannay, Leah Knight, Jessica L. Malay, Leah S. Marcus, Janel Mueller, Heather Wolfe, Susanne Woods, and others, I wouldn't have been able to read, teach, or write about the women at the heart of this book. I am grateful to Brandeis University for supporting my sabbatical leave in 2021–22, and to the Brandeis students in my "Women's Writing in the Renaissance" seminars for expanding my understanding of these literary works. Thanks also to the English departments at Cambridge University and Oxford University for inviting me to give lectures on the book in the fall of 2021, and to Laurie McGuire, Lorna Hutson, and Emma Smith, for making those occasions so engaging. I am very grateful to Richard Ovenden, Bodley's Librarian at Oxford University, for helping me find the rarest of books and manuscripts in the library collections. Jeffrey Marsh generously gave me a tour around Bishopsgate, bringing me to Aemilia Lanyer's parish church. The librarians in Kendal at the Cumbria Archive Centre generously brought me folder after folder of Clifford letters and documents. I want to thank Alina Payne for hosting me in the spring of 2022 as the Robert Lehman Visiting Professor at the Harvard Center for Italian Renaissance Studies, Villa I Tatti in Florence, where I finished the first draft of my book. My fantastic research assistants, Emiliano Guttierez Popoca and Troy Tower, worked tirelessly to track down both historical documents and all kinds of secondary literature; Tali Cohen has been an outstanding reader of the copyedited manuscript.

I also managed to involve a number of friends in the research for this book, forging several unexpected collaborations that extend beyond the chapters here. In an unusual lull brought on by the pandemic, Judith Clark threw herself into the world of Anne Clifford, joining me on a research trip to Kendal, a memorable stay at nearby Appleby Castle, and a panel on Clifford's castles at a conference in San Juan, Puerto Rico, all as preparation for an extraordinary exhibition she is designing on Clifford's architectural and monumental works. Jill Lepore, my model for what it means to write history, helped me think through the structure of this book at its earliest stage. Thomas Laqueur has been my go-to British historian, answering questions of any size (When were girls required to go to church? When did leaden shrouds come into use?) with his usual intelligence and humor. My colleagues Cameron Anderson and Sarah Mead joined me in a project funded by a Brandeis Provost Research Grant to study Ben Jonson's *The Masque of Queens,* and a subsequent collaboration with Eric Nicholson at NYU Florence brought the masque to life onstage.

Less dramatic, but no less important, have been my many conversations about this book with dear friends: Sarah Cole, whom I speak to most days, has been cheering me on from the beginning; Sara Antonelli, Mary Bing, Glenda Carpio, Ophelia Dahl, Joseph Koerner, Meg Koerner, Blyth Lord, Luke Menand, Paul Morrison, Ashley Pettus, Adam Phillips, John Plotz, Kellie Robertson, Catherine Robson, Michal Safdie, Moshe Safdie, Sarah Shoemaker, Alison Simmons, Sara St. Antoine, and Lisa Wyatt have all sustained me in ways too numerous to describe here.

I am very blessed to have spent the years writing this book surrounded by my family. My son, Harry Greenblatt, brings great joy into my life every day, and inspires me to make the world a better place in whatever small ways I can. My husband, Stephen Greenblatt, is my best interlocutor and my dearest companion. The long months of near isolation from the rest of the world when I first began this project were as pleasurable as they could be, thanks to sharing that time with him. And our dog, Marcus, who patiently sits next to my desk while I'm writing, is the most loving and loyal of pets.

To my father, Michael Targoff, who has always given me his unconditional love and support; my stepmother, ShaSha; my brothers, Josh and Jason, and all the members of our wonderful family, I am immensely grateful for their presence in my life. My beloved mother, Cheri Kamen Targoff, led the way for me to write women's history with her own early work, and heard my ideas for this project in her last months; she has been with me in spirit ever since. This book, which begins with Virginia Woolf's fantasy about Shakespeare's imaginary sister, is dedicated to my (thankfully) very real one, Hannah Saujet, whose friendship I treasure.

Notes

Spelling of early modern texts is modernized throughout unless otherwise noted.

INTRODUCTION

For Woolf's full texts, see Virginia Woolf, *A Room of One's Own,* ed. Mark Hussey (Orlando, FL: Harcourt, 2005), and "Donne After Three Centuries" in *The Common Reader,* vol. 2 (London: Hogarth Press, 1951).

For George Clifford, Earl of Cumberland's biography, see Richard T. Spence, *The Privateering Earl* (Stroud, Gloucestershire, UK: A. Sutton Pub., 1995), and his entry in H. C. G., Matthew, Brian Harrison, and British Academy, *Oxford Dictionary of National Biography: in Association with the British Academy: from the Earliest Times to the Year 2000* (New York: Oxford University Press, 2004) (hereafter *ODNB*): Peter Holmes, "Clifford, George, Third Earl of Cumberland (1558–1605), Courtier and Privateer," *ODNB.*

For Vita Sackville-West's account of Anne Clifford, see her "Introductory Note" in *The Diary of the Lady Anne Clifford,* ed. V. Sackville-West (1923; Providence, RI: Women Writers Project, Brown University, 1990).

CHAPTER ONE

For a general account of Elizabeth's death and funeral, see John Guy, *Elizabeth: The Forgotten Years* (New York: Viking, 2016), and Catherine Loomis, *The Death of Queen Elizabeth I: Remembering and Reconstructing the Virgin Queen* (New York: Palgrave Macmillan, 2010). For the description of Elizabeth's final months and illness, see John Chamberlain's letters to Sir Dudley Carleton in *The Letters of John Chamberlain,* vol. I, ed. Norman Egbert McClure (Westport, CT: Greenwood Press, 1979).

For details on Elizabeth I's funeral procession, see W. A. Jackson, "The Funeral Procession of Queen Elizabeth," *Library,* 4th ser., 26, no. 4 (1945):

262–71; for contemporary accounts, Henry Petowe, *Henry Petowe, Elizabetha quasi vivens, Eliza's Funerall. A fewe Aprill drops, showred on the Hearse of dead Eliza* (London: Printed by E. Alde for M. Lawe, 1603), and Henry Chettle, *England's Mourning Garment,* ed. Valentine Simmes (London, 1603; Amsterdam: Theatrum Orbis Terrarum, 1973). For the comment on grief in the streets of London during the funeral, see John Stow, *Annales, or, A Generall Chronicle of England* (London: R. Meighen, 1615). On royal funerals in England and also the role of music in funerals, see Matthias Range, *British Royal and State Funerals: Music and Ceremonial Since Elizabeth I* (Woodbridge, UK: Boydell Press, 2016). For details on the role of the almswomen, see Christine Fox, "The Tudor Royal Almsmen, 1500–1600," *Medieval Prosopography* 30 (2015): 139–76.

On court musicians, see Henry Cart De Lafontaine, *The King's Musick: A Transcript of Records Relating to Music and Musicians, 1460–1700* (London: Novello and Company, Limited, 1909).

Giovanni Scaramelli's letter on the treatment of Elizabeth's corpse is cited in John Guy, *Elizabeth: The Forgotten Years* (New York: Viking, 2016).

Anne Clifford's comments on Elizabeth's death and funeral are from her 1603 memoir, included in Vita Sackville-West, *The Diary of the Lady Anne Clifford,* and in *Anne Clifford's Autobiographical Writing, 1590–1676,* ed. Jessica L. Malay (Manchester, UK: Manchester University Press, 2018), among other editions.

On the Bassano family's background, and on Alfonso Lanyer's role at Elizabeth's funeral, see David Lasocki with Roger Prior, *The Bassanos: Venetian Musicians and Instrument Makers in England, 1531–1665* (Aldershot, UK: Ashgate, 1995).

Arbella Stuart's response to James I's invitation to be the chief mourner is in John Clapham, *Elizabeth of England, Certain Observations Concerning the Life and Reign of Queen Elizabeth,* ed. Evelyn Plummer Read and Conyers Read (1589; Philadelphia: University of Pennsylvania Press, 1951).

For Francis Bacon's comments on a woman's rule, see "In Felicem Memoriam Elizabethae," in *The Works of Francis Bacon,* vol. 11, collected and edited by James Spedding, Robert Leslie Ellis, and Douglas Denon Heath (Michigan: Scholarly Press, 1969); for Knox's comments, see *The Political Writings of John Knox: The First Blast of the Trumpet Against the Monstrous Regiment of Women and Other Selected Works,* ed. Marvin A Breslow (Washington, DC: Folger Books, 1985). For Calvin's letter to Cecil, see Jean Calvin, *Letters of John Calvin: Selected from the Bonnet Edition with an Introductory Biographical Sketch,* ed. Jules Bonnet (Edinburgh: Banner of Truth Trust, 1980).

Elizabeth's 1588 speech at Tilbury is reprinted in *Elizabeth I and Her Age,* ed. Donald Stump and Susan M. Felch (New York: Norton, 2009). Her "Golden Speech" to Parliament in 1601 is in *The Golden Speech of Queen Elizabeth, to Her Last Parliament, November 30, Anno Domini, 1601 with Observations Adapted to These Times* (Dublin: Reprinted, at the Post-Office-coffee-house in Fish-shamble Street, 1698), Early English Books Online, ProQuest.

For Elizabeth's use of wigs and self-presentation, see Paul Johnson, *Elizabeth I: A Study in Power and Intellect* (London: Weidenfeld and Nicolson, 1988). For her wardrobe, and for the French ambassador's response to the aging queen, see Anna Whitelock, *The Queen's Bed: An Intimate History of Elizabeth's Court* (New York: Picador, 2015).

Frances Howard's letter to Edward Seymour, Earl of Hertford, is quoted in Susan Doran and Norman Jones, *The Elizabethan World* (London: Routledge, 2011). Elizabeth's angry wielding of her hairbrush against Mary Shelton is in Whitelock, *The Queen's Bed*. William Fenton's letter about the queen's wanting her women to remain unmarried is in John Harington, *Nugae antiquae: being a miscellaneous collection of original papers, in prose and verse; written during the reigns of Henry VIII. Edward VI. Queen Mary, Elizabeth, and King James,* vol. 1 (New York: AMS Press, 1966).

Elizabeth's 1559 speech before Parliament is in *Elizabeth I: Collected Works,* ed. Leah S. Marcus, Janel Mueller, and Mary Beth Rose (Chicago: University of Chicago Press, 2000); there are two surviving versions of this speech, only one of which has the lines quoted here. Her response to the 1563 parliamentary petition for her to marry is cited in Susan Doran, *Monarchy and Matrimony: The Courtships of Elizabeth I* (London: Routledge, 1996).

On the death of Robert Dudley's wife, see Simon Adams, "Dudley, Robert, Earl of Leicester (1532/3–1588), Courtier and Magnate," *ODNB*.

For the full texts of Elizabeth's translations given to her family members, see *Elizabeth I: Translations, 1544–1589,* ed. Janel Mueller and Joshua Scodel (Chicago: University of Chicago Press, 2009); for her later translations, see *Elizabeth I: Translations, 1592–1598,* ed. Janel Mueller and Joshua Scodel (Chicago: University of Chicago Press, 2009). For Elizabeth's poetry, see *Elizabeth I: Collected Works*.

For an estimate of women's literacy, see Heidi Brayman Hackel, *Reading Material in Early Modern England: Print, Gender, and Literacy* (Cambridge, UK: Cambridge University Press, 2005). This more recent study responds to the often criticized study by David Cressy, "Literacy in Seventeenth-Century England: More Evidence," *Journal of Interdisciplinary History* 8, no. 1 (1977).

For a list of the books that printed the couplet Elizabeth wrote in her imprisonment, see *Queen Elizabeth I: Selected Works,* ed. Stephen W. May (New York: Washington Square Press, 2004).

"*Precationes privatae*" or "Private Prayers of Queen Elizabeth at Court, 1563" is in *Elizabeth I: Collected Works*. "Queen Elizabeth's *Sententiae*" is in *Elizabeth I: Translations, 1544–1589*. This work was originally published in 1563.

GENERAL REFERENCE AND FURTHER BIBLIOGRAPHY

Roger Ascham, *The Schoolmaster (1570),* ed. Lawrence V. Ryan, Folger Shakespeare Library (Charlottesville: University Press of Virginia, 1974).

George Puttenham, *The Art of English Poesy: A Critical Edition,* ed. Frank

Whigham and Wayne A. Rebhorn (Ithaca, NY: Cornell University Press, 2011). *The Art of English Poesy* was originally published in 1589.

Wallace T. MacCaffrey, *Elizabeth I: War and Politics, 1588–1603* (Princeton, NJ: Princeton University Press, 2021).

J. E. Neale, *Queen Elizabeth I* (Chicago: Academy Chicago, 2005).

Anne Somerset, *Elizabeth I* (New York: Alfred A. Knopf, 1991).

CHAPTER TWO

For Mary Sidney's biography, see Margaret Hannay, *Philip's Phoenix: Mary Sidney, Countess of Pembroke* (New York: Oxford University Press, 1990). For the life of her mother, Mary Sidney Dudley, see Simon Adams, "Sidney [Née Dudley], Mary, Lady Sidney (1530x35–1586), Courtier," *ODNB.*

For an account of the lives of the gentlewomen and maids of honor inside Elizabeth's court, see Anne Whitelock, *The Queen's Bed: An Intimate History of Elizabeth's Court* (New York: Picador, 2015).

On Elizabeth's bout with smallpox, see, among others, Edith Sitwell, *The Queen and the Hive* (Boston: Little, Brown, 1962), and Whitelock, *The Queen's Bed.* For the so-called "red treatment," see Donald R. Hopkins, *The Greatest Killer: Smallpox in History* (Chicago: University of Chicago Press, 2002).

Sir Henry Sidney's letter about his wife is cited in Hannay, *Philip's Phoenix.* Jonson's poem "To Penshurst" is in Ben Jonson, *The Complete Poems,* ed. George Parfitt (New Haven, CT: Yale University Press, 1982).

On girls' access to education, see Helen M. Jewell, *Education in Early Modern England* (New York: St. Martin's Press, 1998).

The Sidney children's education is discussed in Hannay, *Philip's Phoenix.* Thomas Moffett's description of Philip's education is in Alan Stewart, *Philip Sidney: A Double Life* (London: Chatto & Windus, 2000).

Elizabeth's letter to Sir Henry Sidney about the death of Ambrosia, and Lady Sidney's letter to her steward John Cockram, are both quoted in Whitelock, *The Queen's Bed.*

For the costs of promotions at court and the acquisition of new titles, see Lawrence Stone, *The Crisis of the Aristocracy, 1558–1641* (Oxford, UK: Clarendon Press, 1965).

A full history of Elizabeth's summer progresses, including the details of her proposed visit to Sir John Puckering, is in John Nichols, *The Progresses and Public Processions of Queen Elizabeth* (New York: AMS Press, 1823; Kraus Reprint, 1969). On the cost of a visit from the queen, see Lawrence Stone, "The Anatomy of the Elizabethan Aristocracy," *Economic History Review* 18, no. 1–2 (1948): 1–53.

On Leicester's architectural improvements to Kenilworth and a history of the house, see Richard Morris, " 'I Was Never More in Love with an Olde Howse nor Never Newe Worke Coulde Be Better Bestowed': The Earl of Leicester's Remodelling of Kenilworth Castle for Queen Elizabeth I," *Antiquaries Journal* 89, no. 94 (2009): 241–305.

For the cost of the entertainments at Kenilworth, see Janette Dillon, "Pageants and Propaganda: Robert Langham's Letter and George Gascoigne's Princely Pleasures at Kenilworth," in *The Oxford Handbook of Tudor Literature,* ed. Mike Pincombe and Cathy Shrank (New York: Oxford University Press, 2011). For the two surviving contemporary descriptions of the Kenilworth entertainments, see *Robert Langham, a Letter,* ed. R. J. P. Kuin (c. 1576; Leiden, Netherlands: E. J. Brill, 1983), and "The princely pleasures at the court of Kenelwoorth" (published anonymously in 1576, later published with Gascoigne's name), in *The Complete Works of George Gascoigne,* ed. William Cunliffe (New York: Greenwood Press, 1969).

For details on Henry Herbert's estate, see Penry Williams, "Herbert, Henry, second earl of Pembroke (b. in or after 1538, d. 1601), nobleman and administrator," *ODNB.*

On Elizabeth I's visit to Woodstock, see J. W. Cunliffe, "The Queenes Majesties Entertainment at Woodstocke," *PMLA: Publications of the Modern Language Association of America* 26, no. 1 (1911): 92–141, and Erzsébet Stróbl, "Entertaining the Queen at Woodstock, 1575" (New York: Oxford University Press, 2012). On her cultivation of her image as a virgin queen, see Roy Strong, *The Cult of Elizabeth: Elizabethan Portraiture and Pageantry* (London: Thames and Hudson, 1987), and Frances A. Yates, *Astraea: The Imperial Theme in the Sixteenth Century* (London: Ark Paperbacks, 1985).

The original manuscript containing Mary's jointure agreement is held at the Houghton Library at Harvard University (MS Eng 725). A summary of the agreement, Henry Sidney's letter to Leicester pleading poverty, and the list of items from Mary's trousseau are all in Hannay, *Philip's Phoenix.*

A record of Mary Sidney's marriage in the Chapel Royal can be found in William Lovegrove, et al., *The Cheque Books of the Chapel Royal: With Additional Material from the Manuscripts of William Lovegrove and Marmaduke Alford* (1872; Aldershot, UK: Ashgate, 2000). The date of the marriage was wrongly given here as 1580 rather than 1577.

On gift-giving at the royal court, see Felicity Heal, "Giving and Receiving on Royal Progress," *The Progresses, Pageants, and Entertainments of Queen Elizabeth I,* ed. Jayne Elisabeth Archer, et al. (Oxford: Oxford University Press, 2007), and Felicity Heal, "The Politics of Gift-Exchange under the Tudors," in *The Power of Gifts: Gift Exchange in Early Modern England* (Oxford: Oxford University Press, 2014).

Mary Sidney's letter to Leicester is included in *The Collected Works of Mary Sidney Herbert, Countess of Pembroke,* vol. 1, *Poems, Translations, and Correspondence,* ed. Margaret P. Hannay, Noel J. Kinnamon, and Michael G. Brennan (New York: Clarendon Press, 1998). Pembroke's celebrations following the birth of William are described in James M. Osborn, *Young Philip Sidney, 1572–1577* (New Haven, CT: Yale University Press, 1972). For the text of the marble plaque, see Brian O'Farrell, *Shakespeare's Patron: William Herbert, Third Earl of Pembroke, 1580–1630: Politics, Patronage and Power* (London: Bloomsbury, 2011).

For Sidney's dedicatory letter to *The Countess of Pembroke's Arcadia,* see Philip Sidney, *The Countess of Pembroke's Arcadia,* ed. Maurice Evans (New York: Penguin, 1977).

GENERAL REFERENCE AND FURTHER BIBLIOGRAPHY

Juan Luis Vives, *The Education of a Christian Woman: A Sixteenth-Century Manual,* ed. Charles Fantazzi (Chicago: University of Chicago Press, 2007).

Pierre Erondelle, *The French Garden, 1605* (Menston, UK: A Scolar Press Facsimile, 1969).

Sidney Family Psalter, Wren Library, Trinity College, Cambridge, UK (ms. R.17.2).

CHAPTER THREE

For Aemilia Lanyer's biography, see Susanne Woods, *Lanyer: A Renaissance Woman Poet* (New York: Oxford University Press, 1999). Any details from Aemilia's life not otherwise cited below are from this biography.

On the history of the Bassano family, see David Lasocki with Roger Prior, *The Bassanos: Venetian Musicians and Instrument Makers in England, 1531–1665* (Aldershot, UK: Ashgate, 1995), and David Lasocki, "Professional Recorder Playing in England, 1500–1740. I: 1500–1640," *Early Music* 10, no. 1 (1982): 23–29.

For Sir William Blackstone's comment on denizens, see *Commentaries on the Laws of England . . . By William Blackstone, Esq. Vinerian Professor of Law, and Solicitor General to Her Majesty,* Book 1 (Oxford, UK: Clarendon Press, 1765), 362. For the census record, see *Returns of Aliens Dwelling in the City and Suburbs of London from the Reign of Henry VIII to That of James I,* ed. R. E. G. Kirk and Ernest F. Kirk (Aberdeen, 1908).

John Stow's description of St. Botolph's is in John Stow, *Survey of London* (1598; New York: Dent, 1956).

On the Italian merchants doing business in the streets of Bishopsgate and for Ascham's comment about Englishmen attending Italian churches to improve their language skills, see Michael Wyatt, *The Italian Encounter with Tudor England: A Cultural Politics of Translation* (Cambridge, UK: Cambridge University Press, 2005).

For the baptismal records of the Bassano children, see Andrew Ashbee and David Lasocki, *A Biographical Dictionary of English Court Musicians, 1485–1714* (Aldershot, UK: Ashgate, 1998).

On common-law marriages, see Amy Louise Erickson, "Common Law versus Common Practice: The Use of Marriage Settlements in Early Modern England," *Economic History Review* 43, no. 1 (1990): 21–39. Sir Edward Waterhouse's contemporary account can be found in Edward Waterhouse, *Fortescutus Illustratus, or, A Commentary on That Nervous Treatise, De Laudibus Legum Angliæ, Written by Sir John Fortescue, Knight . . . by Edward Waterhous, Esquire* (London, 1663).

On Shakespeare's marriage to Anne Hathaway, see Katherine West Scheil, "Hathaway [married name Shakespeare], Anne (c. 1555/56–1623), wife of William Shakespeare," *ODNB*.

For the Bassano brothers' relation to the queen, see Lasocki, "Professional Recorder Playing in England, 1500–1740. I: 1500–1640." The translation from the Italian letter is mine. For Baptista's possible tutoring of Princess Elizabeth, see his brother's *ODNB* entry: David Lasocki, "Bassano, Alvise (d. 1554), musician and instrument maker." Baptista's 1565 gift of a Venetian lute to the queen is cited in Lasocki, *The Bassanos*.

On average incomes in Renaissance England, see Kate Aughterson, *The English Renaissance: An Anthology of Sources and Documents* (London: Routledge, 1998).

Aemilia's account of her father's financial troubles, as well as her account of her childhood years with the Countess of Kent, come from Simon Forman's casebooks. For a transcription of Forman's comments about Aemilia's background, see Woods, *Lanyer: A Renaissance Woman Poet*.

For Baptista's and Margaret's wills, see Ashbee and Lasocki, *A Biographical Dictionary of English Court Musicians*.

On Sir Edward Molyneux's sending his daughters off to become "gentlewomen," see Linda Pollock, "'Teach Her to Live Under Obedience': The Making of Women in the Upper Ranks of Early Modern England," *Continuity and Change* 4, no. 2 (1989): 231. Katherine, Countess of Huntingdon's letter to Sir Julius Caesar is cited in Kenneth Charlton, *Women, Religion, and Education in Early Modern England* (London: Routledge, 1999).

For a full biography of Katherine Willoughby, Duchess of Suffolk, see David Baldwin, *Henry VIII's Last Love: The Extraordinary Life of Katherine Willoughby, Lady-in-Waiting to the Tudors* (Stroud, UK: Amberley, 2015); see also Susan Wabuda, "Bertie [née Willoughby; other married name Brandon], Katherine, duchess of Suffolk (1519–1580), noblewoman and protestant patron," *ODNB*.

For a discussion of the evidence (or lack thereof) connected to Aemilia's time with Susan Bertie, Countess of Kent, and for details of Bertie's marriage to Grey, see Leeds Barroll, "Looking for Patrons," in *Aemilia Lanyer: Gender, Genre, and the Canon,* ed. Marshall Grossman (Lexington: University Press of Kentucky, 1998).

Aemilia's poem to Susan Bertie is in her 1611 publication, *Salve Deus Rex Judaeorum,* reprinted in *The Poems of Aemilia Lanyer: Salve Deus Rex Judaeorum,* ed. Susanne Woods (New York: Oxford University Press, 1993).

On women's wills and the status of widows, see Amy Louise Erickson, *Women and Property in Early Modern England* (London: Routledge, 1993).

For a detailed account of Mary, Queen of Scots' execution, see Garrett Mattingly, *The Armada* (Boston: Houghton Mifflin, 1959).

Details of Henry Carey, Baron Hunsdon's life can be found in Wallace T. MacCaffrey, "Carey, Henry, first Baron Hunsdon (1526–1596), courtier and administrator," *ODNB*. Aemilia's comments to Forman about her relationship with Hunsdon are quoted in Woods, *Lanyer: A Renaissance Woman Poet*.

For details of Raleigh's marriage and imprisonment, see Mark Nicholls and Penry Williams, "Ralegh [Raleigh], Sir Walter (1554–1618), courtier, explorer, and author," *ODNB*.

On affairs between male masters and female servants, see B. S. Capp, "The Double Standard Revisited: Plebeian Women and Male Sexual Reputation in Early Modern England," *Past & Present* 162 (1999): 70–100.

CHAPTER FOUR

All references to the poems, letters, psalms, translations, and miscellaneous works of Mary Sidney, unless otherwise indicated, are from *The Collected Works of Mary Sidney Herbert, Countess of Pembroke,* ed. Margaret P. Hannay, Noel J. Kinnamon, and Michael G. Brennan, 2 vols. (New York: Clarendon Press, 1998).

For Robert Sidney's August 1588 letter to his wife, Barbara Gamage Sidney, see Great Britain Royal Commission on Historical Manuscripts, *Report on the Manuscripts of Lord de l'Isle & Dudley Preserved at Penshurst Place,* vol. 2 (London: HM Stationery Office, 1934).

For the Privy Council's January 1588 letter to Pembroke and the queen's response, see *Calendar of Wynn (of Gwydir) Papers, 1515–1690, in the National Library of Wales and Elsewhere* (Aberystwyth: National Library of Wales, 1926).

Elizabeth's 1588 speech at Tilbury is reprinted in *Elizabeth I and Her Age,* ed. Donald Stump and Susan M. Felch (New York: Norton, 2009). Her "Golden Speech" to Parliament in 1601 is in *The Golden Speech of Queen Elizabeth, to Her Last Parliament, November 30, Anno Domini, 1601 with Observations Adapted to These Times* (Dublin: Reprinted, at the Post-Office-coffee-house in Fish-shamble Street, 1698), Early English Books Online, ProQuest.

For a general history of the Armada, see Garrett Mattingly, *The Armada* (Boston: Houghton Mifflin, 1959). For the celebrations in the fall of 1588, see Roy C. Strong, "The Popular Celebration of the Accession Day of Queen Elizabeth I," *Journal of the Warburg and Courtauld Institutes* 21, no. 1/2 (1958): 86–103, and Arthur F. Marotti and Steven W. May, "Two Lost Ballads of the Armada Thanksgiving Celebration [with Texts and Illustration]," *English Literary Renaissance* 41, no. 1 (2011): 31–63. For Antonio de Vega's report to the Spanish ambassador, see Martin A. S. Hume, ed., *Calendar of Letters and State Papers Relating to English Affairs [of the Reign of Elizabeth] Preserved Principally in the Archives of Simancas: 1587–1603,* vol. 4 (London: HM Stationery Office, 1899).

The Sidney Family Psalter is held in the Wren Library, Trinity College, Cambridge, UK (ms. R.17.2).

Henry Sidney's 1583 letter to Francis Walsingham about the possibility of his remarrying, also known as Sidney's "memoir," is reprinted in Henry Sidney, "Sir Henry Sidney's Memoir of His Government of Ireland, 1583," *Ulster Journal of Archaeology* 3 (1855): 33–357. Philip Sidney's account of having "slipped" into the role of poet is from Philip Sidney, *Defense of Poesy* (1595; Gale ECCO, 2018).

Fulke Greville's comment about *Astrophil and Stella*'s wide circulation is cited in H. R. Woudhuysen, *Sir Philip Sidney and the Circulation of Manuscripts, 1558–1640* (Oxford, UK: Clarendon Press, 1996).

For details on Philip's funeral, see Thomas Lant, *Sequitur celebritas & pompa funeris . . .* (London, 1587), Early English Books Online, ProQuest. For women's participation in men's funerals, see Jennifer Woodward, *The Theatre of Death: The Ritual Management of Royal Funerals in Renaissance England, 1570–1625* (Woodbridge, UK: Boydell & Brewer, 1997).

John Aubrey's comments about Mary and Philip's relationship are from *Aubrey's Brief Lives,* ed. Oliver L. Dick (Boston: D. R. Godine, 1999).

On Greville's editing of Philip's *Arcadia,* see Margaret P. Hannay, *Philip's Phoenix: Mary Sidney, Countess of Pembroke* (New York: Oxford University Press, 1990). For Mary's edition and Sanford's letter "To the Reader," see Philip Sidney, *The Countess of Pembroke's Arcadia,* ed. Maurice Evans (New York: Penguin, 1977).

Edmund Spenser's poem to Philip Sidney, "The Ruines of Time," is from E. Spenser and R. E. N. Dodge, *The Complete Poetical Works of Spenser* (Cambridge ed.) (Boston: Houghton, Mifflin, 1936).

The attribution of "The Doleful Lay" to Spenser is from Charles Grosvenor Osgood, et al., eds., *The Works of Edmund Spenser. A Variorum Edition. The Minor Poems,* vol. 1 (Baltimore: Johns Hopkins University Press, 1943).

For Spenser's "impersonating" Mary Sidney, see Kim Walker, "'Some inspired stile': Mary Sidney, Countess of Pembroke," *Women Writers of the English Renaissance* (New York: Twayne, 1996).

For Philip's relationship to Philippe de Mornay, see Hannay, *Philip's Phoenix,* and Charlotte Arbaleste de Mornay, *A Huguenot Family in the XVI Century; the Memoirs of Philippe De Mornay, Sieur Du Plessis Marly,* trans. Lucy Hill Crump (London: G. Routledge, 1926).

For the question of which work of Mornay's Philip translated, see H. R. Woudhuysen, "Sidney, Sir Philip (1554–1586), author and courtier," *ODNB*.

For Samuel Daniel's dedication of his drama *Cleopatra* to Mary Sidney, see Samuel Daniel, *The Complete Works in Verse and Prose of Samuel Daniel,* vol. 3 (New York: Russell & Russell, 1963).

Bishop John Jewel's comment on Psalm-singing in St. Paul's Cross is in John Hunter, ed., *The Zurich letters, comprising the correspondence of several English bishops and others, with some of the Helvetian reformers, during the early part of the reign of Queen Elizabeth,* trans. Hastings Robinson (Cambridge, UK:

Cambridge University Press, 1842). For a discussion of English Protestant attitudes about singing in church, see my book *Common Prayer: The Language of Public Devotion in Early Modern England* (Chicago: University of Chicago Press, 2001).

For Thomas Moffett's dedication, see Thomas Moffett, *The Silkewormes, and Their Flies: Liuely Described in Verse, by T.M. a Countrie Farmar, and an Apprentice in Physicke. For the Great Benefit and Enriching of England* (London: V[alentine] S[immes] for Nicholas Ling, 1599), Early English Books Online, ProQuest.

For John Donne's poem "Upon the Translation of the Psalms by Philip Sidney and the Countess of Pembroke His Sister," see *The Complete English Poems*, ed. A. J. Smith (London: Penguin Classics, 1977).

John Harington's comments about the impossibility of Mary Sidney's having translated the Psalms by herself are in John Harington, *Nugae antiquae: being a miscellaneous collection of original papers, in prose and verse; written during the reigns of Henry VIII. Edward VI. Queen Mary, Elizabeth, and King James* (New York: AMS Press, 1966). On Mary's not wanting to publish the Psalms, see Debra Rienstra and Noel Kinnamon, "Circulating the Sidney-Pembroke Psalter," in *Ashgate Critical Essays on Women Writers in England, 1550–1700*, vol. 2, ed. Margaret P. Hannay (Abingdon, UK: Routledge, 2009).

For Pembroke's gifts to the queen in 1593, see John Nichols, *The Progresses and Public Processions of Queen Elizabeth,* vol. 3 (London, 1788; Kraus Reprint, 1977).

For a discussion of the relationship between the two manuscripts of Mary Sidney's translation of the Psalms, see Noel Kinnamon, "The Sidney Psalms: The Penshurst and Tixall Manuscripts," in *English Manuscript Studies,* vol. 2, *1100–1700* (1990): 139–61; and Michael G. Brennan, "The Queen's Proposed Visit to Wilton House in 1599," *Sidney Journal* 20, no. 1 (2002): 27–53. For a history of the Tixall manuscript held at the Bodleian Library, see Bent Juel-Jensen, "The Tixall Manuscript of Sir Philip Sidney's and the Countess of Pembroke's Paraphrase of the Psalms," *Book Collector* 18 (1969): 222–23.

John Chamberlain's August 1, 1599, letter to Sir Dudley Carleton about the threat of a second Armada is in *The Letters of John Chamberlain,* vol. I, ed. Norman Egbert McClure (Westport, CT: Greenwood Press, 1979). The Catholic spy William Sterrell's letter of July 21, 1599, about the queen's illness is in *Letters and Papers Sorted and Bound in Date Order,* July 1599 (The National Archives, Kew, SP 12/271/106–108). Cited in the Folger Shakespeare Library digital resource "The Elizabethan Court Day by Day."

Thomas Cecil, Lord Burghley's complaint about wasting meat in anticipation of Elizabeth's long-delayed visit is in "Cecil Papers: July 1599, 16–31," *Calendar of the Cecil Papers in Hatfield House,* vol. 9, *1599,* ed. R. A. Roberts (London: His Majesty's Stationery Office, 1902), 234–56, British History Online.

For an overview of Mary Sidney's literary patronage, see Mary Ellen Lamb, "The Countess of Pembroke's Patronage," *English Literary Renaissance* 12, no. 2 (1982): 162–79. For poets' praise for Mary Sidney, see Hannay, *Philip's Phoenix*. Nicholas Breton's comparison of Mary to Elisabetta Gonzaga, Duchess of Urbino, is in Nicholas Breton, *The Pilgrimage to Paradise, ioyned with the Covntesse of Penbrookes loue* (Oxford: Joseph Barnes, 1592); Francis Meres's compliment to Mary is from Francis Meres, "Comparative Discourse of our English Poets," in *An English Garner*, ed. Edward Arber (London: Edward Arber, 1879), and Thomas Nashe called her a "second Minerva" in his prefatory letter included in his unauthorized edition of *Astrophel and Stella: Sir P.S. His Astrophel and Stella Wherein the excellence of sweete poesie is concluded. To the end of which are added, sundry other rare sonnets of diuers noble men and gentlemen* (London: Printed by John Charlewood for Thomas Newman, 1591).

For Aubrey's praise of Wilton House, see Dick, *Aubrey's Brief Lives*.

Chamberlain's letter to Carleton about Pembroke's death is in McClure, *The Letters of John Chamberlain*, vol. I.

CHAPTER FIVE

For a general account of the history of witchcraft and its persecution in England, see Keith Thomas, *Religion and the Decline of Magic* (New York: Scribner, 1971). For a contemporary account of King James's involvement in the Scottish trial of Agnes Sampson and others, see *News from Scotland* (1591), in *The Demonology of King James I: Includes the Original Text of Daemonologie and News from Scotland*, ed. Donald Tyson (Woodbury, MN: Llewellyn Publications, 2011).

For Elizabeth Cary's participation in her father's witchcraft case, and for all other biographical details unless otherwise noted, see *Elizabeth Cary, Lady Falkland: Life and Letters*, ed. Heather Ruth Wolfe (Cambridge, UK: Renaissance Texts from Manuscript; Tempe: Arizona Center for Medieval and Renaissance Studies, 2001).

For Lawrence Tanfield's biography, see E. I. Carlyle and David Ibbetson, "Tanfield, Sir Lawrence (c. 1551–1625), lawyer," *ODNB*.

On Burford Priory, see Walter H. Godfrey, "Burford Priory," *Oxoniensia* 4 (1939), and Kevan Manwaring, "The Roofs of Burford," *Oxfordshire Folk Tales* (New York: The History Press, 2011), ch. 25.

For the popularity of Seneca's *Letters* among educated Englishwomen, see Mary Ellen Lamb, *Gender and Authorship in the Sidney Circle* (Madison: University of Wisconsin Press, 1990).

Elizabeth's translation of Ortelius's *L'Epitome du Théâtre du Monde* is available in a modern scholarly edition: Abraham Ortelius, *The Mirror of the World: A Translation*, ed. Lesley Peterson (Montréal: McGill-Queen's University Press, 2012).

For Queen Elizabeth's stay at Burford Priory, see the Folger Shakespeare Library's digital resource "The Elizabethan Court Day by Day."

Michael Drayton's poems dedicated to Elizabeth Cary in his 1597 *Englands Heroicall Epistles* are in Michael Drayton, *Poems,* vol. 2, ed. John Buxton (Cambridge, MA: Harvard University Press, 1953).

For Jonson's poem "To Sir Henry Cary," see Ben Jonson, *The Complete Poems,* ed. George Parfitt (New Haven, CT: Yale University Press, 1982).

For John Chamberlain's letter about Elizabeth's marriage, and his letter to Carleton mentioning Henry and Elizabeth's Christmas visit to John Harington's home, see *The Letters of John Chamberlain,* vol. I, ed. Norman Egbert McClure (Westport, CT: Greenwood Press, 1979).

The Lord Mayor of London's condemnation of theater audiences is cited in David Mann, "Female Play-Going and the Good Woman," *Early Theatre* 10, no. 2 (2007): 51–70; John Davies's comment is in "In Cosmum," in *The Complete Poems of Sir John Davies,* ed. Alexander Balloch Grosart (London: Chatto and Windus, 1876).

ADDITIONAL BIBLIOGRAPHY

James VI and I, *The Demonology* in *The Demonology of King James I: Includes the Original Text of Daemonologie and News from Scotland,* ed. Donald Tyson (Woodbury, MN: Llewellyn Publications, 2011).

Reginald Scot, *The Discoverie of Witchcraft,* ed. Brinsley Nicholson (Wakefield, UK: Rowman and Littlefield, 1973).

William Gouge, *Of Domestical Duties* (1622; Pensacola, FL: Chapel Library, 2006).

CHAPTER SIX

All citations of Aemilia Lanyer's poems, unless otherwise noted, are from *The Poems of Aemilia Lanyer: Salve Deus Rex Judaeorum,* ed. Susanne Woods (New York: Oxford University Press, 1993). The spelling has been modernized.

For John Stow's comments about Billingsgate, see John Stow, *Survey of London* (1598; New York: Dent, 1956).

On Simon Forman's unusual life and career, see Barbara Howard Traister, *The Notorious Astrological Physician of London: Works and Days of Simon Forman* (Chicago: University of Chicago Press, 2001), and Lauren Kassell, "Forman, Simon (1552–1611), astrologer and medical practitioner," *ODNB.* For excerpts from Forman's notes on Aemilia Lanyer in his casebooks, see Pamela Benson's digital resource, "Emilia [sic] Lanier," *A Critical Introduction to the Casebooks of Simon Forman and Richard Napier, 1596–1634,* and "Casebooks," *The Casebooks of Simon Forman and Richard Napier, 1596–1634: A Digital Edition,* ed. Lauren Kassell et al.

On Robert Dudley, Earl of Leicester's relationship to John Dee, see

R. Julian Roberts, "Dee, John (1527–1609), mathematician, astrologer, and anti-quary," *ODNB,* and Glyn Parry, *The Arch Conjuror of England: John Dee* (New Haven, CT: Yale University Press, 2012).

For John Chamberlain's letter to Dudley Carleton about Essex's mobilizing troops for his naval campaign, see *The Letters of John Chamberlain,* vol. 1, ed. Norman Egbert McClure (Westport, CT: Greenwood Press, 1979).

For an overview of Aemilia's relationship to Forman, see Susanne Woods, *Lanyer: A Renaissance Woman Poet* (New York: Oxford University Press, 1999). For details of Forman's relationship to Avis Allen, see A. L. Rowse, *Sex and Society in Shakespeare's Age: Simon Forman the Astrologer* (New York: C. Scribner, 1974).

Forman's deliberation over visiting Aemilia and his account of that visit on September 11, 1597, are in Woods, *Lanyer: A Renaissance Woman Poet.* His entry for September 17, 1597, can be read in Pamela Benson, "Emilia [sic] Lanier," in *A Critical Introduction to the Casebooks of Simon Forman and Richard Napier, 1596–1634.*

On Essex's creation of knighthoods, see Lawrence Stone, *The Crisis of the Aristocracy, 1558–1641* (Oxford, UK: Clarendon Press, 1965). Essex's comment about Elizabeth I's being "crooked" is from Paul E. J. Hammer, "Devereux, Robert, second earl of Essex (1565–1601), soldier and politician," *ODNB.* For Elizabeth's comparison of herself to Richard II, see John Nichols, *Bibliotheca Topographica Britannica,* vol. 1 (London: Printed by and for John Nichols, 1780), 525.

For Margaret Clifford, Countess of Cumberland's negotiations with her estranged husband, see Jessica L. Malay, "Positioning Patronage: Lanyer's *Salve Deus Rex Judæorum* and the Countess of Cumberland in Time and Place," *The Seventeenth Century* 28, no. 3 (2013): 251–74.

Margaret's letter lamenting George's losses at sea is cited in Stone, *The Crisis of the Aristocracy.*

Anne Clifford's comments about her parents' disliking one another are from her 1603 memoir, in *Anne Clifford's Autobiographical Writing, 1590–1676,* ed. Jessica L. Malay (Manchester, UK: Manchester University Press, 2018). Her account of her father's mistress is in her entry for George in *Anne Clifford's Great Books of Record,* ed. Jessica L. Malay (Manchester, UK: Manchester University Press, 2015).

Aemilia Lanyer's description of her time at Cookham is from her poem "The Description of Cooke-ham," in *The Poems of Aemilia Lanyer: Salve Deus Rex Judaeorum,* ed. Susanne Woods (New York: Oxford University Press, 1993).

On the dating of Jonson's "To Penshurst" and Aemilia's "The Description of Cooke-ham," see Kailey Giordano, "A Cooke-Ham of One's Own: Con-structing Poetic Persona at Nature's Expense in Aemilia Lanyer's 'The Descrip-tion of Cooke-Ham' and Ben Jonson's 'To Penshurst,'" *Early Modern Culture* 13, no. 1 (May 2018). For Martial's poem on Faustinus's villa, see Marcus Valerius

Martialis, *Epigrams,* vol. 1, ed. and trans. D. R. Shackleton Bailey (Cambridge, MA: Harvard University Press, 1993), Book III, 58.

CHAPTER SEVEN

For Queen Anna's biography, see Leeds Barroll, *Anna of Denmark, Queen of England: A Cultural Biography* (Philadelphia: University of Pennsylvania Press, 2001). For a discussion of contemporary reports regarding Anna's real or faked miscarriage in the spring of 1603, see Clare McManus, *Women on the Renaissance Stage: Anna of Denmark and Female Masquing in the Stuart Court, 1590–1619* (Manchester, UK: Manchester University Press, 2002).

All details from Anne Clifford's experience in 1603 with the new queen and her court are in *Anne Clifford's Autobiographical Writing, 1590–1676,* ed. Jessica L. Malay (Manchester, UK: Manchester University Press, 2018).

For the number of knighthoods in England, see Lawrence Stone, *The Crisis of the Aristocracy, 1558–1641* (Oxford, UK: Clarendon Press, 1965).

On the history of plague in Renaissance England, see Alan D. Dyer, "The Influence of Bubonic Plague in England, 1500–1667," *Medical History* 22, no. 3 (1978): 308–26, and Paul Slack, *The Impact of Plague in Tudor and Stuart England* (London: Routledge & K. Paul, 1985). Thomas Dekker's *A Wonderful Year* (1603) is in Rebecca Totaro, ed., *The Plague in Print: Essential Elizabethan Sources, 1558–1603* (Pittsburgh: Duquesne University Press, 2010).

For a history of English inheritance law, see Eileen Spring, *Law, Land, & Family: Aristocratic Inheritance in England, 1300 to 1800* (Chapel Hill: University of North Carolina Press, 1997), and Amy Louise Erickson, *Women and Property in Early Modern England* (London: Taylor & Francis Group, 1995).

Records from the account book kept by Anne Clifford's governess, Mrs. Taylor, are cited in T. D. Whitaker et al., *The History and Antiquities of the Deanery of Craven, in the County of York,* 3d ed., with many additions and corrections. Edited by A. W. Morant, and with a chapter on the geology, natural history, and prehistoric antiquities by L. C. Miall (Leeds: J. Dodgson, 1878). Anne's description of her mother, Margaret Clifford, Countess of Cumberland, is from *Anne Clifford's Great Books of Record,* ed. Jessica L. Malay (Manchester, UK: Manchester University Press, 2015). For Margaret's interest in alchemy and mining, see Richard T. Spence, "Clifford [née Russell], Margaret, countess of Cumberland (1560–1616), noblewoman," *ODNB.*

For Samuel Daniel's letter complaining about spending his time as a tutor, see John Pitcher, "Samuel Daniel's Letter to Sir Thomas Egerton," *Huntington Library Quarterly* 47, no. 1 (1984): 55–61.

For Daniel's poem to Margaret Clifford, "A Letter from Octavia to Marcus Antonius," first published in 1599, see A. B. Grosart, ed., *The Complete Works in Verse and Prose of Samuel Daniel,* vol. 1 (London: Hazell, Watson and Viney, Limited, 1885).

A full list of the titles shown in Anne Clifford's portrait is in Richard

T. Spence, *Lady Anne Clifford, Countess of Pembroke, Dorset and Montgomery (1590–1676)* (Stroud, Gloucestershire, UK: Sutton Publishing, 1997). For a discussion of Anne's reading, see Leah Knight, "Reading Proof: Or, Problems and Possibilities in the Text Life of Anne Clifford," in *Women's Bookscapes in Early Modern Britain,* ed. Leah Knight, Elizabeth Sauer, and Micheline White (Ann Arbor: University of Michigan Press, 2018).

Anne's comment about her father's refusal to let her learn foreign languages is from *Anne Clifford's Great Books of Record,* ed. Jessica L. Malay (Manchester, UK: Manchester University Press, 2015).

Anne's description of her time with her father at Grafton Regis is from *The Life of Me,* included in *Anne Clifford's Autobiographical Writing.* Margaret's letter complaining about George's efforts to arrange Anne's marriage, and Anne's letter to her mother about the possible match, are quoted in Jessica L. Malay, "The Marrying of Lady Anne Clifford: Marital Strategy in the Clifford Inheritance Dispute," *Northern History* 49, no. 2 (2012): 251–64.

Margaret's disparaging remarks about Anne's marriage portion are in Jessica L. Malay, "Crossing Generations: Female Alliances and Dynastic Power in Anne Clifford's Great Books of Record," in *The Politics of Female Alliance in Early Modern England* (Lincoln: University of Nebraska Press, 2017).

Anne's account of her disinheritance in favor of her uncle is from *The Life of Me.* George's last letter to Margaret explaining his decision is cited in Jessica L. Malay's Introduction to *Anne Clifford's Great Books of Record.* Margaret's letter to the Privy Council is cited in Malay, "Crossing Generations: Female Alliances and Dynastic Power in Anne Clifford's *Great Books of Record.*"

For a history of coverture in Renaissance England, see, among others, Mary Chan and Nancy Wright, "Marriage, Identity, and the Pursuit of Property in Seventeenth-Century England: The Cases of Anne Clifford and Elizabeth Wiseman," in *Women, Property, and the Letters of the Law in Early Modern England,* ed. Andrew Buck, et al. (Toronto: University of Toronto Press, 2004), and Erickson, *Women and Property in Early Modern England.*

For a list of Margaret Clifford's jointure estates, see Spence, *Lady Anne Clifford.* For Margaret's demands on her tenants in Westmorland, see Richard T. Spence, "Mining and Smelting by the Cliffords, Earls of Cumberland, in Westmorland in the Early Seventeenth Century," *Transactions of the Cumberland and Westmorland Antiquarian and Archaeological Society* 91 (1991): 101–17.

Anne's description of her trip with Margaret to the north of England in 1607 is in *The Life of Me.*

Margaret's letter to Lodovick Stuart, Duke of Lennox, is cited in Jessica L. Malay, "Beyond the Palace: The Transmission of Political Power in the Clifford Circle," in *Family Politics in Early Modern Literature,* ed. Hannah Crawforth and Sarah Lewis (London: Palgrave Macmillan, 2017).

For details of Anne's suitors and the negotiations around her marriage, see Malay, "The Marrying of Lady Anne Clifford."

For Thomas Sackville, Earl of Dorset's letter to George More reassuring him that he would respect Anne's right to her inheritance; the contemporary account of Anne and Richard taking a liking to one another during their courtship; and all other details about the Court of Arches case, see Malay, "The Marrying of Lady Anne Clifford."

The 1608 praise of Knole is from the National Trust exhibition at Knole House Visitor Center. Anne's description of her life at Knole and Wilton is from *The Life of Me*. Sackville-West's description of Anne Clifford's life at Knole is from her "Long Preface" to *The Diary of the Lady Anne Clifford*, ed. V. Sackville-West (1923; Providence, RI: Women Writers Project, Brown University, 1990). Virginia Woolf's comment about Knole as "a town rather than a house" is from *Orlando: A Biography* (1928; Orlando, FL: Harcourt, 2006).

For the passage from Ben Jonson's *Volpone*, see Ben Jonson, *Four Plays: Volpone; Epicoene, or the Silent Woman; The Alchemist; Bartholmew Fair*, ed. Robert N. Watson (London: Methuen Drama, 2014).

CHAPTER EIGHT

For Queen Anna's cultivation of the masque at court, see Leeds Barroll, *Anna of Denmark, Queen of England: A Cultural Biography* (Philadelphia: University of Pennsylvania Press, 2001), and Clare McManus, *Women on the Renaissance Stage: Anna of Denmark and Female Masquing in the Stuart Court (1590–1619)* (Manchester, UK: Manchester University Press, 2002).

For the text and illustrations of "The Masque of Queens," see Stephen Orgel and Roy Strong, *Inigo Jones: The Theatre of the Stuart Court, Including the Complete Designs for Productions at Court for the Most Part in the Collection of the Duke of Devonshire Together with Their Texts and Historical Documentation* (London: Sotheby Parke Bernet; Berkeley: University of California Press, 1973). For the prohibition of farthingales in 1613, see John Chamberlain's letter of February 18, 1613, to Alice Carleton in *The Letters of John Chamberlain*, vol. 1, ed. Norman Egbert McClure (Westport, CT: Greenwood Press, 1979).

For the history of women performing as professional actors on the English stage, see Elizabeth Howe, *The First English Actresses* (Cambridge, UK: Cambridge University Press, 1992); a short summary of the topic is in Georgianna Ziegler's article on the Folger Shakespeare Library website, "The First English Actresses," posted on January 22, 2019.

Aemilia Lanyer's *Salve Deus Rex Judaeorum* can be read in full in *The Poems of Aemilia Lanyer: Salve Deus Rex Judaeorum*, ed. Susanne Woods (New York: Oxford University Press, 1993). All quotations from Aemilia's poems are from this edition, with modernized spelling.

On Pilate's wife in *Salve Deus*, see W. Gardner Campbell, "The Figure of Pilate's Wife in Aemilia Lanyer's *Salve Deus Rex Judæorum*," *Renaissance Papers* (Durham, NC: Camden House, 1995), 1–13. For a history of Pilate's wife more broadly, see Aurélia Hetzel, *Témoignage et prophétie: Le rêve de la femme de Pilate*, Classique/Moderne 9 (Paris: Classiques Garnier, 2021).

On Aemilia's ambition in choosing her dedicatees, see Mary Ellen Lamb, "Patronage and Class in Aemilia Lanyer's *Salve Deus Rex Judaeorum*," in *Women, Writing, and the Reproduction of Culture in Tudor and Stuart Britain,* ed. Mary Burke (Syracuse, NY: Syracuse University Press, 2000), and Su Fang Ng, "Aemilia Lanyer and the Politics of Praise," *ELH* 67, no. 2 (2000): 433–51.

Margaret Clifford's letter to Richard Sackville regarding Anne's company during his absence is cited in Jessica L. Malay, "Positioning Patronage: Lanyer's *Salve Deus Rex Judæorum* and the Countess of Cumberland in Time and Place," *The Seventeenth Century* 28, no. 3 (2013): 251–74.

On Aemilia's attempt to gain Mary Sidney's blessing for her own poetic authority, see Barbara Lewalski, *Writing Women in Jacobean England* (Cambridge, MA: Harvard University Press, 1993), and John Rogers, "The Passion of a Female Literary Tradition: Aemilia Lanyer's 'Salve Deus Rex Judæorum,'" *Huntington Library Quarterly* 63, no. 4 (2000): 435–46.

For details on the printing of *Salve Deus* in 1611, see Erin A. McCarthy, "Speculation and Multiple Dedications in 'Salve Deus Rex Judaeorum,'" *Studies in English Literature, 1500–1900* 55, no. 1 (2015): 45–72. For a discussion of the surviving copies, see the "Textual Introduction" in Woods, *The Poems of Aemilia Lanyer.*

For an estimate on the cost of books in seventeenth-century England, see David McKitterick, "'Ovid with a Littleton': The Cost of English Books in the Early Seventeenth Century," *Transactions of the Cambridge Bibliographical Society* 11, no. 2 (1997): 184–234.

CHAPTER NINE

On the formula that Protestant wives should be "chaste, silent, & obedient," see Suzanne W. Hull, *Chaste, Silent, & Obedient: English Books for Women, 1475–1640* (San Marino, CA: Huntington Library Press, 1988). For the Church of England's homily on matrimony, see Gerald Bray, ed., *The Books of Homilies: A Critical Edition* (Cambridge, UK: James Clarke & Co., 2017).

All details from Elizabeth Cary's biography, unless otherwise indicated, are from *Elizabeth Cary, Lady Falkland: Life and Letters,* ed. Heather Ruth Wolfe (Cambridge, UK: Renaissance Texts from Manuscript; Tempe: Arizona Center for Medieval and Renaissance Studies, 2001).

All quotations from *The Tragedy of Mariam* are from *The Tragedy of Mariam, the Fair Queen of Jewry,* ed. Barry Weller and Margaret W. Ferguson (Berkeley: University of California Press, 1994).

Chamberlain's letter of December 9, 1608, to Sir Dudley Carleton can be read in *The Letters of John Chamberlain,* vol. I, ed. Norman Egbert McClure (Westport, CT: Greenwood Press, 1979).

For the meaning of "distractedness" as a mental condition in the Renaissance, see Michael McDonald, *Mystical Bedlam: Madness, Anxiety and Healing in Seventeenth-Century England* (Cambridge, UK: Cambridge University Press, 1981).

Details of Henry Cary's career advancement, and its costs, are from Sean Kelsey, "Cary, Henry, first Viscount Falkland (c. 1575–1633), lord deputy of Ireland," *ODNB*.

All letters concerning Elizabeth's conversion and her marital dispute are reprinted in Heather Ruth Wolfe, *Elizabeth Cary, Lady Falkland: Life and Letters*. The report of Elizabeth's attending Mass with the queen is cited in Wolfe's Introduction.

On child mortality rates, see E. A. Wrigley, R. S. Davies, J. E. Oeppen, and R. S. Schofield, *English Population History from Family Reconstitution, 1580–1837* (Cambridge, UK: Cambridge University Press, 1997), and Gill Newton, "Infant Mortality Variations, Feeding Practices and Social Status in London Between 1550 and 1750," *Social History of Medicine* 24, no. 2 (2011).

On Charles's protracted marriage negotiations, see Mark A. Kishlansky and John Morrill, "Charles I (1600–1649), king of England, Scotland, and Ireland," *ODNB*.

For Queen Henrietta Maria's Catholicism, see Arthur F. Marotti, *Religious Ideology and Cultural Fantasy: Catholic and Anti-Catholic Discourses in Early Modern England* (Notre Dame, IN: University of Notre Dame Press, 2005), and Malcolm Smuts, "Religion, European Politics and Henrietta Maria's Circle, 1625–41," in *Henrietta Maria: Piety, Politics and Patronage,* ed. Erin Griffey (Aldershot, UK: Ashgate, 2008).

ADDITIONAL BIBLIOGRAPHY

Robert Cleaver, *A godly form of household government* (London, 1598), reprinted in Lloyd Davis, *Sexuality and Gender in the English Renaissance: An Annotated Edition of Contemporary Documents* (London: Routledge, 2018).

John Davies, *The Muses Sacrifice* (London, 1612; Cambridge, UK: Proquest LLC, 1992).

William Gouge, *Of Domestical Duties* (London, 1622; Pensacola, FL: Chapel Library, 2006).

James VI and I, *Basilikon Doron, or His majestys instructions to his dearest sonne, Henry the Prince* (London, 1603).

John Milton, *Doctrine and Discipline of Divorce* (London, 1643), in *The Divorce Tracts of John Milton: Texts and Contexts,* ed. Sara J. van den Berg and W. Scott Howard (Pittsburgh: Duquesne University Press, 2010).

William Whately, *A Bride-Bush, or A Wedding Sermon compendiously describing the duties of married persons* (London, 1617), reprinted in Lloyd Davis, *Sexuality and Gender in the English Renaissance: An Annotated Edition of Contemporary Documents* (London: Routledge, 2018).

Henry Smith, *A Preparative to Marriage* (London, 1591).

CHAPTER TEN

All details from Anne Clifford's biography for 1617–19 are from her diaries, in *Anne Clifford's Autobiographical Writing, 1590–1676,* ed. Jessica L. Malay (Manchester, UK: Manchester University Press, 2018).

For James's declaration of his love for Buckingham to the Privy Council, see Roger Lockyer, "Villiers, George, first duke of Buckingham (1592–1628), royal favourite," *ODNB*. For his private letters about Buckingham, see David Moore Bergeron, *King James & Letters of Homoerotic Desire* (Iowa City: University of Iowa Press, 1999).

Evidence of the private passageway from James I's chamber to Buckingham's at Apethorpe Hall is from Kathryn A. Morrison, "The Apethorpe Hall Research Programme: Architectural Investigation and Research," *Newsletter of the English Heritage Research Department* 5 (Winter 2006–7), cited in Jennifer Shun-Yee Ng, *Bedchamber Ritual and the Performance of Stability in Jacobean England, 1603–1625* (ProQuest Dissertations Publishing, 2011).

For the Privy Council's letter to the deputy lieutenant in Westmorland detailing the conflict between Anne and her uncle Francis, see George C. Williamson, *Lady Anne Clifford, Countess of Dorset, Pembroke & Montgomery, 1590–1676: Her Life, Letters and Work* (Kendal, UK: Titus Wilson and Son, 1922). For Anne's appeal to the Appleby authorities for the right to bury her mother and for her altercation with Francis over the tenants at Whinfell Park, see Richard T. Spence, *Lady Anne Clifford, Countess of Pembroke, Dorset and Montgomery (1590–1676)* (Stroud, Gloucestershire, UK: Sutton Publishing, 1997).

Anne's listing Matthew Caldicott as "my Lord's favourite" in the catalogue of the Knole Household is cited in *The Memoir of 1603 and The Diary of 1616–1619,* ed. Katherine O. Acheson (Peterborough, ON: Broadview Editions, 2007).

All letters exchanged between Richard and Anne are transcribed in Williamson, *Lady Anne Clifford, Countess of Dorset, Pembroke & Montgomery, 1590–1676.* The originals are held in the Kendal Archive Centre in Kendal, UK.

The quotation from Psalm 102 is cited from the King James Version of the Holy Bible; all references to the Bible, unless otherwise noted, are from this translation.

For John Chamberlain's letter to Sir Dudley Carleton about Anne's miscarriage, see *The Letters of John Chamberlain,* vol. II, ed. Norman Egbert McClure (Westport, CT: Greenwood Press, 1979). The genealogical table listing the three sons she bore is reprinted in *Anne Clifford's Great Books of Record,* ed. Jessica L. Malay (Manchester, UK: Manchester University Press, 2015).

John Donne's comment about Anne's wide-ranging interests was reported in Edward Rainbow, Bishop of Carlisle's funeral sermon for Anne; see Appendix E in Acheson, *The Memoir of 1603 and The Diary of 1616–1619.*

The book of Turkish history Anne was busy reading in 1617 was George

Sandys's *A Relation of a Journey Begun An: Dom: 1610: Fovre Bookes. Containing a Description of the Turkish Empire, of Aegypt of the Holy Land, of the Remote Parts of Italy, and Ilands Adioyning,* first published in London in 1615.

On the relationship between Anne's diaries and annual chronicles, see the Introduction to *The Diary of Anne Clifford, 1616–1619: A Critical Edition,* ed. Katherine O. Acheson (New York: Garland, 1995).

George Sedgewick's description of Anne's diary-keeping, cited in *Anne Clifford's Autobiographical Writing,* is from his own autobiography: "George Sedgewick, A Summarie or Memorial of my owne Life," in Joseph Nicolson and Richard Burn, *The History and Antiquities of the Counties of Westmorland and Cumberland: By Joseph Nicolson, Esq; and Richard Burn, LL.D. In Two Volumes* (London: W. Strahan and T. Cadell, 1777).

For speculation on the fate of Anne's diaries and their possible destruction at the hands of her grandson Thomas Tufton, Earl of Thanet, see Williamson, *Lady Anne Clifford, Countess of Dorset, Pembroke & Montgomery.*

For the 1684 inventory of Anne's library, see Jessica Malay, "Reassessing Anne Clifford's Books: The Discovery of a New Manuscript Inventory," *The Papers of the Bibliographical Society of America* 115 (2021).

Details of Anne's husband, Richard Sackville, Earl of Dorset's will are in Spence, *Lady Anne Clifford,* and Williamson, *Lady Anne Clifford, Countess of Dorset, Pembroke & Montgomery.*

CHAPTER ELEVEN

All citations from Anne Clifford's 1619 diary are from *Anne Clifford's Autobiographical Writing, 1590–1676,* ed. Jessica L. Malay (Manchester, UK: Manchester University Press, 2018).

For Queen Anna's contribution to England's cultural life, see Leeds Barroll, *Anna of Denmark, Queen of England: A Cultural Biography* (Philadelphia: University of Pennsylvania Press, 2001).

John Chamberlain's estimates of Queen Anna's wealth at her death, and his description of her funeral, are from *The Letters of John Chamberlain,* vol. II, ed. Norman Egbert McClure (Westport, CT: Greenwood Press, 1979); see also M. T. W. Payne, "An Inventory of Queen Anne of Denmark's 'Ornaments, Furniture, Householde Stuffe, and Other Parcells' at Denmark House, 1619," *Journal of the History of Collections* 13, no. 1 (January 2001).

Thomas Lorkin's letter to Sir Thomas Puckering describing King James's lack of ready funds for Anna's funeral is in John Nichols, *The Progresses, Processions, and Magnificent Festivities of King James the First,* vol. 3 (New York: B. Franklin, 1964). Scaramelli's description of Elizabeth's lying in state is cited in John Guy, *Elizabeth: The Forgotten Years* (New York: Viking, 2016).

Mary Sidney's complaints of old age are from Sir Dudley Carleton's August 2, 1616, letter to Chamberlain, in *Dudley Carleton to John Chamberlain, 1603–1624, Jacobean Letters,* ed. Maurice Lee Jr. (New Brunswick, NJ: Rutgers

University Press, 1972). Carleton's description of the Englishmen and -women he met at Spa, including Mary, is from this letter.

The correspondence between Sir Robert Sidney and Sir John Throckmorton is in Geraint Dyfnallt Owen, et al., *Report on the Manuscripts of Lord de l'Isle & Dudley Preserved at Penshurst Place* (London: HM Stationery Office, 1925). The original letters can be consulted at the Kent History and Library Centre in Maidstone, UK, with permission of Lord de l'Isle.

The 1571 Spanish treatise by Nicolás Monardes affirming the medical benefits of tobacco appeared in English in 1577 as *Joyfull Newes Out of the New Founde Worlde* (Constable and Co., Ltd.; New York: A. A. Knopf, 1925). Sir Francis Bacon's comments on tobacco's addictive qualities are from his *Historia Vitae et Mortis,* in *The Works of Francis Bacon,* vol. 2, collected and edited by James Spedding, Robert Leslie Ellis, and Douglas Denon Heath (Cambridge, UK: Cambridge University Press, 2013).

Chamberlain's report of the "suspicion" regarding Mary Sidney's secret marriage to her doctor Matthew Lister is from *The Letters of John Chamberlain,* vol. II. For Lister's biography, see Brian Nance, "Lister, Sir Matthew (bap. 1571, d. 1656), physician," *ODNB.*

For a modern edition of Lady Mary Wroth's play, *Love's Victory,* see *Love's Victory,* ed. Alison Findlay, Philip Sidney, and Michael G. Brennan (Manchester, UK: Manchester University Press, 2021).

The letters attributed to Mary Sidney written to Sir Tobie Matthew are from John Donne Jr., *A Collection of Letters Made by Sir Tobie Matthew, Knight* (London, 1650). On Matthew's life and writing, see A. J. Loomie, "Matthew, Sir Toby [Tobie] (1577–1655), writer and courtier," *ODNB.*

Mary Sidney's *Triumph of Death* is in *The Collected Works of Mary Sidney Herbert, Countess of Pembroke,* ed. Margaret P. Hannay, et al. (New York: Clarendon Press, 1998).

For Sir John Harington's comment on Mary's Psalms, see Jason Scott-Warren, "Harington, Sir John (bap. 1560, d. 1612), courtier and author," *ODNB.*

John Aubrey's comments on Mary Sidney's home at Houghton are from his *Brief Lives,* ed. Oliver L. Dick (Boston: D. R. Godine, 1999).

The observation that the decorative frame of the Van de Passe engraving of Mary Sidney includes quill pens resting in inkwells was originally made by Anne Lake Prescott and is quoted in Margaret P. Hannay, "The Countess of Pembroke's Agency in Print and Scribal Culture," in *Women's Writing and the Circulation of Ideas: Manuscript Publication in England, 1550–1800,* ed. George Justice and Nathan Tinker (Cambridge, UK: Cambridge University Press, 2002). Hannay's article includes a full account of the engraving and its iconography.

Chamberlain's report of Mary Sidney's death is from *The Letters of John Chamberlain,* vol. II.

Aemilia Lanyer's praise of Mary Sidney is from "The Author's Dream to the Lady Mary, the Countess Dowager of Pembroke," in *The Poems of Aemilia*

Lanyer: Salve Deus Rex Judaeorum, ed. Susanne Woods (New York: Oxford University Press, 1993).

CHAPTER TWELVE

Aemilia Lanyer's 1620 petition to the Chancery Court as well as Edward Smith's response have been partially transcribed in Susanne Woods, *Lanyer: A Renaissance Woman Poet* (New York: Oxford University Press, 1999). Other details come from my own examination of the original documents at the National Archives in London.

On Alfonso's hay and grain patent and his ties to John Bancroft, bishop of London, see Leeds Barroll, "Looking for Patrons," in *Aemilia Lanyer: Gender, Genre, and the Canon,* ed. Marshall Grossman (Lexington: University Press of Kentucky, 1998).

For more on women schoolteachers in seventeenth-century England and for details on the records from the diocese of Essex, see Jay Pascal Anglin, *The Third University: A Survey of Schools and Schoolmasters in the Elizabethan Diocese of London* (Norwood, PA: Norwood Editions, 1985). The advertisement for a private academy for women published in 1673 is cited in David Cressy, *Education in Tudor and Stuart England* (London: E. Arnold, 1975).

Thomas More's account of Edward IV's mistress Jane Shore is in More, *History of King Richard III,* written between 1513 and 1518 and first published in 1557. For a modern edition, see *The Essential Works of Thomas More,* ed. Gerard B. Wegemer and Stephen W. Smith (New Haven, CT: Yale University Press, 2020).

A. L. Rowse's edition of Aemilia Lanyer's poems appeared with the title *The Poems of Shakespeare's Dark Lady, Salve Deus Rex Judaeorum* (London: Cape, 1978).

For a list of Shakespeare's plays that may have been performed with the Lord Chamberlain's Men between 1594 and 1599, see Roslyn L. Knutson, "Shakespeare's Repertory," *A Companion to Shakespeare* (John Wiley & Sons, Ltd, 2012), pp. 346–61. Wiley Online Library. See also John Astington, *English Court Theatre, 1558–1642* (Cambridge, UK: Cambridge University Press, 1999).

Tony Haygarth's claim to have discovered Aemilia Lanyer as the subject of the Nicholas Hilliard miniature is in Simon Tait, "Unmasked—The Identity of Shakespeare's Dark Lady," *Independent on Sunday* (London), December 7, 2003. John Hudson's theories about Lanyer's identity and her authorship of Shakespeare's plays are in Hudson, *Shakespeare's Dark Lady: Amelia Bassano Lanier, the Woman Behind Shakespeare's Plays?* (Stroud, UK: Amberley, 2016).

CHAPTER THIRTEEN

Elizabeth Cary's *History of the life, reign, and death of Edward II, King of England, and Lord of Ireland: with the rise and fall of his great favourites, Gaveston and the Spencers* can be read online through Brown University's Women Writers Project (Providence, RI, 1999). It was originally published in 1680.

All letters that Elizabeth wrote or received, as well as all letters and documents concerning her separation from her husband and her kidnapping of her children, are in *Elizabeth Cary, Lady Falkland: Life and Letters,* ed. Heather Ruth Wolfe (Cambridge, UK: Renaissance Texts from Manuscript; Tempe: Arizona Center for Medieval and Renaissance Studies, 2001). All details from her biography, unless otherwise noted, are also from this edition.

Christopher Marlowe's play *The troublesome reign and lamentable death of Edward the second* was first published in 1594. For a modern edition, see *The Complete Works of Christopher Marlowe,* vol. 3, *Edward II,* ed. Richard Rowland (Oxford, UK: Clarendon Press, 1994). For Michael Drayton's "The Legend of Piers Gaveston," see *Collected Poetical Works of Michael Drayton* (n.p.: Delphi Classics, 2011).

For James I's relationship to Buckingham, see David Moore Bergeron, *King James & Letters of Homoerotic Desire* (Iowa City: University of Iowa Press, 1999), and *Royal Family, Royal Lovers: King James of England and Scotland* (Columbia: University of Missouri Press, 1991).

For Raphael Holinshed's account of Edward II's murder, see *The First Volume of the Chronicles of England, Scotland, and Ireland* (London, 1577). Scholars believe Marlowe may have used the second edition published in 1587: Raphael Holinshed, *The Third Volume of Chronicles, Beginning at Duke William the Norman* (London: John Harrison, George Bishop, 1587). A modern edition is cited in the Appendix in Rowland, *The Complete Works of Christopher Marlowe,* vol. 3, *Edward II.*

James I's 1610 proclamation banning Catholics from London and the court is cited in Wolfe, *Lady Falkland: Life and Letters.*

Elizabeth's translation *The reply of the most illustrious Cardinall of Perron, to the answeare of the most excellent King of Great Britaine* (Douai, 1630) isn't available in a modern edition; roughly thirty copies of the 1630 publication are available in libraries worldwide, some with digital access. For a description of the presentation copies, see Wolfe, *Lady Falkland: Life and Letters.* My account of the additional pages is based on the copy in Queen's College Library, University of Oxford, which is the book believed to have been owned by Elizabeth's husband, Henry Cary, Lord Falkland.

For a history of how books were approved and licensed in seventeenth-century England, see Cyndia Susan Clegg, *Press Censorship in Jacobean England* (Cambridge, UK: Cambridge University Press, 2001). On the spread of Catholicism in Henrietta Maria's court and the translation of recusant works, see Malcolm Smuts, "Religion, European Politics and Henrietta Maria's Circle, 1625–41," in *Henrietta Maria: Piety, Politics and Patronage,* ed. Erin Griffey (Aldershot, UK: Ashgate, 2008); and Marie-France Guénette, "Channelling Catholicism Through Translation: Women and French Recusant Literature Around the Court of Queen Henrietta Maria (1625–42)," *Status Quaestionis,* no. 17 (Dec. 2019).

Details of Henry Cary's political struggles both in Ireland and upon his return to England are from Sean Kelsey, "Cary, Henry, first Viscount Falkland (c. 1575–1633), lord deputy of Ireland," *ODNB*.

On the question of Elizabeth Cary's burial, see Frances E. Dolan, *Whores of Babylon: Catholicism, Gender, and Seventeenth-Century Print Culture* (Notre Dame, IN: University of Notre Dame Press, 2005).

For Lucius Cary's biography, see Kurt Weber, *Lucius Cary, Second Viscount Falkland* (New York: Columbia University Press, 1940). Lucius's letter to the Privy Council from December 1636 is included in Wolfe, *Lady Falkland: Life and Letters.*

On Charles I's Personal Rule and the origins of the Civil War, see Kevin Sharpe, *The Personal Rule of Charles I* (New Haven, CT: Yale University Press, 1992). On Charles's execution, see in particular Jason Peacey, *The Regicides and the Execution of Charles I* (London: Palgrave Macmillan, 2001). For a general history of the English Civil War and its aftermath, see, among others, John Morrill, *The Nature of the English Revolution* (London: Routledge, 1993).

On Oliver Cromwell's role in the Civil War, see John Morrill, ed., *Oliver Cromwell and the English Revolution* (London: Longman, 1990); Christopher Hill, *God's Englishman: Oliver Cromwell and the English Revolution* (New York: Dial Press, 1970); and Antonia Fraser, *Cromwell: Our Chief of Men* (London: Weidenfeld and Nicholson, 1973).

Elizabeth's biography was first published as part of a dual biography: *The Lady Falkland: her life from a ms. in the imperial archives at Lille. Also, A memoir of Father Francis Slingsby, from mss. in the Royal Library, Brussels,* ed. Richard Simpson (London: Catholic Publishing & Bookselling Co., 1861).

CHAPTER FOURTEEN

For details on the King's Award, see the Introduction to *Anne Clifford's Autobiographical Writing, 1590–1676,* ed. Jessica L. Malay (Manchester, UK: Manchester University Press, 2018). All references to Anne's life during the 1640s are from *The Life of Me,* included in Malay's edition, as are all references to her yearly memoirs from 1650 to 1675 and her diary of 1676, unless otherwise noted.

Henry Clifford, Earl of Cumberland's final years and death are described in Richard T. Spence, "Clifford, Henry, fifth earl of Cumberland (1592–1643), local politician and royalist army officer," *ODNB*. For Philip Herbert, Earl of Pembroke's activities during the Civil War, see David L. Smith, "Herbert, Philip, first earl of Montgomery and fourth earl of Pembroke (1584–1650), courtier and politician," *ODNB*.

Charles's reading during his imprisonment on the Isle of Wight and other details of his trial and execution are recorded in Mark A. Kishlansky and John Morrill, "Charles I (1600–1649), king of England, Scotland, and Ireland,"

ODNB. For details of his final months, see Jason Peacey, *The Regicides and the Execution of Charles I* (London: Palgrave Macmillan, 2001).

For John Aubrey's description of Philip Herbert, see his *Brief Lives,* ed. Oliver L. Dick (Boston: D. R. Godine, 1999).

Anne's letter to Francis Russell, Earl of Bedford, is cited in Richard T. Spence, *Lady Anne Clifford, Countess of Pembroke, Dorset and Montgomery (1590–1676)* (Stroud, UK: Sutton Publishing, 1997). Her comment about Oliver Cromwell is cited in D. J. H. Clifford, ed., *The Diaries of Lady Anne Clifford* (Stroud, UK: Sutton Publishing, 1992).

For details on Anne's almswomen at St. Anne's Hospital, Appleby, see Spence, *Lady Anne Clifford.* Anne's letter to Christopher Marsh regarding her tenants, written in early December 1649, and her letter to the Countess of Kent thanking John Selden for sending her the book of Chaucer are cited in George C. Williamson, *Lady Anne Clifford, Countess of Dorset, Pembroke & Montgomery, 1590–1676: Her Life, Letters and Work* (Kendal, UK: Titus Wilson and Son, 1922).

On Anne Clifford's habits of reading, see Leah Knight, "Reading Proof: Or, Problems and Possibilities in the Text Life of Anne Clifford," in *Women's Bookscapes in Early Modern Britain,* ed. Leah Knight, Elizabeth Sauer, and Micheline White. I am grateful to Knight for further details concerning Anne's inscriptions in books she read before 1650.

The calculation of the pages in the collected *Great Books of Record* was kindly done by Max Clark, archive assistant, Kendal Archive Centre in Kendal, UK. All details regarding the original manuscripts are from my time in the Kendal Archive Centre in the fall of 2021. For an overview of Anne's work in assembling the *Great Books of Record,* see Jessica L. Malay, "Lady Anne Clifford's *Great Books of Record:* Remembrances of a Dynasty," in *A History of Early Modern Women's Writing,* ed. Patricia Phillippy (New York: Cambridge University Press, 2018).

For Edward Rainbow's funeral sermon for Anne, see Appendix E in Katherine O. Acheson, ed., *The Memoir of 1603 and The Diary of 1616–1619* (Peterborough, ON: Broadview Editions, 2007).

EPILOGUE

For an overview of Renaissance English women writers, see, among others, Danielle Clarke, *The Politics of Early Modern Women's Writing* (New York: Routledge, 2014), and Barbara Lewalski, *Writing Women in Jacobean England* (Cambridge, MA: Harvard University Press, 1993).

For an anthology of Renaissance women's writing, see Randall Martin, ed., *Women Writers in Renaissance England* (Abingdon, UK: Routledge, 2014), and Helen Ostovich and Elizabeth Sauer, eds., *Reading Early Modern Women: An Anthology of Texts in Manuscript and Print, 1550–1700* (New York: Routledge, 2004).

A selection of Isabella Whitney's poetry, as well as poems by Mary Sidney and Aemilia Lanyer, is included in *Isabella Whitney, Mary Sidney, and Aemilia Lanyer: Renaissance Women Poets,* ed. Danielle Clarke (London: Penguin Books, 2000).

Anne Lock's writing can be read in Susan M. Felch, ed., *Anne Vaughan Lock: Selected Poetry, Prose, and Translations, with Contextual Materials* (Toronto: Iter Press, 2020).

Lady Mary Wroth's *Urania* has been published unabridged as *The First Part of the Countess of Montgomery's Urania* and *The Second Part of the Countess of Montgomery's Urania,* ed. Josephine A. Roberts, completed by Suzanne Gossett and Janel Mueller (Tempe: Arizona Center for Medieval and Renaissance Studies, 1999). For her sonnet series, see Lady Mary Wroth, *Pamphilia to Amphilanthus in Manuscript and Print,* ed. Ilona Bell, texts by Steven W. May and Ilona Bell (Toronto: Iter Press, 2017).

For a selection of Margaret Cavendish's works, see Margaret Cavendish, Duchess of Newcastle, *The Blazing World and Other Writings,* ed. Kate Lilley (New York: Penguin Books, 2004). For selected works of Aphra Behn, see Aphra Behn, *Oroonoko, The Rover, and Other Works,* ed. Janet Todd (New York: Penguin Books, 1992).

Index

❈

Page numbers in *italics* refer to illustrations.

A NOTE ABOUT THE AUTHOR

Ramie Targoff is the Jehuda Reinharz Professor of the Humanities, Professor of English, and Co-Chair of Italian Studies at Brandeis University. She holds a B.A. from Yale University and a Ph.D. from the University of California, Berkeley. She is the author of several award-winning books on Renaissance English poetry, as well as a biography and translation of the sixteenth-century Italian poet Vittoria Colonna. She lives with her family in Cambridge, Massachusetts.

A NOTE ON THE TYPE

This book was set in Adobe Garamond. Designed for the Adobe
Corporation by Robert Slimbach, the fonts are based on types first
cut by Claude Garamond (ca. 1480–1561). Garamond was a pupil
of Geoffroy Tory and is believed to have followed the Venetian
models, although he introduced a number of important differences,
and it is to him that we owe the letter we now know as "old style."
He gave to his letters a certain elegance and feeling of movement
that won their creator an immediate reputation and the patronage
of Francis I of France.

Composed by North Market Street Graphics,
Lancaster, Pennsylvania

Printed and bound by Berryville Graphics,
Berryville, Virginia